CITY OF TORRANCE

75th Anniversary
1 9 1 2 - 1 9 8 7

Letters From
WOMEN
WHO LOVE
TOO MUCH

Letters From WOMEN WHO LOVE TOO MUCH

A CLOSER LOOK AT RELATIONSHIP ADDICTION AND RECOVERY

by Robin Norwood

POCKET BOOKS

New York   London   Toronto   Sydney   Tokyo

The actual letters in this collection were sent to the author in response to her book entitled *Women Who Love Too Much*. The names and other identifying characteristics have been changed to preserve the anonymity of each writer.

An *Original* publication of POCKET BOOKS

POCKET BOOKS, a division of Simon & Schuster, Inc., 1230 Avenue of the Americas, New York, N.Y. 10020

ISBN: 0-671-66156-6

First Pocket Books trade hardcover printing January, 1988

10 9 8 7 6 5 4 3 2 1

POCKET and colophon are trademarks of Simon & Schuster, Inc.

Printed in the U.S.A.

A mind might ponder its thoughts for ages and not gain so much self-knowledge as the passion of love shall teach it in a day.

—*Ralph Waldo Emerson,*
"History"

CONTENTS

SEVEN

EIGHT

NINE

TEN

ACKNOWLEDGMENTS

This book, like *Women Who Love Too Much* (hereafter *WWL2M*), has been a birthing process, and two invaluable "midwives" assisted its emergence. First, my editor, Laura Golden Bellotti, whose skills so vitally shaped *WWL2M*, again brought her talent and discernment to bear on this project. With the recent birth of her own son and her consequent plunge into the consuming demands and delights of parenthood, she nevertheless has lost none of her editorial "Golden" touch, the ability to guide softly, firmly and reassuringly all at once. What a blessing it has been to work with her again.

And second, Victoria Raye Starr, whose being carries as much light as her name. As she converted these many letters and my handwritten comments on them to typewritten manuscript pages, she communicated her own richly personal and deeply honest understanding of much of the book's material through innumerable notes attached to freshly typed pages. Often I'd be compelled to go back and rewrite in the light of her cogent comments and probing questions. Our countless conversations helped give me an invaluable perspective on the topics addressed in this book.

While I alone am responsible for its flaws and shortcomings, these two women have contributed immeasurably to whatever is worthwhile in this book, and they have my deepest thanks.

PREFACE

"**S**o, are you going to write *another* book?" It seemed that people began asking that question from the moment *Women Who Love Too Much* was completed, and my reaction was always the same. I felt like a new mother, tired and spent, lying in bed trying to recover from a long and difficult labor while cheerful bedside visitors repeatedly asked, "So, are you going to have *another* baby?" Somehow the very question seemed to vastly underrate the magnitude of the last effort, and I usually answered a little crossly, perhaps as that imagined new mother might have, "I don't even want to think about it right now!" Privately, I was sure nothing would induce me to go through that painful birthing process again.

But the seeds from which this book would grow were sown with the first letter I received in response to *WWL2M*. Even before the official publication date, someone had found the book, read it and been moved enough to write. Her letter follows in its entirety:

> *Dear Ms. Norwood:*
> *Never in my life have I been so moved by a book to put pen to paper to write to the author. Finding, discovering your book came unexpectedly as I was searching for business texts to assist me in my burgeoning new life. I must say your work affected me so profoundly that I*

11

am certain it was the key in fostering an entire positive direction out of so many years of ceaseless pain and confusion. There were times I felt this book was written just for me alone. It was indeed powerful for me. I remember one night sitting on my kitchen floor poring over each page; at times I had to close it and put it by my side until my weeping lessened. God bless you for your clarity, sensitivity, eloquence, and most of all your decision to write it!

I was married to a very powerful man, and I had to leave for my own survival—although he loved me dearly in his way. I see now, through your gifted writing, so many dynamics I never understood.

Beth B.

As I read this letter, I cried. Giving birth to *WWL2M* had taken three years and much sacrifice, but now I knew it had all been worth it. There had been heated moments during the book's gestation when persons who knew the publishing business far better than I insisted that in order to sell, the book needed to be lighter, more positive, less depressing and with far less emphasis on addiction. But I was committed to describing what it had really been like for my clients, my friends and myself as we struggled with the men in our lives. My aim was to depict the frequency with which addiction and co-addiction appeared in so many of our stories and to clarify how very dangerous it was for us to continue our unhealthy patterns of living and relating to men. And I wanted to emphasize what a tremendous piece of work we faced when we decided to change those patterns. Because I had attempted to describe truthfully the often very painful lives of women who love too much, my book did not turn out to be the light, easy-to-read self-help book some people expected; but it was the book I wanted to write.

After reading that first letter from Beth B., I knew *WWL2M* had been of value to at least one person. But there was also something specific in Beth's letter that touched me, aside from the fact that *WWL2M* was accomplishing its purpose. Just like Beth B., I had known so well that experience of sitting on the floor sobbing with pain and relief and gratitude because another woman had honestly described her struggle—a struggle so like my own. In my case, that experience had come after reading a magazine article in the early 1970s in which the author described how it felt to be a woman in this culture—to wake up and finally allow oneself to see and hear all the many ways that women as a class are insulted. When I read that author's words, I knew, with almost a shock, that I wasn't alone anymore. Her writing spoke so deeply and truly of my own need to be unaware and unawake in order to avoid feeling the pain, anger and humiliation that are a part of simply being female in a male-dominated society. But that choice to disregard so many of my experiences and reactions had been costly, and the author of that article spoke to my latent desire to awaken fully, to see and hear and feel everything I experienced, and to no longer silently participate in my own debasement. What was true for her was also true for me, and through her example I was able to set free the feelings I had previously kept hidden even from myself. Her truth had helped me on my way to becoming bigger and braver and more grown up. Now, as I read Beth's letter more than a decade later I was vividly remembering that particular metamorphosis. *WWL2M* had touched another woman to the depth that I had once been touched, and she was now sharing that experience with me. A widening, deepening, brightening circle had been created between us.

That letter was the first of what before long began to feel like an avalanche of responses to the book. By phone (until, because of the sheer volume of calls, getting an unlisted number became an unavoidable necessity) and by letter, women, and some men, too, wanted to connect, to talk about what the book had meant to them. They wanted to pour out their personal experiences, and very often to say thanks. But many also wanted answers to specific questions or had problems they felt weren't addressed in the book.

These questions were important. Some I had heard over and over throughout my career in the field of addiction. Others were raised specifically in response to issues explored in *WWL2M* and came up repeatedly not only in letters but during the lectures and workshops I was giving. As the mail spread beyond my desk to nearly every flat surface in the house and the demand for responses from me weighed heavier, I began to search for a more efficient yet still personal way to answer them all. Though time factors and the sheer volume of letters made it impossible, I longed to answer each of them in detail from my own personal perspective as a woman who has loved too much, indeed who has been a relationship addict most of my life, and also from my perspective as a therapist with many years' experience dealing with addiction and recovery.

But I also knew that the people sending those letters needed much more than a letter from me. They needed each other. These women and men who were sharing so much of themselves with me needed to hear each others' stories, to discover together how the disease of relationship addiction had operated in their lives. I wanted to be able to create for those who had never known it, or had not yet felt its power when applied to relationship addiction, that life-changing experience of hearing how it is for others who share the same problem.

As a therapist, and personally, through my own ongoing recovery, I am convinced of the tremendous value of peer support groups. These groups, made up of people dedicated to speaking honestly with one another about a common problem, and self-led according to simple guidelines and spiritual principles, are in my opinion the most powerful and profound sources of healing available. They provide the basis for recovery from every kind of addiction, chemical and behavioral. These kinds of groups are the hope of every addict for a new, better way of life.

Letters from Women Who Love Too Much is written, then, for two purposes. First, as a practical way of responding in detail to the many, many letters that have common themes and questions. And second, to create an opportunity for those who share the problem of relationship addiction to hear from each other what that struggle has been like and, if there has been some recovery, how it has been achieved.

Obviously, in order to gain the most from this book a reader should have already read *WWL2M* slowly, carefully and hopefully more than once. I highly recommend rereading it before beginning this one. Until that book is *thoroughly* digested this one won't be of much help, as it is not intended to further explain the principles outlined in *WWL2M*. Rather its goal is to explore, through readers' questions and experiences, the implications of putting those principles into action.

When we are lonely and lost we don't yearn simply for company but for our own kind. I am convinced that the advice columns that are so popular are not read for the answers but for the questions. We want to know that we are not alone, that among all those other people whose lives are hidden from us, there are those who struggle as we do. I am grateful that in writing this second book I, too, am not alone. As has always been the case through the years of my own recovery, I have so many of you sharing your stories with me, helping me through the struggle and into the light. Now hopefully, through the vehicle of this book, you will be sharing with each other as well.

To you this book is dedicated.

INTRODUCTION

The letters in this book really do exist, and each is quoted by permission of its author. Many of those whose letters are used herein have expressed gratitude for what they have received from reading *WWL2M*. These thanks, while gratefully acknowledged here, have been consistently edited out to avoid redundancy for the reader. Some further editing has been done for the sake of clarity and conciseness as well as to protect each author's identity.

The letters and responses have, of necessity, been sorted into chapters dealing with specific subjects. However, many of the letters contain multiple questions and problems. Since diseases of addiction, including relationship addiction, tend to overlap in real life, they do so in the letters as well. For instance, the topics of alcoholism and coalcoholism, sexual addiction, incest, compulsive eating and recovery may all be addressed in one letter. Thus any arbitrary sorting of these letters is just that—arbitrary. For this reason, do not expect the content of each letter to be either as narrow or as unequivocal as the chapter headings might suggest.

In answering each letter, I am drawing on fifteen years' experience in the field of addiction and nearly a lifetime of loving too much, thankfully including nearly seven years' recovery. But by no means does that imply that my answers are the "right" ones. They are simply that—*my* answers: incomplete, subjective and biased. I make no attempt to be all-inclusive in my responses. Rather, each letter is answered from the perspective of regarding addiction *as a disease* and each response or comment incorporates my very strong viewpoints on treatment, developed over years of making mistakes and learning from them. The reader may not like my response to any given letter, nor agree with it. That there are many other ways of responding, perhaps more helpful or insightful or to the point than the replies contained in this book, I readily acknowledge. We will each read these letters with our own eyes and our own hearts, like a series of Rorschach ink blots to which we bring our own perceptions, colored by our unique personal histories. The letters will absorb our experiences and reflect back our own projections so, of course, what each of us sees in them, feels from them, will vary. I believe that it is not the answers that matter so much anyway. What counts are the letters themselves, with their pain and pathos, lessons learned, slips backward, progress forward and sometimes even triumphs.

We all want answers to our questions, our fears and doubts and struggles. But the answers must eventually come, not from someone else's advice to us, but from their example combined with our own commitment to changing our life. Setting ourselves upon a path trod by others who have faced the same problems and known the same fears and doubts and struggles, yet who are finding their way, helps us achieve our own recovery. As others share their stories, through their mistakes and victories they help us find our way, too.

Finally, I must state as strongly and clearly as possible that this book is not intended to be a general treatise on love, on how to find the right man or on how to make a relationship work. Quite the contrary, like *WWL2M*, this book is written primarily for heterosexual women who are *addicted* to relationships. Its purpose is to aid women whose lives have become progressively more unmanageable due to an increasingly debilitating obsession with either a particular man or with the latest of a series of men or, if in between involvements, with finding a man. By thus focusing this book I do not mean to imply that only heterosexual women become addicted to relationships, as this is absolutely not the case. Many men are also addictive in their relationships, just as addictive relating is very much a theme for great numbers of homosexual couples. I have chosen to focus on heterosexual women because their experience of relationship addiction is the one I understand best, both personally and professionally.

Although this book primarily contains letters from women who are obsessed with men, it also includes letters from homosexual men and women, straight men, parents who are obsessed with their children and children who are obsessed with their parents. I hope *Letters from Women Who Love Too Much* will be of value to all these populations, as well as to those whose relationships, while troubled, are not addictive. It is, nevertheless, aimed at the woman whose mental and physical health are either at risk or have already begun to deteriorate, whose work performance is potentially or actually suffering, who is likely to be experiencing money problems, whose children, friends and other family members are neglected or abandoned as are her other interests, who is potentially or actively suicidal—who is, as the years go by, becoming sicker and sicker from her dependency on men and on what she chooses to call "love."

As was stated in *WWL2M*, I regard relationship addiction as a definable, diagnosable and treatable *disease process*, akin to other diseases of addiction such as alcoholism and compulsive eating. It shares with these other diseases of addiction the fact that it is naturally progressive (it gets worse) without treatment but that it does respond to specific treatment that addresses its physical, emotional and spiritual components. It is my conviction that a treatment approach that neglects any one of these aspects will not, over time, prove effective.

All this needs to be said in order to explain the uncompromising approach to recovery that I believe is necessary. The most effective approach to addiction in terms of recovery is that taken by the Anonymous programs, and this approach is, in my opinion, the best one for addressing relationship addiction as well. It is the *only* approach I personally can advocate.

ONE

LETTERS FROM
WOMEN WHO . . .

Dear Robin Norwood,

I hated your book.

I hated Women Who Love Too Much.

I hated this book so much that it took me months to read it.

Sometimes I could only read a page a day.

I hated the women that you wrote about. I hated the stories.

I hated what you said.

And then I finished the book.

And then:

—I went to my first Overeaters Anonymous meeting.
—I found Al-Anon.
—I joined ACOA (Adult Children of Alcoholics).
—I got into group therapy.
—I found VOICES* and for the first time in my life talked about having been sexually abused.
—I stopped binge-eating.
—I got a new job.
—I made a budget for the first time (I'm thirty-three).
—I have begun a new life.

I was crazy and out of control. I am five foot three inches and I weighed ninety-nine pounds due to my bingeing and purging syndrome. Now I cannot imagine that there will be a day when I do not have WWL2M *on my coffee table and a second copy in my "personal" drawer at the office.*

I thank you.

Wendy D.

---

*VOICES: Victims Of Incest Emerged Survivors—see the List of Resources at the end of this book.

For me, Wendy's letter just about says it all. Simply reading a book, no matter how deeply it affects us, is never enough in itself to bring about the changes we desire in our lives. At best a book can be a signpost, an arrow pointing out the direction in which we need to travel. It is up to each of us to decide whether or not we will put our feet upon the path. But her letter brings to mind a very important point. When does *recovery* from any addiction actually begin?

Recovery begins when we channel the energy formerly spent on our disease into our recovery.

Recovery begins when we become willing, as Wendy did, to channel the energy and effort formerly spent on practicing our disease(s) into instead pursuing our recovery. Wendy's recovery requires a lot of time and work and dedication, but then being actively addictive cost her a great deal, too. So she made a choice to go to whatever lengths were necessary to get well—and she is continuing to make that choice each day. Thus, she has begun to recover, and her recovery will continue as long as she continues to make that choice.

Where do those of us who have yet to take the first step toward recovery from relationship addiction begin? We begin by becoming *willing* to channel the energy and effort that we formerly spent on trying to bring about a change in someone else into instead changing ourselves. Our initial steps in this new direction may not come quickly or easily, and they may at first seem very small, but we must learn to respect their importance. As we move toward recovery, *no* step we take is really small, because each one changes the direction of our life.

The next letter is a good example of what a first step toward recovery might be. Taking just this small step and sticking with it already has implications for the rest of this woman's life. She has begun the process of change.

> *Dear Robin Norwood,*
>
> *Valentine's Day has always been a tradition I've looked forward to with hope and yet dreaded at the same time, fearing the letdown of a day meant for love when none was received.*
>
> *Two days ago I was thirty pages into* WWL2M. *In my desk drawer was a Valentine's card—sweet, suggestive—for a man who has basically not participated in our relationship for several weeks now. Not sending that card seems like such a little thing, yet it could be the first time I have actively chosen to stop giving to a man and a situation where the feeling of caring is not mutual.*
>
> *I am not finished with the book yet. In fact, it is difficult for me to read because it speaks so clearly to why I have been in one failed relationship after another. This could be the tool that finally begins to liberate me, though.*
>
> *I still have the card. I will not be sending it. Maybe Valentine's Day will become my Victory Day.*
>
>   *Theo P.*

In Theo's case continuing recovery requires that she not only refrain from sending an amorous message to a man who isn't interested in her, but that she do something nice *for herself* to fill the void she has now created. We cannot simply stop an addictive behavior without substituting another (hopefully more positive) behavior to take its place. Otherwise the addictive behavior will only reassert itself. This is because Nature seems to abhor a vacuum as much in the areas of human behavior and emotions as in physics.

Since Theo has the power both to give and receive the gift she has been yearning for from someone else, she doesn't have to wait, empty, until a man comes along to fill her life with pleasure and love. She can become her own supply of love if she is willing to do so. The more lovingly and generously she treats herself the less likely she is to allow anyone else to treat her badly or indifferently.

All this is easy to see but not so easy to do, because nothing challenges us more than having to change the ways we think, feel and act, especially regarding *ourselves*. Theo admits that she hasn't yet been able to finish *WWL2M* because looking at her own patterns of relating is so uncomfortable for her. And yet recovery demands that we change, and the possibility of change begins with awareness. We must be willing to look honestly at our lives, which requires courage; we must be willing to admit that we are not perfect, that we need help, and that we cannot do it alone, which requires humility. So *courage and humility* are absolutely essential in order for recovery to begin.

In the letter that follows, we'll look at what is necessary, after one has begun the process of recovery, for that process to continue.

Dear Robin Norwood,

My parents have a drinking problem, and though I don't drink or use drugs I now realize I have been addicted to men who are self-destructive. I have tried to control the three men I've lived with by threats, bribes, praise, lectures and every other manipulation I thought might work.

I now see that I am equally as self-destructive as they are because I seem to pick only those men who are needy and deficient. I can never stay interested in men who are healthy and competent.

My current boyfriend just called me from the Army brig where he is spending a forty-five-day sentence for possession of pot. He says he is learning a lesson and will stay out of trouble forever now. I told him I was happy to hear that and I hope he takes care of himself. I realize I can only take care of myself and am attending my first Al-Anon and Adult Children of Alcoholics meetings in a couple of days.

I don't know if he and I will ever get back together

and it doesn't really matter, because I'm learning how
to be okay on my own.
    Best wishes from a recovering man-addict.
                      Britt J.

As Britt detaches from her boyfriend's problem, focusing instead on her own unhealthy patterns of behavior and seeking help to change these, she exemplifies the first stage of recovery from relationship addiction. How diligently she continues to pursue her own recovery will determine whether she moves beyond this first stage. As you read the other letters from relationship addicts in this book you will learn that there is no specific amount of pain that guarantees a person will make a wholehearted commitment to recovery. For some individuals, incredible degrees of personal humiliation and degradation do not bring about the surrender that is required in order for recovery to begin. Instead, much like a gambler who cannot stop playing *because so much has already been lost,* these relationship addicts use their abasement to justify their ever more desperate attempts at controlling another person and salvaging a progressively deteriorating situation. In other words, as the consequences of relationship addiction worsen, some people continue to get sicker. But others "hit bottom" and become, at least temporarily, willing to go to whatever lengths are necessary to get well.

It is sometimes difficult to understand that a person can recognize the destructive power of addiction in his or her life and become willing to address it for a time, yet later lose that willingness completely. But this is the case more often than not. This is why distinctions must be made between three phases of recovery: beginning to recognize the disease process that is operating in one's life (this could occur through reading a book such as *WWL2M*); becoming willing to address it as the life-threatening addiction it is (by going to a meeting of an Anonymous program that addresses the particular addiction); and continuing to make one's recovery one's first priority on a daily basis (through regular attendance at meetings and daily reading and prayer). As difficult as it is, launching into recovery is only a first step and is no guarantee that recovery will necessarily continue. Many, many more alcoholics initially become sober than are able to stay sober, and many, many more relationship addicts begin recovery than stay with it.

It is an inexplicable feature of every kind of addiction and every type of addict that no one, no matter how great that person's experience or expertise, can predict who will truly recover from a given addiction and who will not. All that can be safely predicted is that most addictive people will not get well. Yet those who continue daily to want recovery more than they want anything else and who make it their *first* priority will eventually, little by little and step by step, and often with the guidance and support of others who have been through the same struggle, achieve it.

In order to sustain recovery, in addition to the requisite willingness, courage and humility so necessary to begin the process, we must develop two more qualities: a capacity for *rigorous honesty and self-examination,* and a *reliance on a Power greater than ourselves*. This Higher Power certainly doesn't have to fit anyone else's definition of what it is or should be. It can be called God. It can be without a name. It can as likely be found in a support group of peers as in a church or temple. It is a highly personal, individually formulated principle that, when called upon, provides an unfailing supply of strength and solace.

Cecilia's letter exemplifies how necessary this source of strength is as the life-changing process of recovery reshapes us.

Dear Robin,
  I want to tell you about some of the things that have been happening for me since I read your book two years ago. From reading **WWL2M** *I realized my family was*

alcoholic and that it is truly the whole *family's disease. I went to a couple of Al-Anon meetings and began to understand myself and my choices much better. I felt "cured."*

It was truly just the beginning.

Having had an unhappy early marriage and then a disastrous affair with a man who had a long and sordid criminal record, I was able, with what I had learned, to make a healthier choice for myself. Now I am married again, this time to a wonderful man who treats me like gold. Sometimes I get angry when he tells me he loves me. Sometimes I pick a fight. I am more comfortable being angry. I don't yet know how to be loved.

Something in my past has been buried for years and now, with the help of God, I have recently been allowed to remember it all. Five months ago when the memory came back I thought at first I'd die from the pain. I remembered that when I was four years old my Dad molested me. When I could finally acknowledge that, suddenly so much made sense to me. I have always hated and pitied my mother but now I have begun to understand her. Of course she drank. What else could she do? Face the truth? Hardly. There was nowhere to go with it.

I have lived in a state of denial for so long. I want to tell you how strong *denial is. As the true circumstances of my childhood have surfaced, I have experienced some physical ramifications. I began having "heart attacks" during which my chest hurt and I felt as though I was going to lose consciousness. I had an EKG/ treadmill test and the doctor told me I had no indications of heart trouble. To the contrary, I have a very strong heart. So that wasn't the problem. But the panic attacks continued to happen even when I wasn't thinking about my Dad or Mom. I was still trying to push it all down. I didn't want to remember. I didn't want to know. It felt like everything I had believed about my family was a lie. I thought I was losing my mind. Growing up in my house you learned to lie even though the truth was hitting you in the face. Now I believed nothing, I knew nothing.*

During this horrible time, God asked me in the most gentle, loving way not to drink. With all my agony over my parents' craziness, I was resorting to a very fine pinot noir to take away the pain. I had already decided I was not ever going to be like my parents, so I didn't catch on to the fact that I was an alcoholic too, just like both of them. Now I am grateful that I was delivered from three generations or more of alcoholism.

Not drinking left me naked. I had used alcohol, sarcasm, dirty fighting and staying angry so that I wouldn't feel the hurt inside me anymore. Now God asked me to give up those other tactics as well.

Throughout all of this my heart palpitated and I began to have migraine headaches three to four days a week. The desire to deny my past created a war in my body which left me tired and sad.

I have cried so much lately, something which I could never do as a child. Getting in touch with the tears and the grief has been frightening. Sometimes I've felt as though I would never stop crying.

I'm writing to you, Robin, because I think it is important for you to know what some people may be going through from reading your book. The pain of true change is the most immense agony I have ever known or ever hope to know. It hasn't come over me all at once and it isn't healing overnight either. It will probably take me years and the love of God to come to terms with this devastating family secret, accept it, heal from it and forgive everyone involved. It is such hard work and the cost of looking at these things is high. But the cost of not looking is even higher.

Please let people know that.

I am doing very well right now. I hurt and I cry and I'm healing. I have given up that mindless "Gidget Gets Remarried" image I was trying to portray. My need for approval from every living, breathing soul is slowly lessening, and I am setting realistic goals and loving boundaries for myself. I no longer have to save every damaged person I run into. It is becoming okay to take care of myself first. It is even becoming okay to be loved!

I always thought I just wanted to be loved and the reality is I chose only people who weren't capable of loving me. I have chosen better this time and am learning how to hold still and accept that love.

God has taught me so much in such a short period of time and has told me He will hold my hand the rest of the way no matter how long it takes. The heart pains are lessening and the migraines are going away, and I am accepting what happened to me and mourning for my lost childhood when I need to.

My most wonderful husband holds me and hugs me and even understands why it is so hard for me to receive his caring. I see him struggle with me and I wish it were over and I were healed for his sake, too. So you see, your book was only the beginning—a very helpful, gentle, loving beginning . . .

Cecilia

If self-honesty were easier, more comfortable, perhaps we wouldn't need help from a Power greater than ourselves in order to achieve it. But as Cecilia's letter demonstrates, looking honestly at ourselves and our lives can be so excruciatingly painful that most of us cannot face the task with only our limited human resources.

Trying to recover without faith is like walking up a steep hill backward and in high heels.

Trying to recover without faith, for someone who has none and wants none, is not impossible, but it is more difficult. It means doing recovery the hard way—kind of like walking up a steep hill backward and in high heels. You still may get where you're headed, but there is a faster, more efficient, less strenuous way to make the journey. But faith itself is surprisingly easy to cultivate if a person is willing to do so—willing to act as if there is a greater Intelligence than one's own operating in the universe. However, nothing, *nothing* could be more personal than a quest for faith, and none of us can tell another how to conduct that quest. We each discover our God alone and in silence.

———————

There would be no point in assembling letters from women who love too much unless, taken together, these letters can help promote recovery in those who read them. Yet recovery from relationship addiction is a far more subtle, less definable achievement than recovery from most other addictions such as alcoholism, compulsive spending, compulsive gambling and even compulsive eating. Throughout this book you will need to evaluate for yourself what constitutes recovery from relationship addiction, what promotes it and what prevents it, why it happens for some and not for others. All these questions and their answers will matter deeply to you if you want to recover yourself.

Theo and Britt are just beginning to explore recovery. Wendy and Cecilia are well on their way because the steps they are taking to promote their healing are now an established part of their daily lives. But starting the journey and then continuing on it is up to each of us, alone. No one, nothing can do it for us. We must find the courage and the humility, as Wendy has, to take the necessary first steps and then the honesty and a source of spiritual strength and guidance, as Cecilia has, to face the specific issues that are on our path.

Throughout this book women (and men) who have read *WWL2M* will describe their lives, their situations, their relationship addiction and very often their other addictions as well. Sometimes, as with these four women, we'll hear about the steps they've taken in order to begin and sustain their recovery. Hopefully, the steps taken and the progress made by those who are recovering will be a source of inspiration and guidance to those of you who are beginning that journey yourselves.

Two

. . . HAVE YET TO RECOVER

The roots of relationship addiction can inevitably be traced to emotional traumas in childhood—loss, pain, abuse and abandonment—and the patterns of relating developed in consequence of these traumas. The details of these traumatic experiences vary among individuals, as do the corresponding "styles" of addictive relating that are developed and later practiced in adulthood as relationship addiction. For instance, women who come from violent homes tend to choose violent partners, women who grew up in alcoholic homes tend to choose chemically dependent partners, and so on. But one dynamic is always present and operating in relationship addiction: the unconscious drive to re-create the struggle from the past and, in confronting it again in the present, to emerge triumphant. Stated more simply, it is a compulsion to play the game again and this time to *win*. The struggle to prevail over what defeated us in our past becomes an obsession. As long as this motive is still active, relationship addiction is still present, whether or not there is a current partner.

This chapter comprises letters from women who acknowledge their relationship addiction and also recognize some of the contributing factors from their childhood experiences. But awareness of the conditions and events that predisposed one to developing a pattern of addictive relating is by no means tantamount to mastery over that behavior pattern.

Each of these women believes herself to have recovery more firmly in hand than is, in my assessment, actually the case. In order to understand my reservations regarding these particular reports of progress, keep in mind the factors that promote recovery. Courage and humility are required, as is the development of a capacity for rigorous honesty. One must be willing to go to any length to get well. In order to maintain the healing process it is usually also necessary to surrender to an Intelligence greater than one's own for guidance and comfort.

Awareness by itself is not enough to promote and support the massive changes necessary for recovery to take place. When that awareness is coupled with self-willed determination to overcome addictive behavior, the possibility of recovery becomes even more remote, because the addict is bringing to bear on her disease the same unhealthy attitudes and behaviors she has used for so long on other people. Nothing has truly changed. She is still operating from the conviction that she, of herself, has the answer to her problem and the power to force herself to change. It is natural at first (and comforting) to believe that merely making up one's mind to change will end the problem, but if that were all that were necessary there would be no such thing as addiction. Self-willed control doesn't work in the face of addiction of any type because all diseases of addiction are diseases of control. We try and try to control what we cannot and we get sicker in the process. Addiction is not amenable to self-will, only to surrender, to admitting it is bigger than we are and that we cannot overcome it alone.

The following letters are presented to help you more readily recognize relationship addiction as well as to help identify self-will in operation. Self-will is always a feature of relationship addiction and presents a tremendous impediment to achieving recovery.

Dear Robin Norwood,

Your book was so difficult for me to finish. I actually put it down several times and told myself that I couldn't continue with it—it hurt too much to read the truth about myself. Every time I would try to put the book in a bottom drawer, face down, I would turn to page four, where I had underlined the words "you will change from a woman who loves someone else so much it hurts into a woman who loves herself enough to stop the pain." I would then persevere and continue to read. I know I cannot stop my pain overnight, but to finally admit that I am indeed in pain is a beginning.

I am thirty-three, have two children, have had two husbands and just this evening ended a year-long relationship with a married man. Reading WWL2M gave me the strength to end the relationship. All of these men have needed "fixing" and I have even carried my "fixing" into my career. I teach severely emotionally disturbed senior high school students. I have received many awards and so much praise for working with these kids, but now I have a new perspective on what I've really been doing all these years. When people used to ask me why I chose to work with crazy kids I told them that I didn't choose my work, it chose me, almost like a calling. How wrong I have been! What better profession for a compulsive "fixer"! I am not going to run away from my job, but when I return in September, it will be with a new awareness and a healthier attitude.

You write about dysfunctional families and alcoholism. My own family was dysfunctional, not because of alcoholism, but because of the death of my only sibling, a brother, nineteen months younger. He became ill at the age of five, with a terminal brain tumor. He died a little bit every day for three years, and my mother, my father and I all died with him. He died in January, my parents divorced in February, my mom remarried in November and my father in May. I have spent the last twenty-five years trying to "fix" all of us up again, but never realized this until I read your book. In the meantime, I have hurt two good men and my own children as well. If you write another book, please write about what the death of a child does to a family. There must be so many others like me who have lost a brother or sister and don't recognize what it may still be doing to them. The parents of the dead child receive the sympathy but the siblings know only that they can never "fix" that loss for the family that is left—they can never be good enough, smart enough, pretty enough, or strong enough to fill the void. They can never love enough or be perfect enough to justify their own existence and the fact that they are still alive while their sibling is dead. Please try to help the unwitting survivors of a sibling's death who may feel these same feelings I have. You can reach so many people and I cannot.

I graduated from college with a cumulative average of 3.98 and remember thinking how proud my parents would have been if only I hadn't gotten that one "B" which kept me from a perfect 4.0. Somehow I was sure I had let us all down.

I hope that I have cried the last of my tears for a while, that I will wake up in the morning, look in the mirror and say, "Moira, you are loved so much, especially by yourself." Then, I will go ahead and have the courage to mail this letter.

Moira D.

Moira's first letter describes so well one of the many ways children can be damaged enough to develop into serious relationship addicts in adulthood. The loss of a child through death inevitably delivers a deep and lasting blow to the remaining family members and will to some extent always affect their continuing relationships with each other. The surviving family members are very fortunate if they are able to explore their guilt and pain and fear of yet more loss and to use their shared grief to forge deeper and more honest bonds with each other. All too often instead there is a shutting down, a closing off of feeling due to the very natural fear of loving and losing again. When this happens, the burden assumed by the remaining child(ren) for restoring the family's well-being can be a tremendously heavy one.

Moira's feelings of guilt for surviving, along with her need to be perfect in order to recompense the family for its loss, are both common reactions in children whose sibling has died and tend to be exaggerated to the degree that the family is unable to confront the pain of a child's death. But in Moira's case the loss she suffered was far greater than even her brother's death accounted for. Her family, her entire support system, in essence died right along with her brother. The agony of his long, slow dying stressed her parents' relationship to the breaking point. Unable to mourn both their son's illness and his death, Moira's parents each sought solace and relief in relationships outside of their marriage. Their divorce from each other and quick remarriages left Moira emotionally abandoned. She tried to stifle her own desperate feelings of loss and grief by focusing on remedying her parents' pain. When her efforts to be perfect in order to save them all and restore all that had been lost inevitably failed, she redoubled her efforts out of her own pain and need . . . and her sense of failure grew.

Alcoholism doesn't cause problems; it just exaggerates the ones that are already there.

There is a very wise saying in the addiction treatment field that "alcoholism doesn't cause problems in a person, a relationship or a family. It just exaggerates the ones that are already there." This axiom applies not only when alcoholism is present but when any profoundly stressful condition occurs in a family and cannot be openly recognized and discussed. It certainly applies to Moira's family and to Moira individually as well. I think it can be safely assumed that her family had difficulty with intimacy and honest communication even before her brother's death. These events simply exaggerated the effects of their inability to be genuine with one another. And I would guess that Moira already had a highly developed need to be "good" before her brother's illness. His death exaggerated this need from a characteristic into a character defect. Her perfectionism was an attempt to control the uncontrollable (in this case, the deterioration of her family). She inevitably carried her fear of uncontrollable situations (and her accompanying attraction to them because of her need to fix them) into every area of her adult life. She brought her repertoire of tools for tackling this old, familiar struggle to her relationships with men, her friendships, her parenting and her career.

Moira's next letter (written in response to my request to use her first letter in this book) begins with a concern, so common to women who love too much, for her daughter's possible predisposition to relationship addiction. When not focused on a partner, relationship addicts will very often turn to a child and do their (to use Moira's word) "fixing" there.

This next letter quickly makes clear that power and control issues have long been themes in Moira's family history and that, under the guise of "helping," she has adopted these approaches to relating to those close to her. Indeed, her letter is a study of a will of iron operating in interpersonal relationships. It also demonstrates that this iron will can be concealed, at least from oneself, by assuming alternately the roles of helper or victim.

Moira is caught in what is by now a very old pattern of relating. It doesn't work, it doesn't bring the happy results she longs for, yet she cannot stop. The pattern itself creates pressure, and under pressure it is all she knows how to do.

> *Dear Robin,*
>
> *My children have just returned home after spending three weeks with their father. They have not seen him since I was divorced from him five years ago. The three-week separation was good for all of us, especially me, since it gave me time to think about what my "too much loving" has done to them. Your request to use my letter has made me think that I need to tell you about this, as it seems that this disease can become generational. My daughter was my firstborn and my redemption for staying alive, becoming married and having a family, when my brother was not allowed to reach his teenage years. She weighed ten and a half pounds and was twenty-four inches long at birth. Every nurse and many doctors I didn't even know stopped by my hospital room to con-*

gratulate me on having this wonderful baby. I was in heaven. I was showing my parents that I could do everything perfectly, even giving birth. She was the perfect baby. She was beautiful. She did everything early and perfectly. Strangers would stop us in the supermarket and on the street to fuss over her. My father was crazy over her, but my mother acted as if she wished she had never been born and wouldn't allow herself to be called "Grandma."

I see now that I would not allow my husband to have very much to do with the baby. In my mind, he wasn't capable of giving her what she needed. Only I could give her the right kind of love and teaching. Poor dear. When she began school, she was immediately put in gifted classes and again was validating my existence. I wasn't excited or even much impressed, because I expected this of her. After all, she was my child. How could it be any other way? When she was in sixth grade, I went back to school to work on my master's degree. She insisted that I convert all of her report card grades into a grade point average so that she could compare them to mine. I, of course, got all A's. She got a couple of B's. Her teacher called me in to school. She didn't think my daughter was as happy as she could be. Something was beginning to go wrong.

Now at fifteen she is no longer the perfect child. She failed two subjects last year. She refuses to believe that she is beautiful even though the boys swarm around her like bees to the hive. I have tried and tried to tell her how great she truly is, but coming from me, she refuses to believe it. Robin, do most of the women like me pass this disease on to their daughters? It's frightening to think that we might. My daughter doesn't seem to love enough, herself included, but I suspect that she, like me, "loves too much." Please tell me if you have found this to be so. I feel so guilty. I love her so much and am frightened for her. She is very much against going to any kind of counseling so I am waiting to see what this school year will bring and whether my new insights into myself will help her too, before insisting that she get help.

Also, I have to tell you about how I picked my husbands, because I have recently realized what I have done. I married my first husband when I was seventeen and he was thirty. My father is very wealthy and I married a man who worked at a gas station. That says a lot right there. I thought I could make this man into something, and of course we both suffered for my trying. My father moved us across three states so that my husband could go to work for him with the idea that he would take over some of my father's businesses. There was no way this would ever happen. My husband would never be good enough, either in my father's eyes or mine. He was uneducated for the task and could not become a male version of me or replace my dead brother, but God, how we pushed him! He buckled under our pressure and became physically abusive to me. The marriage finally disintegrated even though it lasted eleven and a half years.

I was only single for one month when I met my second husband. He had been married before, when he was only eighteen, and had been single for seven years when I met him. He also had a fourteen-year-old son, who had lived with his dad since he was seven. Two people to "fix"! Both my husband and his son were drug addicts, although I didn't realize it at the time we met or else I just didn't want to see it—I don't know which. Cocaine is their drug. My stepson has been in trouble with the law for selling drugs and my husband has not worked in almost a year due to his addiction. Although I stayed married to him for five years I finally knew that I had to get away. This husband, too, was physically abusive and I had to be hospitalized for surgery when he punctured my eardrum by hitting me in the head during an argument. I can see all of this now and I understand why I chose both these men. They were lacking so much and both of them (in my opinion) needed to have someone like me to look after them!

I'm writing all this to you because I know that you understand. My friends would be appalled if they ever guessed that I could be so messed up. They're always

calling me for help. It's so nice to let someone know that
I am far from perfect.

Moira D.

After reading in Moira's second letter that both her present husband and stepson are cocaine addicts, I wrote back urging her to attend Al-Anon meetings* where she might not only better understand chemical dependency and her powerlessness over it but also learn how to let go of her daughter's problems and focus on herself. Her reply, which follows, reveals the extent of her disease both in terms of how unmanageable her life has become and her unwillingness, as yet, to surrender her own self-will in order to receive appropriate help. Although ready to insist that her daughter get help, she wants to believe that she can manage her own problems alone and in secrecy.

Dear Robin,
The thoughts I write to you are thoughts that have rattled around inside of me for so many years that I've thought that I would explode. I've always felt that no one else would really understand what I was feeling until I read WWL2M. *The things we suffer are things I believe only other sufferers can truly understand. I used to believe that it was impossible to love or care too much and just kept thinking that I had to pour out more and more love, never realizing that there was a bottom to the well of my heart and soul and very being. I guess that some of us are unable to look up into the daylight until we've hit the bottom with a thump. I have a close friend who always shakes his head and cynically describes me*

---

*I recommended Al-Anon (for the families and friends of alcoholics) to Moira rather than Nar-Anon (for the families and friends of addicts) or C-Anon (for the families and friends of cocaine addicts) for two reasons. First, it is more likely that Al-Anon is available in her area as it is a much more widespread program than either of the others at present. Second, because Al-Anon has been around so much longer some of its members are likely to have a greater depth of recovery than might be found in newer programs. The principles of recovery are the same in each of these programs and attendance at all of them would be ideal.

as "a do-goodin', long-sufferin' so and so." He appears to me to be quite callous but seems very happy with himself, so who's to say? I would sure like to find the middle ground between the two of us.

The major kink in my recovery at this time relates almost directly to your mention of Al-Anon. My second husband has been wooing me unmercifully. When we separated last March it was with much bitterness on his part and much sadness on mine. I was defeated and exhausted from living with a father-and-son addict team, while trying to protect myself and my children from Will and Billy's addictions. My children, at fifteen and twelve, were at such vulnerable ages and my job as a senior high school teacher is also at risk through my having any connection with drugs or drug users. Both Will and Billy had been physically abusive to me and the children at times. Will did one thousand dollars' worth of damage to my new car with a baseball bat while my son and I were locked inside of it. Right before we separated Will took twenty thousand dollars from a joint savings account for a drug deal. Anyway, I have not seen or heard from him until last month. Billy has been sent to his natural mother in Arizona, as he has been arrested twice on drug charges and was in serious trouble. He has not seen her since he was seven years old. Will is alone now and has been giving me back some of the money and belongings which he took. He's calling and begging almost every day, telling me he's changed, realizes what he's lost etc., etc., etc.—He's killing me! My son's thirteenth birthday is Monday and Will has given me a gift for him, although he always was so jealous of my love for my son and went out of his way to be mean to him. On one occasion we had told the kids they could have no more iced tea after dinner. Will caught him with a big glassful and dumped it over his head. How cruel and humiliating for a child! What mother could continue to let her children live like that? When I begin to feel sorry for Will, these are the images I try to conjure up. I try not to see a sad, lonely man but rather one whose addiction has hurt so many. I've been having a recurring nightmare where I'm at the bottom of a deep hole with

Will. I keep trying to climb up the sides but Will pulls my leg. My fingernails are all broken and bleeding. All the children, even Billy, are at the top crying and telling me I promised to take care of them. Sometimes even the stupid dog is up there with them. Will's at the bottom pulling and telling me how much he loves me. I wake up exhausted. He's still unemployed and still using drugs although he says he hasn't since July. I can hear the cocaine in his voice—I know it well.

The second kink is my first husband. Now that I have separated from Will he is sending child support, which he hasn't done since I remarried. This summer he saw the children for the first time since we were divorced. He calls at least twice a week, talks forever to me and then I have to ask him if he wants to speak to the children. He says, "Yes, but tell them to make it fast. This is long distance." He tells me to consider my marriage to Will a five-year vacation from him and "let's get back together." Both these men are driving me crazy. I'm still dating other guys, but have tried to slow it down somewhat as I'm tired of men right now.

Now to Al-Anon. Robin, my greatest fear is that of not being in control. That's why I don't drink and have never been tempted to try any kind of drug. I realize that Al-Anon is a support group, but I've seen people become so dependent on Alcoholics Anonymous, religious groups, etc. I hate to give up the control of my own life. I sort of feel that way about any kind of therapy right now. I feel that it's like admitting defeat and I don't feel that way yet—defeated. I think I'll feel stronger if I can go it alone for as long as possible. It's funny—I've always had men so I wouldn't be alone, never realizing how very alone I was while with them. Now, I'd truly like to be alone with Moira for a while, just to see how it feels. Sometimes it's great, I feel so strong and capable. Once in a while, I slip a little, but not for too long. In the midst of all this writing I almost forgot to thank you for your advice about my daughter. I'll try to let go, but it's so difficult—flesh of my flesh and all that. I'll keep trying—thanks.

Moira D.

Throughout adulthood, Moira has always been involved with one man or another or, as is presently the case, with more than one at a time. Whether these men were married to someone else, addicted to drugs, violent or merely inadequate, they have always been her central focus. They have provided her with a distraction from her own life with its long-standing pain and guilt. If proof were needed that Moira is very much in the throes of relationship addiction her last letter provides it, containing as it does far more emphasis on all of "them" than on herself. As long as she continues to use her involvements with men to avoid holding still and developing a deeper relationship with herself, she will never heal. Moira needs to leave men and their problems alone until she has fully embraced her *own* life. When she understands, to the core of her being, that one man or another will *never* be the answer to her difficulties, she will no longer be the prisoner of her patterns.

Resistance to involvement in a recovery program has more to do with our illusion of control than with fear of becoming dependent on a source of help.

It is not surprising that someone who has been as dependent on, as addicted to men as Moira has would nevertheless express fear of becoming too dependent on a particular approach to recovery. There is an incredible irony in Moira's refusal to seek help because to do so feels to her like giving up control of her life. A life more patently out of control than hers would be difficult to imagine. However, she is sure that very soon she will be able to control the problem on her own by sheer exertion of will. Every addict can control the addiction *for a while,* but all my experience both professionally and personally tells me that permanent control through self-will is a deadly illusion, and that recovery comes only after surrender. To most people in this culture, self-will denotes strength and determination while surrender implies weakness of character. Up to a point that is the case, but for many of us there come times in life when we must acknowledge that all our personal resources are not sufficient to bring us through our difficulties. We need to be able then to turn to others who understand and to share our secret with them. This is not weakness. This is humility, and through humility we find there is incredible strength available to us. I must predict that Moira, on her own, will not be able to make the massive changes that are necessary in order for her to recover. Without the support of others who have been through the same struggles she faces, she lacks the resources necessary for sustained recovery.

Fear of becoming dependent on a particular source of help is a concern commonly expressed by addicts of all kinds. Alcoholics, for instance, often claim that they are afraid of becoming "addicted" to Alcoholics Anonymous and therefore don't want to involve themselves in that program. But the concept of addiction only applies when life is becoming progressively more unmanageable. If involvement in a Twelve-Step program makes life more manageable rather than less so, that's not addiction, that's recovery. The resistance to involvement often has more to do with unwillingness to surrender our illusion of control and with issues of pride and self-will than with genuine fear of becoming too dependent on a source of help. Another reason for resisting involvement in a program of recovery is that we simply are not yet ready to give up the addiction itself.

———————

The next letter makes a clear case for the generational aspects of the diseases of addiction and co-addiction, and for the attraction that those from addictive and otherwise dysfunctional backgrounds hold for one another. The letter and my response to it indicate what a long and demanding task recovery is.

Dear Robin:

I am in the process of breaking up with my third husband (first and third are alcoholics, second was a married man in whom I lost all interest once we were married, while he in turn became a wife-beater). My current husband is a recovering alcoholic with nearly four years in Alcoholics Anonymous. Our marriage is four and a half years old. He has moved from active alcoholism to active workaholism, and I have responded with the anger, violence and efforts to control that are described in WWL2M. All in all, the relationship has given me little or nothing emotionally, sexually or intellectually other than financial security. Now that you know I qualify as a relationship addict, let me give a quick overview of my childhood:

Born to parents who divorced when I was an infant. Mother abandoned me, father got custody. Paternal grandmother (married to alcoholic second husband) raised me until age of five, when father married a woman who was raised in an alcoholic home. Father and stepmother began abusing me by locking me in the closet in the basement for punishment. This continued for years. Simultaneously, paternal grandfather (grandmother's first husband) began sexual abuse of me that continued for years. My father, who was very violent, also beat me and my five half-brothers and sisters. I had an inordinate amount of responsibility and rarely was allowed to do the things that children and teenagers are allowed to do. My real mother went on to become alcoholic, then was sober in Alcoholics Anonymous seven years but is back out drinking again in recent years. My father remains actively alcoholic, without treatment. The family continues to be very dysfunctional. Children have gone on to marry addicts and alcoholics. There have been suicide attempts, etc. One son is actively alcoholic at twenty-two.

Now the good news. Because of your book and my therapist who I have seen up to three and four days a week and my years in Al-Anon, I am well on my way to recovery.

My two sons (from my first marriage) and I are in the process of leaving my present husband and will move out soon. Neither myself nor my husband have filed for divorce yet but I am moving on with my life. My relationship with him is over. I am not closing the door on the possibility that a new relationship could form out of the ashes of the old, but unless he would consider launching into therapy on his own for at least six months, I would not consider staying with him.

Today I am freer and happier than I've ever been.

Holly L.

Dear Holly,

I want to help you bring the focus back to yourself, where the healing must take place, before *you* are able to relate to another person with closeness and trust. You are angry to the point of violence with your present husband because after becoming sober he submerged himself in his work in what appears to be a conscious, deliberate attempt to avoid you. But Holly, you married him when he was drinking! He couldn't have been available then, either, so this unavailability is nothing new and your rage over his workaholism doesn't quite make sense.

You have come a long way in understanding the contributions your family history has made in determining how your life has developed and who you are today. But you must realize that your present husband is not your main problem. He is simply the man you married because the limited amount of closeness he was capable of (along with the drama and chaos that accompanies active alcoholism) was comfortable for you. Your present self-understanding and awareness of your family history are still not enough to teach you how to be intimate with another human being. None of us can radically change our style of relating in one lifetime. Indeed, we are incredibly blessed if we can stretch to even a small degree our ability to trust, to be close in an honest, nonmanipulative way and to simply and graciously accept another's caring for us. You are demanding something from your husband that you probably wouldn't be able to handle right now if you got it.

A very wise friend of mine, an Episcopal priest, told me once that when people asked him if he believed in divorce he answered, "Sometimes people need to be apart. But you should not separate until you have learned the lesson that the relationship is trying to teach you. If you don't learn the lesson you will have to face it again in the next relationship and perhaps again in the one after that." Sometimes, Holly, after the lesson is learned we realize that whether we stay or whether we leave hasn't been the real issue after all. Instead, we have faced a much simpler and yet far more difficult task— learning how to hold still and live with ourself and with another human being in all our separate and shared imperfections.

When you've perfected holding still, the staying or the leaving will take care of itself.

As long as you are demanding more attention from your present husband than he is capable of giving, he will naturally withdraw even further in self-defense, fear and anger. That driving, compelling need to do *some-thing*—to effect some change in another person—is one of the most destructive elements in co-addiction. Rather than acting on that need to change someone else you can learn to quietly hold still with your own anxiety or anger or frustration or desperation or whatever emotion is gripping you. Follow it to its source in *you*. Allow the emotion to happen, even welcome it if you possibly can, feel it, experience it, explore it and let it teach you about yourself, your history and your pain. Because, Holly, *no* relationship can save you from the pain of your history. No partner can provide you with enough distraction or enough love to keep it covered up. You must face it, go into it, accept it and allow your Higher Power to help you heal from it and forgive it and go on with your life.

Then you'll be learning the lesson my friend was talking about.

When you've perfected holding still, if you can call on all you've learned in Al-Anon and all you've learned in therapy to bless your husband and accept him *exactly* as he is, without anger or resentment, without wanting to punish him or change him, without taking what he does and doesn't do personally, you will have truly deepened your soul and received the gift this relationship has been trying to give you. After that, the staying or the leaving will take care of itself, I promise you.

Relationship addiction is most often practiced with a spouse or lover. Sometimes the addict believes she has recovered because the relationship with the person on whom she focused addictively is now over. But, as the next letter demonstrates, such a change in circumstances in itself rarely constitutes recovery.

Dear Ms. Norwood,

I just purchased a copy of WWL2M *and I have had to stop reading it at work because my cries of "Oh, my God!" are disturbing my boss. For twenty years I have been married to a man who, when not actively drinking, is on a dry drunk—angry, critical and full of mood swings.*

I used to compare my husband to a wild eagle that was trapped in a cage and beating his wings against the bars. I was a plump little tame duck content in the cage. Every so often the eagle would break free of the cage; the duck would fly with him and be happy. But she was always content to return to the cage. The eagle would return too, but in a short while, he would be beating his wings against the cage again.

Two months ago my husband ran away with my ex-best friend. He's out there somewhere living in a fantasy with her. When he left, my first thought was, "If he doesn't want me, who will?" Sound familiar? I was thirty-five pounds overweight, which he claimed never bothered him, yet he told friends he wished I would slim down. Throughout our marriage I have always felt he was more intelligent, more attractive, more everything than I, and that I was lucky to have him. How could I exist without him?

Two years ago, I was hired for a job I love where I was considered smart, innovative and resourceful. I began to sing and act in local theater productions too, to very positive reviews. I began writing again, but at home I was still seen as stupid, crass and boring. Our two older children, then teenagers, blamed me for all their problems. I was crazy, didn't I know that? How could I exist in the outer world when I was crazy?

Last fall our fifteen-year-old daughter ran away from home for two days. She was using alcohol and pills heavily. I pulled my attention away from my husband and threw all my support into helping her. His attitude was that we should throw her into the streets. He didn't want to handle any of the problems. My reply was, "She is our child. I will not throw her away!" Through counseling, she began to straighten out while my relationship with my husband deteriorated. I could see him drawing closer and closer to my ex-friend, but I was trying to save my daughter, and had nothing to give to him.

There was nothing I could do. In twenty years, he has let me be close to him six times, once every three or four years. This is not much shared love and understanding. For ten years I have gone to counseling, trying to find what I was doing wrong, how I could change to make things better. After all, wasn't it all my fault?

When he left, a friend showed me some information about chemical dependency and how it affects families. Suddenly, pieces began to fit, pieces I have been searching for throughout all these twenty years! I have begun going to Al-Anon and that has helped immensely.

🌿 *If my husband doesn't want me, someone else will. I'm not dumb, I'm not ugly, and I do have something to offer. I have lost twenty-five pounds through this, and am continuing to exercise and diet. Food, especially sugary food, is no longer so important to me. I'm continuing with my acting and singing. I work my program, and am surviving without him.*

My daughter, however, is back on drugs and alcohol and is becoming violent. She is spiraling downward and I am seeing the same pattern in her as in my husband. Monday I made the decision to place her in a six-week alcohol and drug rehabilitation center for teens. Tonight she will be confronted with the decision. She is living with a counselor friend of mine for the time being. She has run away twice in the past week, and we agreed that if she was unhappy at home, an agreeable place should be found for her to stay for a while. If she runs away tonight, there is not too much I can do except call the police. I know if she goes to treatment she will stay. She is really crying for help.

A month or so ago, I would have been living in total panic, wondering what I had done wrong to this child to have made her act this way. I'm learning the hard way to let go, and to survive these crises with reasonable sanity. I'm getting better, thank God.

I don't know what will happen in the future for me, but for now, I am more at peace with myself than I have ever been before. I like myself. I'm okay. I don't have to depend on my husband to survive. Thank you for your book. It has opened my eyes, and helped me to find the elusive pieces of myself.

Willow D.

Dear Willow,

While I want to applaud the progress you've made in understanding yourself and recognizing your family situation, I also want to offer a warning. With an appreciation of the power of relationship addiction, which in your case is of the co-alcoholic variety, it becomes easy to see why you were not able to remove your focus from your husband until you could switch it to your daughter.

Now that your husband is out of the house the tendency to concentrate on your daughter will become all the more compelling. So often when the relationship addict's partner is out of the picture there is the compulsion to go to work on the next closest person. Often this means that one or more of the children now receive the brunt of the relationship addict's attention. When the relationship addict is a co-alcoholic and the alcoholic partner is no longer present but an alcoholic offspring is, the need to help, manage and control that offspring's life *appears* to be a perfectly justified effort rather than the continuation of the disease process that it really is.

People do not stop abusing alcohol and other drugs in order to make other people happy or comfortable, whether these others are their husbands or wives or parents or children. If they stop, it is because the consequences of their addiction have become intolerable to them.

At the risk of drawing down upon myself the wrath of parents everywhere who are thus dedicated, I want to say to you that your first job is not to find the solutions for your teenage daughter. Your job is to take care of yourself. The better job you do of taking care of yourself and not allowing your life to be made unmanageable by your daughter's behavior, the greater favor you will be doing her as well as yourself.

It is a very high form of love to allow someone for whom we care deeply to suffer the natural consequences of his or her behavior and thus to have the opportunity to learn the particular lessons that behavior will teach. When, out of our fear and guilt, we short-circuit those consequences and therefore those lessons, it is more for our own sake than for the ultimate sake of our loved one. When we feel responsible and we cannot bear our guilt or others' disapproval, we need help *in managing our own uncomfortable feelings,* not help in managing someone else's life. Basically, we need to become able to sort out what is our problem and what is someone else's. I urge you to leave the responsibility of your daughter's abuse of alcohol and drugs where it belongs—with her.

When you attempt to force a solution to her problem you are, as a co-alcoholic, practicing your disease. Your own recovery is still so new and you have so much to learn about not managing and controlling those around you.

People do not stop abusing alcohol and other drugs in order to make other people happy.

Over and over again I've watched teenagers and young adults who were trying to take responsibility for their lives and recover from addiction (the first is necessary to the second) actually *beg* their parents not to continue to rescue them or bail them out or give them money or a place to come home to or *find them help,* but rather to let them make it on their own. And over and over I've heard these parents tell their children that this help was their parental duty and besides they couldn't bear to watch them suffer, that even if it were in the child's ultimate best interests, they could not stop "helping." I've also heard both recovering compulsive eaters and recovering alcoholic/addicts say, "My parents spent more than a million dollars trying to get me well. It wasn't until they finally stopped trying to fix me that *I* decided to do something about my life." The best rule of thumb for dealing with addicts is to scrupulously avoid doing anything for them that they could do for themselves *if they chose.*

In many ways we relationship addicts are actually very dangerous people, because we *need* to have someone else be our project, our focus, our reason for being, our distraction from ourselves. Our great attraction to another's dependency or inadequacy causes us to romanticize addiction rather than see it as the disease it is. (Your comparison of your husband to a "wild eagle" is an example of this.) We can actually sabotage the development of self-respect and growth in others when we either take too much responsibility for bringing it about or pay too close attention as it unfolds. Willow, do your daughter a great, great service of love by taking your focus off her and her recovery and putting it on yourself.

———————

Many people yearn to be the best at something, to be distinguishable in at least one noteworthy way from everyone else on the planet. It is a common desire, though not necessarily one that always leads to the greatest peace of mind. For instance, when relationship addicts experience this longing to be different, to be special, it may evolve into an overidentification with the most negative aspects of both their history and their disease. The conviction (and telling the stories to support it) that one has had the *saddest* childhood or the most *dangerous* lovers or the most *shocking* experiences can become a person's chief way of feeling important and getting attention from others. Once this gambit has been developed, giving it up and trading it in for the tranquility and composure of recovery can feel uncomfortably like settling down to obscure mediocrity. But if one is to recover, giving it up eventually becomes absolutely necessary, because inherent in such an overdramatized identity is either self-pity or self-aggrandizement or both; it is a resolute determination to win the prize in the "Best Worst" category of life. Endeavoring to achieve such a goal is an empty pursuit indeed when compared to the rewards of putting one's life in perspective, accepting the past, forgiving it, learning from it and going forward with greater wisdom.

The following letter contains a definite bid for the "Best Worst" award and reveals Hedy's relish for her costarring role in the recurring dramas and melodramas that, strung together, have made up her life. In the second half of her letter she is beginning to test the possibility of living a calmer, saner existence. Quite a bit of her pride may have to be relinquished if she is to truly make the transition.

Dear Robin,

Pardon the informality of this letter, but you may never see this letter if I have to drag out the typewriter!

I read your book as though I was an avid baseball player at Yankee Stadium. I read it everywhere and told so many men and women about it!

I am a woman who has loved (and maybe still loves) too much. I've been through nine years of therapy—enough to pay for my therapist's baby's college education. I gave it all one hundred and ten percent and begged for communication, feedback and encouragement from others but got cruel discouragement instead. Now I can put it all together. Before now I was ready for a big leap, but I wasn't sure how to make it or really what actually was my problem.

Of course, my stories and anecdotes could have been the high point of shock to your readers. I have dated and slept with the most incredible variety of men. They came from every ethnic background, age group and profession imaginable. Once in a while there was a nice guy thrown in; those were the ones I had no respect for. They seemed weak.

So now that I'm thirty-six years old, I've decided that it's time to pull it together. I've looked at my life as I read your book and thought it amazing that I've been able to obtain a license as a physical therapist, a degree in dance and theater, two teaching certificates and be a certified hypnotist, a certified massage therapist, and hold down a full-time job in a hospital. I'm also very concerned about my health and exercise on a daily basis. I also have a million friends!

As I read your book, phrases such as, "I need you to accomplish my dream," and "You've really let me down," came to mind from my situations with men. The manipulations of these men are now apparent to me. (It's difficult for me to admit to my manipulations!) In looking at my own childhood I see how my parents and I have danced the same dance. They saw my sister as the important one and I was conceived in order to provide her with a playmate. My mother has told me how disap-

*pointed she was when I didn't live up to their expecta-
tions in this area.*

*As you say, families don't change! My parents still
expect me to pay for the long-distance calls to arrange
for six people to stay in my one-bedroom condo for ten
days. Why not? I've done it before. Now it's expected! I
think that those of us described in your book are often
encouraged by society, family and friends to continue
our cycle.*

*My life is exciting (like a roller coaster—people love
to visit and watch it)—always a different lover, a different restaurant or event—always that "high." People are
amazed that I can stay up all night and work the next
day with incredible energy, or quit my job on the East
Coast to marry a West Coast bookie twenty-nine years
my senior who I didn't even know. I used to tell these
stories with humor and pride. Everyone marveled at me.*

*When I began reading your book I was dating a
"nice guy" (maybe) and another man I described as
"charismatic." The nice guy happened to be an osteopath with a lot of kindness and patience but with whom
I feel no fireworks. Mr. Charisma was absolutely flattering in such a sincere(?) way. He was so romantic that
when he banged on my door at three a.m., I would
always have time to talk* and *make love. As time went
on, Mr. Charisma was always around when he was
hungry, complimenting me on my cooking, of course. (I
just know he meant it!) Then he'd only show up in the
middle of the night. Who else would let him in? And
when his headlights were out for two weeks, he called
telling me to pick him up and bring him to my place. (Of
course, it was* only *one a.m.) He was a gifted songwriter
who only went out to Hollywood to work for a weekend
now and then in order to earn money for rent and for
cocaine.*

*I kept slighting the osteopath, doing things like
checking my answering machine from his house. If Mr.
Charisma even called to demand where I was, I'd run
home and sit by the phone.*

When I finished two-thirds of your book, after forc-

ing myself to stay home nights and read, I realized whatever needs to be done must be done by me.

Robin, you know how hard it is!

Some of the techniques I've used may help some of your patients. I started asking small favors of Mr. Charisma. For example, a collect *long-distance call because I needed him to pick something up for me or come give me a ride or whatever. I managed to leave my answering machine on in order to screen calls. Then I spoke to him only by phone for two weeks. Then I wanted to see him to have some fun and I called him for a specific event, making sure I had an appointment two hours later. (We met in public.) All these maneuvers gave me distance from him without causing me to feel that I'd closed the door on the relationship completely. But as I was able to distance myself, I was changing my perceptions of him, remembering the tennis lessons he never gave, the sailing we never did, the bicycle rides we never took. I began asking myself what I was getting. The answer? Sex and flattery. I pictured his brain smoked out and coked out, so when he would talk to me, I'd tell myself how dumb it really sounded. He tended to be a little bald, so I focused in on that shiny head (silently), and his diet was not sound, so his soft body became the Pillsbury Dough Boy's. When I spoke of him, I called him "The Charismatic Jerk."*

He called the other night—two-thirty a.m., three a.m., three-thirty a.m., four a.m., four-thirty a.m. and five a.m., with such demanding messages, I was relieved to be justified (although justification wasn't necessary) to call it quits. I actually hesitated over whether or not to pick up the phone, saying to myself, "What will he think of me if I don't?!" (Recovery is a slow process!)

There will always be a "charismatic jerk." The hardest thing is to stick with the nice guy. I find myself saying, "Is this all there is?" And then the other little voice says, "What do you expect? This nice man is an ordinary human being. You've taken a great step, now stay with it." My osteopath friend may not be "it" for me but he's good practice!

When I find myself panicking, I identify it and ask myself what I want. I try to hold still to see if the panic will dissipate. It always does.

I'm putting my energies into my work now. I've always said that if I spent as much time on my work as I did on my relationships, I'd be famous! People are incredibly drawn to me. I'm blessed with lots of social and professional friends and contacts, so I can develop in the directions I want to pursue.

I'm willing to make decisions (a big risk) and realize I know what's best for me. It's fun to observe the reactions and the nonverbal behavior when I do. What a sense of power! Centered and calm power. It feels wonderful!

Hedy P.

Dear Hedy,

The key to the life patterns described in your letter is contained in the paragraph about your relationship to your parents and your sister. In reading that I understood everything else, because in every area you describe— your work, your friendships, your dating and marriage— I hear a compulsive striving to overcome the identity given you by your family. Their persistence in defining you as some kind of auxiliary to your sister and their corresponding inability to recognize you as a separate, distinct, unique and valued person in your own right must still carry a very painful sting, since you go to such extreme lengths both to prove yourself likable, accomplished, interesting and attractive and to distract yourself from what I would guess is a fear that their assessment is correct. At the end of your letter you mention the panic that overtakes you when you're not frantically engaged in one pursuit or another. You seem to be gearing up for a bout of workaholism to provide the distraction that, up to now, the drama of your love life has created. You may change from one compulsive pursuit to another but you will not *recover* from being compulsive until you can find the courage to focus on yourself rather than a man (exciting *or* boring!) or a new kind of work, or another degree or certificate, or a party, or a social event, or a family get-together, or whatever other distraction you can find.

You may need help to hold still like this, help from people to whom you will have to admit that you cannot do it alone. I hope you can find the courage that this kind of surrender on your part will require, courage to admit that your life is not as exciting and wonderful as you have tried to make it. Also, if you are to recover, you must face and accept the fact that you may never be as special in your family's eyes as you would like to be. Then you need to stop taking their assessment so personally. Their perception of you says much more about who they are than who you are. When you realize this, you may be able to let go of trying so hard to win their attention and approval and love. After all, by now it isn't *their* lack of appreciation and acceptance that is driving you to frantic lengths and frenzied exploits but your own. You can change this, but it will require great humility to do so since your self-rejection is so carefully masked by activity and accomplishment.

If what we have been doing all along really worked, we wouldn't need to recover, would we?

I cannot imagine a greater challenge to someone of your personality structure than the cultivation of humility. Action and power have been your favored defenses against your pain, and humility embodies their opposite: surrender, letting go and acceptance of the fact that none of us has all the answers or resources and we must therefore wait and be guided by Something greater than ourselves.

For so many of us, Hedy, the key to our recovery is in learning to do the opposite of what we've always done. Frightening as that may be, if what we have been doing all along really worked, we wouldn't need to recover, would we?

———

Dear Ms. Norwood,

I have spent the better part of thirty years actively trying to find out what this life of mine was all about and why it was always such a mess. My library consists mainly of self-help books. My courses in college were almost all in sociology and psychology. I have been involved with various kinds of groups and have had a lot of individual therapy, but nothing has ever really hit the nail on the head or explained me to myself.

My two ex-husbands could not have been more dissimilar, or so I thought. One was kind, gentle, fun-loving, a self-starter with projects and interests inside and outside the home. He was loved and respected as a good, decent person. My second husband was a loner who had few friends, no hobbies or projects, but who loved to have me all to himself. He didn't want me to be out of his sight and resented my having people around me. He was a comedian at times with a marvelous sense of humor.

Why the attraction to these two men who were as different as night and day? And why did both marriages burn out and end unhappily? I didn't think there was a common denominator until I read WWL2M and then suddenly there it was! Lack of real availability. They were both preoccupied—one with outside interests and the other with self-obsession, but with both of them I took a back seat. It was exactly the same when I was growing up! It was what I was used to.

I grew up with a father who was preoccupied and unavailable. He was a physician and a drug addict and alcoholic as well. His character and health deteriorated slowly until after being bedridden for two years he died of a stroke. Prior to his death my mother did everything for him, accepting no help and finally developing a heart condition as a result of her martyrdom.

I watched my mother suffer when I was growing up. She said she loved him although I could never understand why, since he was exceptionally mean to her and to my older brother and myself. She told us kids that it came as a shock to her when my father told her outright that he no longer loved her. She had failed to see the danger signals, or had chosen to ignore them. She told us that she had stayed with him because of us kids. My brother was grateful but I thought it was insane. I knew I would have been far better off with him out of my life. Instead, through watching them, I was taught how to suffer and even learned how to put my mother's facial expressions on my own face. I saw *myself doing it. By the time I was in high school I had the whole act down pat. In my own right I was sad, but I took on* her *sadness as well. I told myself that I loved her and then I tried to make her into the kind of mother I wanted her to be. I made myself react to her as though she* was *that fictitious person I'd invented and it seemed to work. I felt a little better.*

Both my mother and my father were very strict without knowing why. They would automatically say no to everything and anything. They had baseless fears and reacted to them, not to who I was or what I was all about. I never was asked how life was for me. I don't remember ever being asked a question of a personal nature from either of them. They acted together upon assumptions and most of the assumptions were negative. They agreed on nothing else. They fought silently and assumed my brother and I could not be affected. If, now and then, their rage would bubble to the surface it would quickly get squelched. Nice people did not fight like cats and dogs. To do so was common, and they were not common.

As we were growing up my brother and I had a very hostile relationship and earnestly tried to harm each other, feeling pleased when the other got hurt or was ill. My brother, three years older than I, never stood up to Dad and I hated him for that. He also behaved stupidly. He would speak at the wrong times and trigger my father's temper. I, at least, knew when to shut my mouth, so I learned to have no respect for my brother. But, when I married my first husband, he and my brother got along well, so I began to learn to enjoy my brother a little bit too.

I married the only man of whom my father really approved. I knew at the time that it was my way of getting closer to the father who had always ignored me or had made life intolerable in one way or another.

My marriage to my first husband began to deteriorate almost as soon as it started. When the children came along I saw that my husband was not available to them either and I began to get nervous. I didn't realize that history was repeating itself. I just knew it felt familiar, too familiar. I felt trapped in the marriage because of the two small children and as a result found myself becoming closer to my mother. Even though she was a great deal older than I, we had in common that we were both married and both had children. We shared silently that we were both unhappy women.

I began to go out after the children were older. I encountered a man on whom I had had a crush many years before. He was unavailable due to a marriage which he always complained about. He had two children, older by far than mine were, and a drug addicted wife whom he had first started on diet pills. Her habit progressed to forged prescriptions for amphetamines and then on to alcohol abuse. He and I began to have a serious relationship. He paid a great deal of attention to me and since I had not had any of that, I felt like I was on cloud nine. He, in turn, felt good with me because I was not a substance abuser and he could rely on me for everything. He eventually became my second husband. I was everything he had never had and he was everything I had never had. It seemed at first like a marriage made in heaven. Well, maybe not exactly. There were hints of the problems to come, but I was sure they could be managed because so much was good in the relationship. I was wrong! I began to drink to get some of the pressures off until one day he told me point-blank he would leave me and never look back if I was going to be a drunk like his first wife. I knew he meant it. I stopped drinking. I kept my promise. I asked him in turn to get a grip on his anger and to look at his coldness, but he never kept his end of the bargain. Things went from bad to worse.

While all this was going on, I was going for counseling, and I was trying to get him to go as well. He joined me for only a few disruptive sessions. I couldn't salvage this marriage by myself, but I made the effort because I loved him so much. The pain of this relationship was like no other pain in the world. It nearly crushed me. Twice I went to a lawyer and began divorce proceedings. Twice I pulled back and went on. I was not convinced it couldn't be saved, and I was trying to scare him into acknowledging the reality of what was happening to us, thinking the marriage was as important to him as it was to me. Wrong again!

I began to get MS-like symptoms. After every possible test, two doctors said I had multiple sclerosis while two other doctors said I didn't. But I could tell that no one really knew what was wrong with me except that I was a very sick woman.

I still have the symptoms. I am divorcing my second husband after years and years of trying. I am happier now than at any time in my life in spite of all the incredible unknowns—money? The house which I had put in his name, too? The car? On and on and on. I finally reached a point in my life when I had been battered emotionally for THE LAST TIME. I didn't care if I wound up being a bag lady. I wanted to be free of all the sadness, all the pain and everything and everyone who had gone along with it. I had said all this before. This time I meant it from my very core. It is still this way today.

I'm sending this letter to you, mistakes and all, because I think you will want to have it no matter what.

Leslie S.

Dear Leslie,

A family in which both parents are sick, as yours were (one through his progressively worsening alcohol addiction and the other through her increasingly desperate and ineffective efforts to control him), produces a child whose needs for attention, affection and emotional security have been almost wholly neglected. That child almost inevitably develops into an adult who is virtually insatiable in her need for reassurance that she is loved. But at the same time she is incapable of trusting another's willingness and ability to love her. This condition, along with her probable inability to choose a healthy partner, makes for some predictable dynamics when she enters into marriage. Soon the early glow of hope that everything is going to be all right, every need is going to be met and every wound from childhood healed begins to fade. That pit of emptiness is back, demanding to be filled. She feels a gnawing sense of betrayal because her marriage, her partner, cannot make her feel safe and lovable. Eventually, her partner is no longer flattered by her constant need for his company. What he at first perceived as her depth of love and attraction for him now feels like the all-engulfing need that it is, framed by the lack of trust that darkly tints her perception of their every contact.

We all tend to choose as partners those people who are capable of the same level of intimacy as we are. Thus both partners in a marriage often share similar backgrounds that either well prepared or ill prepared each of them for sustained closeness and commitment with another person. Indeed, partners who have been damaged in childhood find full commitment or an occasion of true intimacy far from welcome; for them, such situations seem claustrophobic and intensely threatening. An atmosphere of sustained tension and frequent battles of opposing wills soon dispels the threat of unfamiliar, unwelcome closeness. Now the marriage, which was supposed to be the solution to old problems and old pain, seems to both partners to have become the biggest problem of all.

The battle lines are drawn and the opposing strategies are chosen. One participant may choose the role of pursuer, hungrily and then angrily chasing after the other who has, in turn, become the distancer, fleeing from the perceived threat of engulfment. Should a crisis be reached and a breakup appear to be inevitable, this pair may switch roles, the distancer now pursuing the partner who, at least temporarily, has given up the chase in despair. This switching of roles accounts for many reconciliations, which are based not on a profound change in either partner's willingness or ability to give and receive love but simply on a temporarily reassuring change of battle tactics. Such reversals still serve ultimately to maintain the status quo of an absence of true intimacy.

Should the discouraged former pursuer, now pursued, find her resolve to leave undermined by the cajoling attention of her previously unavailable partner and recommit herself to the relationship, the tables will be turned again fairly quickly. Soon they each will resume their old, more familiar roles and behaviors, those which guarantee that their capacity for trusting each other and relating intimately will not be stretched unbearably.

In your first marriage it appears that you were the pursuer while in your second you were, at least in the beginning, pursued. I would guess that your second husband was a co-alcoholic in his family of origin, as you were. The biggest clue is the fact that he married one woman who developed a chemical dependency and next chose a partner whose drinking became a problem to him. Incidentally, whenever someone stops using a drug to placate another, as you did when you stopped your drinking to keep him from leaving, that person feels enormous resentment. The partner who has given up the drug expects the one who demanded sobriety to "make it worth it." Your letter indicates that your second husband was never able to adequately recompense you for not drinking.

The less we need *from a partner, the more able we are to choose someone who isn't so needy himself.*

When you describe your attempts to get from each husband the caring and attention you craved, and how seriously ill you finally became in the process, you reflect a basic underlying assumption that each man *could* have given you what you wanted and needed if only he'd cared enough about you to make the effort. I want to suggest that this premise is faulty, that each man gave as much as he could and when that wasn't enough each withdrew both out of fear of being overwhelmed and anger at feeling inadequate. It's as though someone in your position were in need of water, picked up a bucket, went to the well marked "husband" and lowered her bucket down. When she pulled it back up and found that the bucket wasn't filled, she felt hurt and angry and kept lowering the bucket down over and over again, each time spilling a little out and drawing up less and less water. Feeling desperate, she may have turned to another well marked "family," but with similar results—little or no water produced growing hurt, anger and resentment. Meantime, there are perhaps a dozen other wells around from which she could, if she chose, get various amounts of water so that she would have enough to satisfy her needs. Her mistake is in insisting *that a particular well provide her with her total supply.*

Your family of origin and then each of your husbands could only give a small portion of what you wanted and needed. Because of their own lack, their own emptiness, they could not fully supply you. But as adults each of us has a responsibility for taking care of ourselves and making sure our needs are met. There are many sources to which we can turn to supply our needs if we are willing to let go of self-will and self-pity; that is, if we are not too determined to extract all our supply from a given source.

One of the primary features of relationship addiction is tremendous dependency, often but not always masked by apparent strength. The dependency is extreme because so many unmet needs have been brought forward from childhood. Those of us who are relationship addicts will never be able to forge a healthy partnership until we become willing to approach more than one appropriate supply for our needs. We need other wholesome sources such as friends, interests, a spiritual practice, etc., to validate us, support us, and fill our emptiness and heal our dependency. If we neglect to take responsibility for meeting our needs in this way, we will find ourselves again and again struggling with relationships in which we either present our (pseudo) strength and choose a man who presents his need or we present our need and choose a man who presents apparent strength. But that "strong" man is very likely to be another dependent person like ourselves, pretending to have strength enough to support the burden of our need, yet actually masking equally deep dependency needs of his own.

As you leave this second marriage behind, I suspect that you are turning to friends for some of your needs for affection and that you are expanding your horizons to make sure that you include in your life opportunities for creative expression and positive interaction with others. This expansion of your circle of supply will serve you well in any future relationship. It will help you to see a possible future partner as he is, with all his strengths *and* weaknesses. You will not be so blinded by your own need when the two of you come together because your own need won't be so great. The likelihood of some sort of blind bonding between the two of you is greatly reduced when you take good care of yourself. The more we heal our own damage and the less we *need* from a partner, the more able we are to choose someone who isn't so damaged or needy himself. It then becomes possible for us to be both truly happy from within and grateful for that which we are freely given.

The next two letters should be read together in order to understand the degree of self-will usually operating in a relationship-addicted woman. It is not difficult to read between the lines and see the anger and contempt toward men that Wynne brings to her adult "love" relationships. As her first letter indicates, these feelings have their roots in the past. Her bitterness toward her father must be healed in order for her ever to know a relationship with a man that doesn't degenerate into a contest of wills.

Although these parts are edited out, in her second letter Wynne also writes in great detail about books (including specific page numbers) which she tells me I should recommend, sends printed material she thinks I should use in the preface of my next book (along with a name and address where she suggests I "verify the quote" she has provided). She advises me to appear on a specific television program and finally offers to proofread my writing! Wynne's need to control others under the guise of being helpful is very typical of the relationship addict.

Ms. Robin Norwood,

I am not the product of an alcoholic home but I am the daughter of a selfish man/child who competed with me, and I with him, for my mother's attention. Because of his accusations that I caused my mother's illness I tried even harder to win his approval and love. All of the emotional involvements since have been toward unattainable men. Of my own choice I just "Dear Johned" a going nowhere relationship after a year-and-a-half struggle. I was in love with an idea but he was not reciprocating or validating my giving and my love. God, I am torn. I know I did right, but I really wonder if I would know how to react to a loving and caring man. I find that type weak and boring, not a challenge.

Wynne F.

Dear Robin,

It has been almost a year since I first wrote to you. I continue to recommend your book and I continue to reread my copy.

For an update of my progress. After programming for a perfect mate for twenty-one days, the "rattlesnake" with whom I've been involved called me and I did get together with him, but I saw him differently. He is still a hard number to get over. He floats in, stirs up the hormones and disappears again. Meanwhile my programming resulted in the reappearance of a very nice man in my life. I had known him about three years, just as a friend. He really possesses all the qualities I have been looking for (and have been programming for) but I had just brushed him off as another ordinary man, nice but boring, not the challenge I've always liked and certainly not a man I lusted for. He is a good man, good to me and good for me and although my intellectual, rational mind knows this, my emotional sexual/chemical self still lusts for the "rattlesnake."

I know I need to reprogram certain ideas in my mind in order to release the "rattlesnake." It is not that I want him. I just want him to want me. (The same was true of my relationship with my ex-husband years ago.) It hurts my ego that he did not come back after the Dear John letter and say, "You are a great gal, and I want you, need you, love you!" Then I could say, "Sorry." So you see the challenge is to my ego.

Unfortunately, the "rattlesnake" gets into my head and into my bed, figuratively, when I am with the nice man.

Science of Mind or Mind Control advises us to watch what we program or ask for because we will get it. Because the "rattlesnake" did not want me I asked God for a man who wanted me more than I wanted him. The nice man fits that bill, therefore I am going to do another twenty-one-day program and ask that the relationship be equally and mutually one of caring and loving. I need to release the "rattlesnake" and grow to love and lust for the nice man.

I have lived through trying to win the acceptance and approval of at least three men in my life . . . therefore I know of what you write! I have benefited and grown!

Wynne F.

Dear Wynne,

I want to address two points your letters bring up. One I would term "self-will versus God's will" and the second has to do with the hostile components of lust and seductiveness.

Let's begin with the second point. You obviously do not like the man you refer to as the "rattlesnake" although you claim to have loved him and to still find him very attractive sexually, while you feel little or no sexual attraction for the nice man. This is a very common phenomenon among relationship addicted women, and it is not at all difficult to understand if you let go of the mistaken idea that your high degree of sexual attraction or lust has, or ever did have, anything to do with love. Your sexual feelings are probably much closer in principle to the excitement a hunter feels when closing in on the animal being pursued than to anything actually related to love, which is a deep and tender acceptance of and caring for another person. There is a predatory element in the sexual chase, a desire to subjugate another person through one's own desirability. It is a highly charged struggle for dominance, control and, of course, ultimately victory.

There is a predatory element in the sexual chase, a desire to subjugate another person through one's own desirability.

Learning to interact sexually with another person in an intimate, rather than competitive and essentially hostile way, is a tremendous piece of work for the relationship addicted woman. It only becomes possible *after* a great deal of recovery has been achieved, at which time dramatic, difficult relationships are no longer appealing. When our primary aim becomes protecting our own serenity and well-being—rather than finding the right man—then and only then are we able to begin to choose companions with whom we can be friendly and who can also care about us in a wholesome way. Sexual involvement for those who are achieving recovery is based on the tenderness of truly caring about another human being and the excitement of shared intimacy rather than on the struggle to make a conquest of an impossible lover.

Now to the first point, self-will versus God's will. It seems evident from your letter that you are involved with what is often referred to as "New Thought," a religious/philosophical orientation that emphasizes among other things the use of affirmations to produce the desired results in one's life. What follows is, of course, only my opinion, but I want to share it with you.

I wholeheartedly believe in and advocate the use of affirmations to bring into manifestation more positive conditions (for example, "Each day I grow more serene"), and the use of denials to cancel out adverse conditions (for example, "I no longer suffer"). I think, however, that we make a great mistake when we put our order in to our Higher Power for a specific result, whether we are asking for a man to appear and be our partner or whether we desire that a certain event take place or that we receive a certain material thing. Since we can never know as well as that Higher Power does what truly is for our highest good we may, with our very specific affirmations (or to use your word, "programming"), actually limit our own growth and our own good. Our affirmations should always be invitations for spiritual principles to guide us rather than self-willed demands for this or that specific thing, event or person. For instance, by programming for another man to be in your life you may actually be letting yourself in for many more months or years of struggle in a relationship, time you could better spend healing instead.

Most of the women I have worked with who have led lives similar to yours could not ever hope to have a wholesome relationship with any man until they spent enough time working toward greater understanding and acceptance of themselves and of all the others who had already been in their lives. They needed to learn to live without having their focus be on a man as either their problem or their solution. They needed to bless and forgive and, at least in their hearts, *ask forgiveness from* all the men (and the women, too) with whom they had ever struggled and fought in the past.

This is very demanding spiritual work. It requires a steady focus on our spiritual path, humility and complete willingness to surrender old and often dearly held anger and self-righteousness. It often takes months, even years of patient work. And yet, when the willingness is finally truly genuine, there is frequently a great breakthrough of understanding and insight as the pain of the past drops away. Sometimes these breakthroughs happen all at once, sometimes in steps or stages. Sometimes they are painful stretchings of the soul and sometimes they bring pure joy. But there is always a sense of letting go of something hard and frozen and, heretofore, immovable— something incredibly old and immeasurably deep. I believe that through this work of forgiveness we learn the lesson for which our soul has chosen this lifetime.

Your anger with your father is old and deep and bitter, and until you choose to heal that relationship your dealings with men will to some extent always be tainted by your unhealthy relationship with him. But deciding to heal your relationship with him doesn't mean that you go to your father and tell him how terrible he's been to you in hopes that he will be sorry and apologize. To do so is another exercise in self-will and puts *you* and your well-being at risk because you *need* him to respond to you in a certain way. The more any of us need a specific reaction from another person, the more dependent we are on that individual, and yet the more likely we are to encounter only his defenses. If, in order to protect himself, your father gets angry or tells you that you're crazy or denies everything you're saying or tells you he doesn't remember it that way at all, you will probably respond in your most practiced and familiar way. If your tendency in the face of frustration is to become angry, then under these conditions you will be furious. If you have a penchant for depression you may become suicidal when your father doesn't react as you want him to. If you deal with being thwarted by feeling hurt you will probably dive into self-pity. If it is your style to get even you may find yourself calling him every name you can think of. Obviously, you cannot afford to stake your serenity on his reaction. You must learn not to need anything from him.

What is required then is that you do your spiritual homework and pray daily to be able to forgive your father *completely* for everything he ever did or didn't do that hurt you or made you angry. As you work at this you may find more unhappy memories coming back to you through dreams or in your waking hours. It is as though, when it hears our prayers, the psyche becomes willing to cooperate with our efforts at housecleaning and brings forth the buried pain of the past so that it can be consciously released. I repeat: This is hard work. You will often feel tired from the effort. You must respect the enormity of the task you are tackling and the energy and time (often years) it will take. You must say lots of prayers for the willingness, the strength and the courage to look honestly at your past—to feel all the feelings, recognize your own role in your life so far, forgive yourself and others, release the past pain and let it go. In your heart you need to become willing to ask your father's forgiveness for all of the anger, resentment and ill will you have borne toward him all these years. If it is possible for you to ask his forgiveness in person, you need to become willing to do so. If it is not appropriate because of possible harm to yourself, to him or others (or impossible for other reasons), the fact that in your heart you are making amends to him will still in its own way move mountains in both your lives. Even if your father is now dead, it is not too late to make amends. You need, when you are ready, to begin to work toward doing so for the sake of his soul and your own.

Wynne, it is my personal belief that we manifest on this earth plane many, many times and that as our souls try to learn their lessons in order to draw closer to perfection they choose the life conditions that will give them the opportunity to do so. But, as in your case, in order to learn certain lessons we must be plunged into the very conditions that would naturally produce in us just the opposite effect from what we are trying to learn. It is in overcoming our natural response to our conditions that the lesson is learned. For example, if I am truly to learn patience I must have my patience tried to the most extreme degree. Then I *may* learn patience finally, through a surrender of my impatience, or I may not. But the opportunity to learn patience only comes through having my patience tried. If my lesson is to learn to forgive, I must experience the unforgivable and then, through the self-destructive effects of carrying my bitterness, perhaps I will become willing to forgive. But if I don't forgive the unforgivable, where is the lesson? Where is the soul-stretching, soul-redeeming growth?

A woman who attended a seminar I gave said that her therapist had told her that the only people who never have to forgive are incest victims. In my opinion no one *has* to forgive, but we must, eventually, if we truly want to get well ourselves. Forgiving doesn't mean we go back and allow ourselves to be hurt by these people again. It means we detach from them enough to no longer take their actions toward us so personally. We lean on a Higher Power rather than on them for our personal validation. We realize that they were probably very damaged themselves and that they did the best they could even if their best was deplorable. We remember that their journey is in God's hands just as ours is, and we bless them and release them and let them go *so that we may live*.

When you write, "release the 'rattlesnake,' " by your name-calling you are actually binding yourself to this man more strongly than ever. Anger and hatred toward another person tie us to that person with bonds of iron. This is one of the reasons why both forgiving and asking to be forgiven are so important. It is through forgiveness that we release and are released. Without it we return to the person or to others like him and act out our drama over and over again. Far from making us weak people who can be stepped on by others, forgiveness frees us so that we never have to allow ourselves to be treated badly again. We have *given* good *for* bad (*forgiven*) and we are finished with it.

There is even more to the act of forgiving than all of this. The reason it is such an enormous piece of work, in my experience, is that what we are accepting, forgiving and releasing in another we are also accepting, forgiving and releasing in ourselves, perhaps from this lifetime, perhaps from another. The following is an example of how entwined self-forgiveness and forgiveness of others can be. That Sue's story includes dreams that revealed her experiences of past lives is not an essential point in her recovery, although these dreams were highly illuminating for her and ultimately constituted part of a deeply spiritual experience. Many people reading this may object that past lives have nothing to do with reality. As with everything else that is written in this book, please take only what is acceptable and helpful to you and disregard the rest.

Anger and hatred toward another person tie us to that person with bonds of iron.

Now in her early thirties, Sue had a severely traumatic childhood history of physical and sexual abuse, most severely at the hands of her father but also with her mother, her grandmother and one of her stepmothers. She grew up to be both very compulsive sexually and alarmingly careless of her personal safety. She was raped more than once and often found herself in extremely dangerous situations. After having over a period of about ten years what were primarily sexual encounters with a great number of men, most of whom she very deliberately seduced, she then met a man several years her junior who was sexually compulsive himself. The first time she visited his apartment she found the floors strewn with pornographic materials. Both before and during their marriage he constantly pursued other women and conducted secret affairs, as well as continuing to be heavily involved with pornographic materials, which as time went by, focused increasingly on bondage, subjugation and violence. After several years of escalating compulsivity on his part—more affairs, more hidden materials, more time spent evading her and practicing his disease—and escalating attempts to control him on her part, accompanied by declining sexual contact between the two of them, she finally ended the marriage.

A spiritual practice including prayer, meditation and reading had always been very important to Sue. In the pain of her marriage ending she turned to these sources of comfort and healing with more diligence than she had in years. She also began focusing on her co-alcoholism in Al-Anon, since her mother was a drug addict and her father, grandmother and husband had all abused alcohol. She made the Twelve Steps of Al-Anon a central part of her daily spiritual practice.

Sue continued, however, to find herself involved with men who were both chemically dependent and sexually addictive. Each consecutive man also had an increasingly severe penchant for violence. Also, again and again, when she was out in public she would run into men who exposed themselves to her or were otherwise overtly inappropriate in a sexual way.

During this time Sue's father died. As she struggled with her conflicting feelings of anger toward him and grief over losing him, in the aftermath of his death, she had the first of a series of vivid dreams. In it she saw clearly that she had lived in another lifetime as her father had lived in this one. She, too, *knew* the experience of being an alcoholic who was violent and sexually abusive. That knowledge helped her to stop judging her father so harshly and to begin to forgive him.

Prompted by further dreams, which directed her attention to her own present behaviors and feelings, Sue was able, albeit with tremendous fear and shame, to begin to confront her own sexual compulsiveness. As she became willing to look at how *she* had been completely out of control sexually and had then married a man whom she could try to control rather than face the escalating problem in herself, her day-to-day experience of reality began to change. After a while she no longer ran into men exposing themselves. The very unhealthy men to whom she had been attracted both before and after her marriage lost their appeal for her and she for them. They, too, began to disappear from her life.

All the dreams taken together helped Sue recognize, accept and forgive her own sexual compulsivity. In doing so she was able, as well, to forgive those who had abused her. At the same time Sue became increasingly able to choose to say no to the unhealthy people and situations that had inexplicably ensnared her previously. Finally these people and situations ceased to manifest in her life because the lessons she had to learn with them were completed.

Sue's series of powerful and pointed dreams was her psyche's gift to her, sent to promote her healing. They came in response to her own commitment to recovery and her dedication to following spiritual principles. She wisely accepted these dreams but did not use them to launch a provocative yet distracting pursuit of further past life material. She recognized that the reason we aren't ordinarily aware of past lives is because they are not what we ought to concern ourselves with in the present. We are meant to concentrate on what is happening now, in *this* life. What an irony it is that we want to travel backward and forward in time and from one end of the globe to the other searching for enlightenment when our soul's work is always right in front of us. Even without the dreams Sue's work of self-forgiveness and forgiveness of others would have been the same. The dreams came only as a kind of bonus explanation after she had already made a commitment through her spiritual practice to achieving that forgiveness.

What difficult, threatening, painful and all-consuming work this entire process of self-exploration and healing is simply cannot be overstated. But the alternative for Sue was a life—and quite predictably an eventual death—inextricably bound to her disease.

Nothing is meant to stay the same, and if we don't progress forward we decline. We are here to grow and to learn and to wake up. This is why there are no accidents in everyday relationships. We are inexorably drawn to the partners with whom we can either learn our personal and relationship lessons or become more caught in the web of our own unhealthy patterns of living and relating, patterns that will eventually bring more pressure to bear on us to change our ways. It is, equally, my belief that there are no accidents as to which souls we manifest with—whether it be our fathers, our mothers or the others with whom we have compulsory attachments. With all the difficulties they may embody for us, they are nevertheless gifts to our soul. They bring us an opportunity to learn the next spiritual lesson. We either learn it or become more soul-sick and, religious practice notwithstanding, more out of touch with our essential spirituality.

So you see, Wynne, our work is ever with ourselves, with changing our own hearts and becoming willing to give up our identification with that role which has served us long and, in some ways, well—the role of victim, martyr, rescuer or self-righteous avenger, or perhaps all of these in turn. Obviously, this is a much greater challenge than simply going out and finding another man and hoping this time he'll be the "right" one. No man will ever be right until we heal that in ourselves which has been attracted to a battle of wills and has needed to win or to lose and then point the finger of blame at another for our troubles.

———

Those who are thoroughly familiar with both addiction and recovery are almost constantly faced with two very trying situations: encounters with people who are addictive but try to prove they are not; and encounters with others who insist they have recovered but who have not. The first type of encounter occurs most often with those whose ongoing addiction carries a great deal of stigma while the second type happens more frequently when the addiction carries little or no stigma. Admitting to having struggled with relationship addiction (whether that specific phrase is used or not) tends to evoke sympathy rather than condemnation in this society today, as it is the most romanticized addiction of all and is believed by most people to have little in common with such sordid conditions as drug addiction or alcoholism. Further, because recovery from relationship addiction requires such rigorous effort and yet is so difficult to measure effectively, it is far more common for relationship addicts to claim recovery than actually to achieve it. Statements such as, "This time I've really learned my lesson," or "I could never go back again. I'd be too humiliated," or "I'll be fine now. I have other things that will keep me too busy to chase around after him," tend to be signs of the presence of disease rather than the achievement of recovery. Nothing in these statements acknowledges either the incredible power relationship addiction has over those of us who suffer from it or the discipline and work required to overcome it.

Recovery will always be a process, never a finished product.

It is so tempting to see ourselves as recovered when in fact we have barely begun what will be a lifetime process of change and growth, struggle and self-discovery. The key is in recognizing that recovery will always be a process, never a finished product. Each day of recovery is both a priceless gift and a splendid achievement.

Three

. . . ARE BATTERED

Here is a working definition of addiction: In spite of ample evidence that something isn't good for us we cannot stop our involvement with it. We do not stop, even though we have experienced negative consequences both emotionally (through humiliation and degradation) and physically (through declining overall health and the possibility, occurrence or recurrence of serious illness or injury) and those who best understand our condition (professionals who understand addiction or others with similar histories who are now recovering) tell us that as unhappy and unhealthy as we already are, unless we change our behavior we will get even worse. Receiving more information doesn't take care of the compulsion to repeat our behavior; nor does further suffering, no matter how great that suffering is. This is addiction.

This definition runs so contrary to the everyday rational approaches most people try to apply to most problems that it is incomprehensible to many addicts and many of those who deal with them but who don't understand addiction that any aspect of human behavior could be so uncontrollable. Addictive persons are blamed for being stubborn or stupid both by those who are trying to change them and by themselves.

It is only from a thorough appreciation of the nature and power of addiction that this great portion of otherwise inexplicable human behavior can be understood and, if the addict is willing, treated. One of these areas of seemingly inexplicable behavior is that of the battered woman. The following letter from Meg articulates so well the irrationality of relationship addiction as it operates in the woman who is battered. Only when the concept of relationship addiction is applied to her condition does it become possible to understand her and effectively treat her.

Meg perfectly fits the profile of the battered woman that I've seen again and again in my practice. She comes from a family of origin that was violent; she is highly attracted to drama, chaos and excitement; and she had suffered physical violence at the hands of her partner *prior* to making a serious commitment to him. It is very important to recognize these factors when they are present (as they have been with *every* battered woman I've counseled) in order to move away from seeing the battered woman as a naive victim of a brutal man. To do so is to guarantee that her treatment will fail.

At the risk of being redundant I must repeat that we naturally choose in relationships that with which we are already familiar. The word "familiar" is derived from the concept of family. Thus, what we have known in our family of origin will always be what is most familiar and comfortable to us no matter how unhealthy that family of origin was. If what we've known is violence, then in adulthood we will automatically choose a partner and a situation in which violence is again a factor, both because it "fits" for us and because its continuing presence offers us chance after chance at what we want most—to *win*. When we have been traumatized in any way there is always the (usually unconscious) drive to re-create the traumatic situation and this time to prevail, to gain ascendancy over what defeated us before. The greater the trauma, the more powerful this drive to surmount it.

Battered women come in many varieties, but always *there is a rage inside that comes from having been exploited and abused as a child.*

Battered women come in many varieties, from helpless and hopeless, to apparently competent in every other area of life, to self-righteously aggrieved and aggressive. But always, *always* there is a rage inside that was already present and burning long before there was any involvement with the current partner. That rage comes from having been exploited and abused as a child, when one is helpless to defend or protect oneself. Acknowledging that rage, experiencing it consciously, examining the methods used to deny it or suppress it or vent it are all necessary if the rage is to be healed and the patterns of relating changed.

I want to make clear that by urging that we recognize these factors I do not mean in any way to impute blame on the battered woman for having been beaten. Any perpetrator of violence is always responsible for that act. But both the woman who was battered and those who would work effectively with her must be able to acknowledge that the powerful attraction she feels toward violent men has contributed toward her condition. Those who work with victims of domestic violence, including members of the criminal justice system and the helping professions, see that time and again this obvious attraction on the woman's part has defeated their best efforts to counsel and protect her. This attraction must be acknowledged and addressed.

Actually there are three areas that every shelter and every program for battered women would do well to address with their clients: the client's definite relationship addiction, her very probable co-alcoholism and her quite possible chemical dependency. About eighty percent of those who batter have the disease of alcoholism, which automatically makes their partner co-alcoholic. (Also, most women who are battered are daughters of violent alcoholics.) Further, about half of the women who seek shelter from their battering husbands or boyfriends are themselves chemically dependent. Shelter personnel and others who work with battered women often hesitate to address alcoholism and drug addiction in their clients out of fear that if they do so the women will not stay in treatment. But no treatment can hope to be effective if it ignores the presence of alcohol and other drug addiction in the client. When battering is taking place no woman who is actively chemically dependent herself can possibly develop the tools necessary for her recovery from relationship addiction. Facing chemical addiction when it is present is the unavoidable first step in the treatment of these women.

Through attendance at Alcoholics Anonymous meetings or other Twelve-Step programs that address chemical dependency, battered women will be exposed to the healing power of a spiritually oriented support group. This experience will serve them well in every other recovery they face, including recovery from relationship addiction. Similarly, attending meetings of Al-Anon will benefit all the battered women who qualify as co-alcoholic because they are with an alcoholic partner or come from an alcoholic family or both. If alcoholism is not present in the woman or her partner, she can find appropriate help in the Twelve-Step approach taken in Relationships Anonymous (see Chapter 9) and other Twelve-Step programs that address relationship addiction. Whatever the particular case, *every* battered woman qualifies for at least one Twelve-Step program. Involvement in the appropriate program(s) must represent a primary source of recovery from her condition.

Recovery from relationship addiction, especially the variety from which the battered woman suffers, is a very difficult, one-day-at-a-time process requiring a tremendous desire to get well. This disease is as cunning, baffling and powerful as is alcoholism and has an even lower recovery rate, perhaps because of the multiple addictions so often present. (Besides alcoholism and drug addiction, compulsive eating and sexual addiction are frequently present in the battered woman.)

Working with battered women is discouraging both because of their low recovery rate and because recovery often takes so long, sometimes many years. The frightened, endangered, damaged and despairing woman who has been abused almost inevitably "hooks" that part of the counselor that wants to rescue her, help her, control her. But in order to really be of service one must always remain aware of the specific principles of recovery and share those with the client.

In reading Meg's letter, for instance, one can hardly help but want to do what she asks and give her advice about whether to stay or to go. However, such advice is as pointless and ineffectual coming from a therapist as it is coming from her friends, because *in the face of addiction, advice doesn't work.* The only appropriate reply is to invite Meg to begin to address her own relationship addiction, one day at a time.

Dear Robin Norwood,

I am reading your book, and I am identifying with these women.

I am twenty-four years old and have been married for three months. My parents separated when I was eleven and were divorced when I was sixteen. When Dad was home he was a disciplinarian more than a father and used beatings more than heart-to-heart talks to keep us in line.

When I was eighteen and a senior in high school, while living with my Dad in Massachusetts (Mom and the rest of the family live in Ohio) I had a romance with a twenty-four-year-old guy who drove a fancy car and lived at home. He became irrationally violent when I told him I was going to leave him. Usually if I got sarcastic during an argument he would hit me hard enough to knock me down. One night he tried to kill me "so no one else would have me if he couldn't." I managed to get away and flag down a patrolman who drove me home. My father was outraged at the shape I was in and left with a gun. He came back later and gave me an ultimatum: press charges or he'd shoot this guy. I pressed charges, but told my Dad I would not show up on the court date. I didn't. I went back to school and never saw this guy again.

During college I had no serious attachments. After graduation I got a temporary job and needed a place to stay. I was planning to go home to Worcester so that Dad could help me settle down. He was going to get me an apartment as repayment for the student loan money he took from me my freshman year. But I met Tim and tried to find a way to stay where I was in New Rochelle.

I asked to move in with him and for the next three months I was unemployed. Then my former employer called me back for a second temporary assignment. I went back to work with high hopes of a permanent position.

Things between Tim and me were stormy. Some nights we argued all night long, and he would hit me, too. I would cry and let him console me. Then we would make up and have sex.

I was always threatening to move out though, which kept me forever packing and unpacking. My friends warned me to dump him. I more or less dumped them instead.

Finally Tim drove me to my Dad's in Worcester and we argued throughout the whole trip. He even hit me in the face with a newspaper for driving in and out of the lines.

I stayed with my Dad for a month and he badgered me about my weight and how long it was taking me to find a job. Tim (believe it or not) would console me on the phone and ask me to "come back home."

Finally Tim got fed up with New Rochelle and came to Worcester to visit. We argued and I threw him out. He got right back on the highway and went home. I agonized over it and had crying spells for eight hours until I reached him on the phone.

He agreed to move to Worcester entirely but was two weeks late coming. Actually he had disappeared and no one, not even his mother, knew where he was. He later said he went to Mexico and California to try to forget me.

In the meantime I had a quick one-week affair with a security guard at my office. When Tim finally showed up I ended it after a few last secretive visits.

Our life in Worcester was also plagued with fights, both verbal and physical. I asked him to move out. He did. Then I begged him to come back. We agreed to date.

Then we decided to get married—my idea. He got my engagement ring out of the pawn shop (he still had the ticket) and we were married two months later.

After one month of marriage I became depressed and attempted suicide with pills. The psychiatrist suggested marriage counseling. Tim agreed, but later refused to go.

Recently he bought a gun to defend himself at his part-time job at night. He's been robbed twice. I am scared that this gun will become part of our domestic fights. The other night he woke me up (I was asleep in the second bedroom) and demanded I leave the house at twelve midnight because he was so angry he knew he'd hurt me.

I went to my Dad's where I am today trying to decide if this can be worked out??!!??

The argument was about my signing for a certified package from a lady who has my husband's son and is looking for him for child-support. He also said I should leave because I slam doors after he told me not to.

Now he wants me to come home again. I told him my Dad was helping me to get a new place and that I would soon have an annulment.

Tim says he'll be more sensitive, nonviolent, go to marriage counseling, etc., etc., etc.

Robin, the outer edges of my intelligence tell me that this relationship is past hope. Do you think even marriage counseling can help? Are Tim and I better off apart?

On the other hand when we aren't arguing we have long talks about society, religion, family, children. Usually we go to the movies every week or do something fun.

Still, he is not very giving and forgot my birthday during the first year I knew him when we were living in New Rochelle. He's been halfhearted on other present-giving occasions.

In spite of all this is there hope? With marriage counseling? Or should I turn my back and give up on the marriage?

> *Trying to do the*
> *best thing,*
> *Meg C.*

Dear Meg,

You suffer from one of the deadliest types of relationship addiction. Not only your physical health but your very life is in danger, as you surmised when Tim purchased his gun. However, if I were to say to you (as I know others have) that you should stay away from Tim, that advice would not make it suddenly possible for you to do so. So instead, I am urging you to get help with *your* addiction to Tim—not help for him or help for the marriage but help for yourself and your own unmanageable life. Getting this help is not predicated on your staying away from Tim. You need it whether you go back to him or stay away. Unless you address your own addiction there will always be life-threatening violence in your life. You won't just "get over it" one day. Instead, whether it's with Tim or someone else, the situations will become more dangerous, the encounters more deadly and the physical harm more serious. Both your relationship addiction and your partner's addiction to violence are progressive conditions that naturally escalate over time.

Many, many violent men are also alcoholic and many, many abused women come from homes that were both violent and alcoholic, so most women who are or have been in a battering situation qualify for Al-Anon. If you do, you are very fortunate, because there is not a better place to learn to face your powerlessness over another human being's actions and mood swings. When you fully grasp your powerlessness over him you can then begin, with the support of the people and the tools in the program, to take better care of yourself and eventually heal that part of you that up to now has *needed to choose dangerous men and dangerous situations*.

Like many women who have been abused by their fathers, you are still very closely tied to yours (as is he to you). You enter into various "deals" with him that keep the two of you hooked into each other. Since your father was your first batterer, each time you leave another man and return to him, his home, his rules, his advice, his criticism, his "protection," you are in essence jumping from the frying pan right back into the fire. You are constantly reacting either to him or to another violent man, seeing each of them in turn as either your "resource" or your "problem." To learn to do otherwise—to sit still with yourself so that you can face your *own* rage, heal it and eventually learn to live a calmer life—will be a far greater challenge to you than continually coping with the repeated physical assaults and geographic relocations with which you are already so familiar. But in the long run learning to hold still and heal will save your life.

Learning to hold still and heal will save your life.

You will not be able to make these changes alone or with just the help of a therapist. You need a constantly available source of support. You need people who will share their own tools for recovery with you but who will not indulge you in any of the obsessional behaviors that are part of the disease (your calling him, searching for him, trying to control or punish him, talking about him, launching into affairs with other men, etc.). You need people who, by their own example, help to guide your thinking toward those concepts which promote recovery, including a reliance on a Higher Power, rather than Tim or your father, to solve your problems and take away your pain.

Please remember, Meg, that knowing why you do what you do, while helpful, is not enough to cause you to change. Surrendering to the acknowledgment that, by yourself, you simply cannot overcome your compulsion to choose men who are violent, and then joining together with others who are working toward healing from that same compulsion is your necessary path toward a sane and serene life. I hope you seek help from a shelter in your area and that they, in turn, put you in touch with a group that uses the Twelve-Step approach to recovery.

Dear Robin,

I was brought up in a very conservative, straight environment where there were no drugs, no liquor, no cursing, or much of anything else other than criticism, harsh, violent discipline and severe punishments. I am now in a marriage that I know is not healthy or nurturing and must be, I'm certain, an addiction for me and I ask myself every day, why, why, why, am I still here?! The verbal, emotional and psychological abuse from my husband has gone on for years and years (at least five or six) and he finally (although I never thought he would) crossed over that line into physical violence. As bad as that is by itself, I have also been physically assaulted twice now in less than a year by his fifteen-year-old son (from my husband's first marriage) and I am certain it will happen again. I have had two marriage counselors (one secular, one Christian) as well as two psychologists tell me to leave the marriage. My husband has now seen three psychologists and we have spent tons of money trying to "get him well" all to no avail. Everyone (friends, family, the law enforcement officials, the local county women's counseling center, etc.) seems to think that I need to leave my home. Not because I'm dealing with one abuser, but two! At this point, the son has been more abusive than his father, and our home is like a battleground. It is like gasoline looking for a match. Yet I am still here!

There are many other factors entering into this situation as well that compound it and make it very complicated. One of the things that meant the most to me in your book was that you specifically addressed spirituality. As a Christian woman I have been having the hardest time finding some kind of middle ground or compromise between what I felt were two extremes. I have been attending an excellent program for battered women through the YWCA here and yet I hear so much "Leave the bastard," "Screw him," "Get the hell out," "File for divorce," etc. that it seemed to be the only line of thought, and quite frankly it disturbed me. The other extreme, which I am exposed to through church, a women's Bible study and most Christian friends, is that you stay in the marriage NO MATTER WHAT. You never give up. Divorce is the supreme no-no. The marriage comes before my personal safety(?!?!) It has become obvious to me that these people clearly want me to become a martyr and actually give up my entire life or any possibility or hope of any happiness whatsoever. I have had a very hard time buying either one of these approaches and as yet our problems go unresolved. Your mention of spiritual development as part of recovery seemed so refreshing to me. I know all too well how important it is to have Someone Else to turn this all over to when I'm reaching the heights of my own personal maximum frustration and exasperation levels. So many people seem to be running from God these days that I was almost shocked to find Him even mentioned in a book that I did not buy in a religious bookstore.

Fay K.

Dear Fay,

The relationships I've seen that are similar to yours in that they are highly combative struggles between two people who call in lots of reinforcements in the way of family, friends, clergy, counselors and the law are just that—highly combative struggles between *two* very angry and self-willed people, each determined to change (control) the other. What makes it so very hard for them to stop relating in a combative way and no longer go round after round in the battle is each partner's determination to win, to prevail over the other. This is as true of the one battered as of the batterer.

One of the most powerful weapons you have in this ongoing conflict with your husband and his son is the way you use your religious affiliation. Because to be a Christian implies meekness, humility and surrender to God's will, you may believe that your concern for your husband's attitudes and behaviors arises from a lovingly Christian impulse toward him. I want to suggest that something very different may be operating in you. I suspect that, like many others, you may be using your "Christianity" to mask your own self-willed determination to change *him* by implying that God is on your side in all your efforts. Can you honestly say that every attempt to pressure your husband to change has been loving rather than coercive and manipulative? Remember, when we feel we have the answer for other people, that they are wrong and we are right, we are being *self-righteous*, a state that cannot coexist with the spiritual principles of humility and surrender.

Being self-righteous, believing that we know exactly what the truth is regarding right and wrong, can unfortunately serve as one of the most impenetrable defenses against waking up to the truth about ourselves. I hope you can begin to acknowledge that you came to this marriage full of anger over the treatment you received in your family of origin and that the battles with your husband have provided some outlet for that rage but have also contributed to it.

Can you honestly say that every attempt to change your husband has been loving rather than manipulative?

Since people can divorce each other and still continue to fight for years, the answer is obviously not as simple as either staying or leaving. If you truly want to recover from your relationship addiction, you must take responsibility for the fact that you *chose* this partner and realize that there are lessons for you to learn in this relationship. The first lessons will be how to let go of the determination to change another person. Then you must learn how to take responsibility for healing the damage done to you in the past. This is the work you need to be paying attention to and from which, all this time, your husband and now your stepson have provided a great distraction. When you become willing to address this work you won't allow them to pull you off course. You will take better care of yourself and you will leave each of them to God.

In recovery we are no longer calculating what we say and do in terms of how the other person will react—

whether he'll "hear" us and change or be sorry or get angry or go away, or whatever. Rather, we do what we do and say what we say (and we usually say a *lot* less) with one purpose in mind—to hang on to our own peace of mind. We stop *our* half of the battle and when we do so the battle is over. You see, Fay, recovery isn't winning—it's not playing. Usually, as we begin to let go of trying to force a change in another person and to concentrate on our own recovery instead, a period of terrific tension ensues while we're working to learn these new ways of thinking and behaving. Our partner may be trying to get us hooked back into the battle, and a part of us may really want to go back and make all the old familiar moves, too. Sometimes, when things cool off we find that while we were taking care of ourselves, our partner and the relationship did some healing too. But sometimes not. Ironically, it is *easier* to leave, if that's what we finally need to do, after we have some recovery under our belt. As we learn to shift the focus from trying to change another person to taking care of ourselves, we naturally become more detached from the struggle with that other person, more accepting of who he is and less angry. Remember, it is anger, not love, that keeps most people in unhealthy relationships. When we let go of our insistence that *he* take care of us emotionally and *we* take care of ourselves instead, we become less dependent and naturally more able to let go. Then, when we are with him we're no longer empty, desperate, angry, frustrated and despairing. We can allow him to be who and what he is and we can choose what is right for us.

In order for you to obtain support for the kinds of changes that you will need to make in order to recover, attendance at Relationships Anonymous meetings in your area will be most helpful. Although in most parts of the country this program is very new, it is also very widespread. But keep in mind that because it is new, most members, unless they have long-standing affiliation with other Twelve-Step programs, are new to this approach themselves. It takes a long time for any Twelve-Step program to develop a core of individuals who have well-practiced recovery to share with newcomers.

The very simple (but not always easy) Twelve-Step approach taken in the Anonymous programs will not conflict with your religious values. In fact, it may well serve to further illuminate them for you.

———

The purpose of *WWL2M* was to introduce as persuasive an argument as possible for regarding relationship addiction, like alcoholism, as a progressive and ultimately fatal disease process. Nan's letter, which follows here, supports this theory with shattering clarity. Her brief letter makes obvious that she was trapped in a pattern of relating that she could not control on her own and that with the passage of time this pattern was becoming a more damaging and debilitating force in her life. Put simply, if she had not gone for help *and then stayed with it* she would very likely have died of her disease.

Though it may be tempting to see her violent husband as the actual threat to her well-being, her candid report of her history shows that he was only one of a series of dangerous partners whom, due to her disease, *she chose*.

Robin Norwood—

I met Mr. Wonderful on May 1st and he moved in on May 31st. Two weeks later he tore the earlining to my right ear. After repeatedly hitting me, forcing a broom handle up inside me and spitting in my face I finally had him arrested. Oh yes, he lit my hair on fire and put lit cigarettes on my face and arms, too.

Robin, after three marriages and divorces I didn't want another failure so when he got out of jail after six months and came to see me I let him in the house. He hit me again but the District Attorney dropped the charges I made against him this time, even though he had broken probation and harassed me.

From reading your book I was able to end a lot of relationships (four) within the last few months that I had begun because I was lonely. I've been able to stay away from my husband, as well as a man who is on downers, a man who is married and a man who abuses drugs and alcohol.

I'm beginning to understand how I got this way. I was adopted. My adopted Mom worked while her son abused the rest of us children a lot.

I'm going to counseling through the District Attorney's victim-witness program here. They are terrific. I'm getting a lot of help.

My husband goes to court soon and he wants me to be on his side. But I can't or won't take any more abuse. I'm going ahead with my divorce from him. I'm lonely but I don't want to go back to the way I've been living.

Wish me luck. I'm beginning to know God loves me.
Nan G.

When Nan returned her signed contract allowing me to use her letter, she wrote on it that her divorce is now final, that she again had to have her husband arrested for harassing her, that she is continuing with therapy and that she now knows daily that there is a reason to live.

At this point Nan is learning to take care of and protect herself. If she continues to work on her recovery she will eventually have to face and heal the violent aspects of her own personality that have attracted and been attracted to those men who manifested violent behavior. When her pain and rage are acknowledged, confronted and healed, encounters with her husband and with others who are violent will no longer be part of her life.

It is a spiritual principle that we will continue to encounter others who will embody the opportunity for us to learn our most pressing lesson. When we learn to overcome the problem *in ourselves* our "teachers" will fade away.

Very often those who counsel battered women are drawn to this work because of their own unresolved and often even unrecognized rage toward others, especially men. If this is the case they will not be able to guide clients toward what should be the ultimate goals of their work together—the healing of that rage and true detachment from (as opposed to wanting to prevail over) the violent situation. For every one of us, client and counselor alike, our most important work is always with ourselves.

———

Dear Robin Norwood,

After hearing about WWL2M I ordered it sent to my office. I told my secretary I was taking a course (indeed I was!) and had to study uninterrupted at lunch time. My red eyes could have given me away but apparently they didn't. After three months I continued "the course" with a noon Al-Anon meeting once a week, and a noon once-a-week appointment with a certified alcoholism counselor at a local rehabilitation center. By the time another three months had passed, the counselor and I decided that I would have to leave the area in secret in order to avoid a possible confrontation with my violent alcoholic husband. With help of some movers and the presence of a constable, I packed a U-Haul, took my eight-year-old daughter and our cat, and moved to Washington where two of my sisters live.

I have since found a good job in my highly specialized field and am seeing another specialist in alcoholism and co-alcoholism with plans to "graduate" to group therapy soon. My daughter is well, despite some fears which might be expected. I take her to a child psychiatrist occasionally about that. We rented a house directly across the street from my favorite sister who provides a lot of emotional support.

My ex has not bothered us and occasionally (not as often as I would like) writes to my daughter. He is pretty far gone, using marijuana extremely heavily along with lots of beer and cocaine, and has a precancerous colon. I am hoping that a way will open for me to take Amelia down South to see him sometime before he is gone, and after I am strong enough to do it well.

I am happy being alone, and at the same time working on myself so that I can someday have a good relationship with a man if one comes along. It is a true miracle to see the change in me from one year ago! And the circle spreads: my sisters are making cautious inquiries about the Adult Children meetings I now attend! I am so excited for them to begin, but don't say a word unless they bring it up.

WWL2M has probably made as big an impact on my life as my parents did—and it was what got me grown up at last. Thank you.

Kathryn F.

It is encouraging to end a chapter of letters from battered women on such a positive note. Kathryn is making all the appropriate efforts to recover and they are working well for her. However, if she were my client I would encourage her most seriously to examine her motives for making any trips with her daughter to visit her ex-husband.

At the risk of sounding heartless to all those who feel this daughter "needs" her father, let me make two points. First, this man is a late-stage alcoholic/addict. As long as he is drinking and using drugs, any visit is at best going to be confusing and dismaying to his daughter and at worst dangerous. Second, it is a most serious mistake to think that he is the only one with the problem and that Kathryn can safely visit him with no risk to herself. I am not just referring to her physical safety here, although that is certainly an important consideration. Since Kathryn, like every other victim of domestic violence I have known, is a relationship addict, her visit to her ex-husband is as dangerous to her recovery as taking a drink is to a sober alcoholic.

Within each of us is an incredibly strong need to make things turn out the way we would like, to somehow wring a happy ending from even the most disastrous situations. But for those of us who are relationship addicts, such maneuvers come suspiciously close to manipulation and the forcing of issues.

We who are relationship addicts must always question very closely our motives for reengaging with those people who have been our "drug." Sometimes our reasons sound so plausible, even humanitarian, and yet at their core they are rationalizations for practicing our disease again. If a visit between Amelia and her father is going to take place it should be his project, not Kathryn's. It seems unlikely that he will be able to carry out such a project unless he is sober. His daughter already knows what he is like when he is drinking and using drugs. A visit will not magically change anything unless he has changed.

Alcoholism, like death, represents a tremendous loss of the dream of how we would like things to be. But, as is the case with death, what alcoholism has taken away cannot be changed by any action on our part. It must be accepted. Kathryn must acknowledge that her daughter's path includes coming to terms with what is and what isn't a part of her childhood. As her mother, Kathryn does not owe it to her daughter or her ex-husband to find a way to reunite them. That is better left in God's hands.

Living with diseases of addiction and co-addiction requires that the rules of etiquette be suspended and the guidelines for recovery be followed instead. That is one of the most difficult aspects of recovery from co-addiction. What we must do to protect our own recovery doesn't always appear to others as the "nice" thing. We may be judged as selfish, thoughtless, ungenerous. But we owe it to ourselves and to those we love to go to any lengths to recover. This mother's truest gift to her daughter is her own ongoing recovery. As Kathryn heals, Amelia will see again and again what it is to make health-promoting choices rather than the "easy" ones, the ones that appear to be kind and of which others often approve but that are really part of the disease of relationship addiction.

It will not be what her mother tells her but rather how her mother acts and feels that will make up Amelia's most formative lesson in what it is to be a woman. Kathryn's recovery will be no guarantee that Amelia won't become a relationship addict herself, but given all their shared history together Kathryn's recovery provides the best insurance against the progression of the disease in her daughter. It is a comforting principle of recovery that the better care we take of ourselves the more we create the opportunity for true healing in others.

Four

. . . HAVE EXPERIENCED SEXUAL MOLESTATION AND/OR SEXUAL ADDICTION

Sexual addiction is not the same thing as relationship addiction. A woman may pursue sex addictively with little or no thought to establishing a relationship, or she may pursue relationships obsessively in order to have the framework she requires to practice her sexual addiction; both of these styles of behavior still amount to sexual addiction. Relationship addiction is the driving need to have another person on whom to focus. Sexual addiction is an obsession with sexual thoughts and/or activities. These two addictions may coexist together, just as other diseases of addiction may, for instance compulsive eating and compulsive spending or compulsive drinking and compulsive gambling. But each disease of addiction is separate and requires a separate recovery even though the tools employed to recover may be essentially the same.

Sexual addiction may be practiced with only one partner and within the sanctified framework of marriage just as well as with innumerable faceless partners or with no partner at all. What is important is to be able to identify it when it is present as an addictive disease and to understand the most effective approach to its treatment.

Very little up to now has been written about sexual compulsivity and sexual co-dependency. It was in reading letters from readers of *WWL2M* that my own education was begun regarding this particular aspect of addiction and co-addiction. Today it is my privilege to know people who are recovering. They have continued to educate me about the level of denial that operates in sexual addiction and co-addiction, the ways these diseases

107

manifest themselves in "normal"* people and the level of self-honesty required for recovery.

What are the specific elements of sexual addiction? Styles of sexual compulsivity, like drinking behaviors in alcoholics, may differ from one addict to another but there are always components that all addicts have in common no matter what the addiction.

Some of these are:

- that the addiction is causing life to become progressively more unmanageable;
- that although practicing the addiction brings temporary relief, the behavior ultimately causes more discomfort than it relieves;
- that the behavior is destructive to one's emotional well-being and, in time, to one's physical health;
- that it is supported by dishonesty with oneself and others;
- that there are constant attempts to control it—to not do it again—and those attempts usually fail;
- that there is shame about both the behavior and the inability to stop;
- that the unconscious defense mechanisms of *denial* (the lack of awareness regarding the reality of one's behavior and its frequency) and *rationalization* (the invention of excuses, especially the blaming of others for one's behavior) are constantly operating, preventing the addict from accurately assessing his or her condition.

When these criteria apply to sexual behavior, then sexual addiction is present. We say of alcoholism that it isn't what someone drinks or how much or how often, but the effect of the person's drinking on his or her life that defines alcoholism. The same is true with sexual addiction. It isn't necessarily how often one has sex or with whom (with the exceptions of rape and the seduction of children) or in what way or under what conditions that defines sexual addiction. It is rather a question of how one's

---

*We as a culture tend to make what is actually a rather arbitrary distinction between those who are "abnormal" because they have been incarcerated for criminal sexual offenses and those who are "normal" because this has not (yet) happened to them—especially since so many perpetrators of incest are never arrested or prosecuted.

sexual behavior is affecting other areas of one's life and if, in the face of problems due to one's sexual behavior, one is unable to stop or to change. Those problems might include the fact that one's sexual activity is not promoting healthy relationships with others but is either preventing them or destroying them. The threat to one's health and, in the face of the AIDS epidemic, to one's life is also a very possible problem. That a person may be risking arrest, prosecution and incarceration for certain sexual activities and yet continues to practice them is another indication. Not all of these criteria need apply. Any one of them is sufficient to diagnose sexual addiction.

From time to time, many people choose to use sex as a drug to numb themselves to whatever else is going on, just as many choose to use alcohol or food or a shopping spree or a gambling excursion for the same purpose. But when the need for and use of sex (or any other behavior or substance) creates greater problems than the momentary "high" it affords can justify or compensate for, the addictive nature of its pursuit should be investigated. Addiction develops when reliance on the drug, substance or activity evolves from being a choice into being a compulsion. When the addiction is sexual one moves from choosing (whether consciously or unconsciously) to use a certain sexual activity as a diversion from discomfort to *having* to indulge in that activity in order to avoid being overwhelmed by anxiety. Ultimately, in sexual addiction as in all other addictions, the ever-increasing burden of anxiety that the addict must manage is partially due to the cumulative weight of unfaced difficulties from which sex has served as a distraction, partially due to historical traumas that are threatening to emerge, and partly the consequence of past episodes of the addictive activity itself.

Women whose "drug of choice" is sex or who choose sexually addicted partners do not, in my observation, make either (or both) of these choices by accident. Their own childhood experiences of sexual traumatization, especially sexual molestation, predispose them to the development of this particular form of addiction and/or co-addiction. Indeed, sexual compulsivity and sexual co-dependence (being involved with a sexually addicted partner) are often two interchangeable aspects of the same disease—obsession with sex. Whether it is with one's own sexual activity or with another's, the obsession is still with sex and its roots are still the same: sexual traumatization in childhood. Sexual seduction is a hostile, aggressive act, whether it is practiced by a sexual addict or by a co-dependent who is trying to control the addict. The constant need to prevail sexually over another person is rooted in shame and rage at having been exploited oneself.

Perhaps the development of sexual addiction in consequence of sexual abuse is actually the psyche's way of trying to bring about a healing of that past trauma. Such experiences from childhood are almost always either so deeply buried or so emotionally disowned that a force as agonizing and dangerous as sexual addiction may be required in order to force their acknowledgment. Because healing from sexual addiction requires that one's past sexual traumatization be faced, emotionally relived and finally forgiven, the addiction itself serves as the key to the sufferer's past. Anything less than a full commitment to recovery might allow the sufferer to employ all the popular rationalizations for her preoccupation with sex and continue to keep at bay the reality of her unpleasant family history.

Several factors make it difficult to objectively discuss sex itself, much less addictive sexual behavior. One difficulty is that the subject is unavoidably titillating to some degree, either creating discomfort or encouraging a kind of voyeurism. Another factor is our culture's tremendous ambivalence regarding sexual expression. We have no real cultural consensus as to what kind of behavior is appropriate or inappropriate, wholesome or degenerate, liberated or immoral. Although we have cultural rules and values about sexual expression, scarcely anyone follows them. We have yet to decide whether breaking them is deceitful, immaterial or an expression of greater honesty than the rules permit. What is written here is not intended to address those questions. Addiction of all kinds is, in my opinion, never immoral but simply amoral, as is any other disease. It is not right or wrong any more than cancer is right or wrong. Diseases of addiction imply both the violation of one's own value system and the inability to stop or change one's behavior through one's own efforts.

I received the following letter from a woman physician who has been a respected professional and yet whose own life became unmanageable due to sexual addiction and co-addiction. She describes her own recovery as a sexual co-addict as well as her viewpoint (which I share) that the Anonymous programs provide the *primary* source of recovery from addiction and co-addiction. Counseling can serve as an adjunct—not vice versa.

Her letter is a good introduction to the concept of sexual compulsivity.

Dear Ms. Norwood:

I read your book, WWL2M, with great interest. I think it is an important addition to the understanding of women co-addicts. As a physician and a member of an Anonymous group, I was impressed by several points that your book made:

1. Such women need to be involved in a Twelve-Step program in conjunction with whatever professional counseling they receive.

I was so glad to read that you insist that your clients who belong in Alcoholics Anonymous, Al-Anon, Overeaters Anonymous or any other Anonymous program must attend the appropriate meetings in order to stay in therapy with you. I have been distressed at the number of counselors in my community who see Twelve-Step programs as an alternative to counseling rather than as part of the self-healing process. In fact, many counselors, psychologists and psychiatrists appear to be threatened by these groups, as though they fear that they will lose business if people go to self-help groups. Furthermore, there seems to be a feeling in the psychiatric community that self-help groups may be okay for people who have minor problems, but for real help you need a professional rather than *a self-help group. I have col-lected a list of counselors in my community who work along with Anonymous groups, and I refer my patients to such counselors whenever appropriate. I hope that your book gains wide dissemination and that it has a significant impact on those who counsel "women who love too much."*

2. It is no accident that certain women end up involved with alcoholics and other addicts.

About two years ago I joined a Twelve-Step group for spouses of sexual addicts. I heard other women telling their stories, and it was clear that they had a life-long pattern of hooking up with inappropriate, addicted men. When I heard them I realized that I, too, had a long history with this problem, starting with my choice of a homosexual for my first romance to my current marriage to a man who is addicted to affairs. As one woman in my program put it, "We were volunteers, not victims." This knowledge helped me greatly in forgiving my husband for the pain I experienced as a result of his affairs.

3. The particular addiction that someone develops may vary, but the dynamics are the same.

You mention alcohol, food, drugs, gambling and work. I agree with you 100%, and I would like to tell you about another addiction which you mention briefly in your book. On pg. 115, you state that "sex may thus be substituted for the use of a drug to relieve the anxiety that is typical in early sobriety." True, but sex can itself be a primary addiction, with all the dysfunctional fea-tures of the other addictions. The definitive book on this subject is The Sexual Addiction, *by Patrick Carnes, now published under the title,* Out of the Shadows: Under-standing Sexual Addiction.*

Several Twelve-Step groups are in existence around the country that address this issue. The one my husband belongs to is called Sexaholics Anonymous. As Al-Anon is to Alcoholics Anonymous, S-Anon is to Sexaholics [SA], and I am an S-Anon member. My husband has no

---

*See the Recommended Reading list for more information.

*other addiction; connecting with other women has al-
ways been his "drug." I found him exciting, dynamic,
sexy, sensitive, etc.—and until he joined SA and I joined
S-Anon, our life together was chaotic. I can identify with
everything that is said at Al-Anon, and I realized long
ago that no matter what the particular addiction, the
problems are the same. For almost two years my husband has been "sober" and working his program, and I
have been working mine, and our lives are much, much
improved.*

*Incidentally, multiple addictions are a common fea-
ture in SA circles. Many members first achieved sobriety
from alcohol and then realized that their sexual addiction was out of control and was threatening their chemical sobriety.*

*I'm so sorry you weren't familiar with sexual addic-
tion and its Twelve-Step groups when you wrote your
book, as I'm sure many of your readers are struggling
with this issue and would be glad to know that help is
available.*

                                        Sharon J., M.D.

This letter describes clearly the parallels between sexual
addiction and co-addiction and other addictions and co-addic-
tions, including the effectiveness of a Twelve-Step approach to
recovery. It requires no comment other than my thanks to the
woman who wrote it. After receiving her letter I was able to
send those of my clients who were sexually addicted or co-
addicted and interested in recovery to SA and S-Anon. These
groups are growing in number, as the need is great.

Meanwhile, an appropriate attitude toward diagnosing and
treating sexual addiction is barely beginning to appear among
members of the helping professions. While problems with lack
of sexual desire or inability to perform sexually are seen by
therapists as legitimate areas of concern, only recently have
professionals recognized compulsive sexuality as an addictive
disease process that, like other diseases of addiction, responds
best to a Twelve-Step approach. Nor has our training been of
much help. It has been my observation that many of the profes-

sionals who specialize in teaching about and treating sexual problems are, themselves, sexually obsessed (which is why they have chosen this particular field of work). Due to their own denial, rationalization and other defenses against recognizing the condition in themselves, they naturally have difficulty diagnosing the condition of sexual compulsivity in their clients. There is as yet an even less clear definition of what constitutes compulsive sexuality than what constitutes compulsive drinking, and for many of the same reasons. We, as a culture, have ways of "dressing up" addictions to make them look like free choices rather than the compulsions they really are.

It was primarily from alcoholics that professionals finally learned (when they were willing to be taught) to understand alcohol addiction and its appropriate treatment. I would predict that the same will be true for sexual addiction and its treatment. Those who are admittedly sexually addictive and are actually recovering and maintaining sexual sobriety will be the source of true understanding of this disease process. Similarly, recovering co-dependents will be the ones to shed light on their component of this disease. From them professionals will learn that sexual addiction and co-addiction, like alcoholism and co-alcoholism, require that the physical, emotional and spiritual aspects must all be addressed in order for treatment to be effective.

We, as a culture, have ways of "dressing up" addictions to make them look like free choices rather than compulsions.

Although there does not seem to be any particular career or field of work typically chosen by the alcoholic, it has been my observation that certain other kinds of addictions often tend to lead a person to very definite career choices, ones that are, in fact, reflections of the disease itself. For instance, relationship addicts most typically are attracted to the helping professions, with careers in nursing and counseling being their most common choices. Their next most common career is teaching, especially when the "helping" aspect is emphasized as with handicapped or emotionally disturbed students. Compulsive debtors (or spenders) tend to be drawn to work that involves the management of money, such as banking, accounting, tax preparation, the loan and credit industries and bookkeeping. Compulsive eaters typically pursue work that is somehow food-related. They study nutrition and food preparation, they work for diet centers or write cookbooks or teach cooking, or are employed as waiters and waitresses. Those who have been abused physically and have tendencies toward violence themselves are often drawn to careers in which violence is a major, albeit controlled, component, as in the fields of law enforcement or the military. And those who are sexually compulsive tend to choose careers that focus on human relations, especially in the area of morality. They typically are involved in some aspect of the ministry or in an otherwise religious life where, frequently, they counsel others. Professions where there is the opportunity to work with others' bodies, as in the medical field, are also commonly chosen. (In describing these observations, I do not mean to imply that all those who work in these fields are addicts of one sort or another but only that these various careers tend to appeal to people who have synchronous addictions.)

It is not difficult to discern that each of these types of addicts is seeking a way to constantly be involved with and yet to *control,* through effort and education and expertise, the substance or behavior that is causing his or her life to become progressively more unmanageable. These addicts are also trying, ever more desperately, to use their careers as a defense against their addiction. How, after all, can one have a problem in a given area when one is an expert in that field?

But addiction being what it is, the result of all these efforts to maintain control is exactly the opposite of what is hoped for. Control repeatedly fails and there is an increasingly alarming disparity between one's public image and one's secret, private behavior. Because of pride and fear, the career that was meant to be the greatest defense against acting out the disease instead becomes the greatest impediment to surrender and recovery.

Keep this concept in mind while reading the following two letters from Catherine N., a minister. Her letters provided some of the strongest impetus for assembling this book, because she describes so well both the progression of the disease of relationship addiction (in her case specifically sexual co-dependency) and the humility, surrender and perseverance necessary in order to achieve recovery.

Dear Ms. Norwood,

I read your book and have all the chronic symptoms of a WWL2M—panic attacks, claustrophobia, use of tranquilizers, severe anxiety, depression, suicidal thoughts, a constant, *tormenting feeling of emotional pain that is lodged in my chest and throat, and outbursts of crying daily, usually many times during the day. I can't relieve the pain and I can't identify the crying. Before I read your book I thought I was going crazy. No one knew what was wrong with me, especially me. I am thirty-seven years old with three children, ages nine, eleven, and thirteen, and have been married fifteen years to a man who is a good-looking, macho type who has been addicted to illicit sex since he was twelve. He carried his addiction through our marriage and I always covered up for him and felt it was my "duty" to keep forgiving him. I knew how to do that really well after having lived with a physically and emotionally abusive, alcoholic mother. (Typical, huh?)*

We are both ministers. What an image to live up to! Six weeks ago I was three chapters into your book when my husband confessed another "slip" and I left him. Now I'm back home with the kids and I told him to get another place to live. I don't want him back unless he seeks help from a therapist and a support group and tells the elders at our church what's really going on. He is agreeable, has already reached out, admitted he's ad-

dicted and powerless and can't do it alone. He has broken through emotional walls and is crying for the first time in twenty years. In the meantime, I'm wracked with this emotional pain and I need help so bad. Sometimes the pain gets so bad I don't know what to do. I can't work, take good care of my kids (give them any quality attention), or my house. I cry all the time and can't go anywhere because I get there and have to cry.

The pain and crying have been this intense for a year and a half, no let up, even when we separated six weeks ago. I trust you know what I'm talking about.

Catherine N.

Dear Robin,

I want to let you know I was so thankful you answered my letter last December and that I am recovering. After leaving my husband last November, in December we attended a three-day seminar for helping professionals given by Patrick Carnes, author of Out of the Shadows: Understanding Sexual Addiction. *It was at this seminar that my husband identified his problem and began to see a marriage and family counselor we met there. I also further identified my problem of sexual co-dependency and began therapy. Dr. Carnes, in his recovery program, suggests a period of abstinence for the sexaholic which we agreed to and it did me just as much good as it did my husband. It took away his "drug" (sex) and my "drug" (him). In your letter you advised me to go to S-Anon, which I found through my husband who had started Sexaholics Anonymous, and I have been going every week since. At the same time our counselor advised us very strongly to stay separated, which we did for seven months.*

All through that time I continued to grieve and cry, and the depression got worse at the reality I had to face. I began to work through some issues connected with growing up with alcoholism, reading It Will Never Happen To Me, *by Claudia Black* and attending an eight-*

---

*See the Recommended Reading list for more information.

week seminar on the subject given in my area. I felt suicidal and very fearful of my husband. All the tears I had never cried were coming out as though a dam had broken. I kept saying "things went too far for too long (fourteen years) with my husband and it will never work again and I don't know if I can ever get over it." The impulse to run away was a driving force inside me and all I had to hang on to were the words in your book, ". . . as you recover you will realize that staying is not the problem and leaving is not the answer." I sat in bed day after day isolating myself under my quilt, crying and surrounding myself with self-help books. Getting up to do the dishes felt like being asked to climb a mountain. I thought I'd never feel normal (emotionally healthy) again. The only thing that kept me functioning was going to my aerobics class.

But I began to learn I had a disease, too, and just this past month, eight months later, I am beginning to know what it means to exercise some restraint over myself, not to obsess over, control, blame and manipulate my husband. He now has nine months "sobriety" and has become one of the role models and sponsors of his program. (Because of the newness of the Sexaholics program there are very few long-time veterans.) My disease seems even more subtle than his as it can try to hide itself very well inside me. At first, instead of concentrating on myself and my program I kept up my old tricks of working his program for him. Now, we have been back together for almost three months and I'm just starting to relax. The depression is beginning to break up and I have three to four good days in a row. I have not had one panic attack since I read your book and left him to recover, nor any chronic anxiety. I had panic attacks for sixteen years and chronic anxiety for twelve. I tried to cover my anxiety and depression problems up the same exact way any good co-addict would cover up the drinking or the sexual acting out, but the guilt over being so unstable was tremendous. Once I learned to say it out loud, admit it, accept it and humble myself to receive help in each area, I began to get better. I always had to be the top dog—always the doctor, never the patient. My obsession went so far I even thought I had to find my own answers in stacks of books on psychology. I learned ages ago in my church life that self-willed self-sufficiency meant that I was not relying on God. I had a theology in my head about surrendering to Him but not in my heart and no action to back it up. The Twelve-Step programs can really teach the clergy a lot about spiritual practice! I'm just learning to truly look to my God who I have always known but never trusted.

I've also learned that one of the dynamics of my depression was the desire to continue to punish my husband for what he had done to me. I finally saw that I was only continuing to hurt myself with this need for revenge and when I owned the responsibility for what I've done to myself the depression began to lift.

Now, as I sit here today writing you this letter I feel peaceful inside and filled with hope. Recovering together with my husband has been the best. *How fortunate I am I had a husband who would do so. If he had not gone for help and stayed with it for a substantial amount of time I would never have gone back. I'm expressing my feelings, reporting my needs and staying assertive with him. He has thanked me a number of times for leaving him and for saying, "This is no longer acceptable behavior to me."*

Catherine N.

There is very little to add to Catherine's two letters. They clearly reveal for both therapists and other women who love too much the behaviors, feelings and dynamics of co-addiction and the tremendous pain and struggle inherent not only in the disease process but in the recovery process as well. After a lifetime of unhealthy relating, the co-addict in the beginning stages of recovery will often feel worse even as she begins to get better. This is because she is in withdrawal from her old patterns of thinking and behaving, *all* of which must change in order for her to get well. As she learns to withdraw her obsessive attention from another person's behavior and welfare, she is left without distraction from her own problems, which may be massive. These may include one or more of the following: panic attacks and chronic anxiety (such as Catherine experienced); phobias; a lifetime struggle with endogenous (physically based) depression; deep feelings of self-hatred, guilt and shame (often connected to a history of physical and/or sexual abuse); serious behavioral compulsions (spending, cleaning, etc.); an alcohol or drug or food or sexual addiction of her own.

No wonder many of us choose as partners men with such blatant problems of addiction. We do so knowingly, even though we might at first consciously deny that we are aware of their propensities toward behaviors we find unacceptable. Only the increasingly dramatic severity of *their* problems can provide enough of a distraction from our own. Should they begin their own recovery, we are robbed of that focus "out there." We are either left to embrace our own disease and our own recovery or forced to find another person or problem of equally great magnitude to distract us. No wonder, again, that so many co-addicts subtly or not-so-subtly sabotage their partner's recovery! It is sad but true that for many of us being with a very sick partner is easier than facing our own disease and embarking upon our own recovery.

Every recovery is nothing less than a miracle.

Catherine's case is very typical in that her career choice has provided both a distraction from and a defense against her own particular disease. She has not yet identified the roots of her own preoccupation with sex. Until now it has been expressed as concern with her husband's behavior. That identification will be an important part of her further healing. As with the careers we choose, the choice of a partner with a particular addiction to whom we then become relationship addicted or co-dependent can be a tremendous defense against examining our own unacceptable impulses and our own painful history. As difficult as this examination is, it is absolutely vital in order for us to achieve the fullest recovery possible from our particular variety of co-dependency.

All of us, therapists and lay people alike, need to remember that most behaviorally and chemically addicted people do not recover and that most co-dependent or co-addictive people *do not recover either*. This is not written to be discouraging but simply as a reminder to be realistic. Most people eventually die of their diseases. Catherine's letter clearly illustrates why this is true. The magnitude of surrender necessary for recovery from co-addiction fully matches that required for recovery from any chemical or behavioral addiction. Her story makes clear that every recovery is nothing less than a miracle—a miracle that happens by grace but not by accident. We must be willing to go to any lengths to recover. Like Catherine, we need to find the courage to show up in all the places where recovery is offered and to face what we learn about ourselves there. When we do that, and as long as we continue to be willing to surrender our self-will, a Power greater than ourselves will take care of the rest.

The following letter illustrates the premise that sexual compulsivity is a *learned* behavior in both sexes, that its strongly addictive component arises out of the drive to reencounter and reenact the overwhelming but often suppressed and forgotten traumatic sexual experiences from childhood. Sandra's letter also delineates the appropriate treatment approach, which is, again, a support group of peers who share similar histories from childhood and similar disease processes in adulthood. When this group work is augmented by the skills of a therapist who understands sexual molestation and sexual addiction issues thoroughly (ideally through his or her own ongoing recovery as well as professional training), then the climate most conducive to healing is created. In my opinion, nothing—no other training or reading or research—can ever compare with a therapist's own experience of *and recovery from* an addiction as preparation for working realistically, compassionately and appropriately with clients who face the same struggle.

Dear Ms. Norwood,

I am a two-year member of Parents United which is a support group for those of us whose children have suffered from incest, either at our own hands or our partner's or at the hands of other close relatives. The therapist I see for individual sessions recommended your book to me, as it addresses all of the major issues that I am working on right now. I was molested at the age of five, but did not remember this until two and a half years ago when I did some regressive therapy outside the program of Parents United. That therapist, untrained in the dynamics of molest recommended that now that I knew, I should put it behind me and go on with my life. That sure dove-tailed with what I wanted to do, which was to ignore what had happened, how I felt about it and all the ways that experience was affecting my present life! Well, six months after my realization, I finally left my second husband, and then found out that he had molested my fifteen-and-a-half-year-old daughter. Her molest was important enough to propel me through the doors of Parents United.

Although I saw myself in one way or another in every chapter of your book, the part that really clicked for me was about childhood roles. I recognized that I was the original "invisible child." Just before I read your book, I worked in group (I am in "Recontact" right now, which is made up of adults molested as children, perpetrators—both male and female—and mothers of molested children) on finally expressing some anger by pounding on a pillow with a bat. As I was working, I remembered another detail of my molest—my perpetrator pinning me down with his knees on my chest (something which my first husband—an alcoholic who was verbally, physically and sexually abusive—did to me and which immobilized *me). Although I was scared to death, I made myself go on with the memory and then take comfort from the female therapist leading the group. The scariest part of the whole session, even though it was also the most beautiful, was looking into her eyes as she tried to make a point, realizing that she saw me and cared about me and was there for me, and seeing myself reflected back as a real person, finally feeling the hurt and dealing with it. Before this the only way I could deal with my invisibility, my non-personhood, was to get drunk and pick up strangers in bars (the only touching I ever knew was sexual) and then when that didn't work, to marry a man as sick as I was and to numb myself by stuffing my face rather than drinking!*

My therapist has been working with me on my inability to forgive myself or feel any compassion for myself, and for always choosing flawed, dangerous, withholding, forbidden (married!) or otherwise unhealthy men. I always felt that the part of me that made those choices was really sick and tainted. Something clicked as I read your book and finally I understand that what I was seeking each and every time was the "sameness" of feeling which being with these men engendered, those same feelings I had experienced being in a nontouching (except for incest), nonsupportive, noncommunicative family. No matter what I did, whether it was grades, housework, etc., etc., it was never good enough for my parents. So, of course, I chose men who further validated my badness by beating me up, raping me, verbally and emotionally abusing me. They just confirmed both the overt and covert messages my family always gave me. Anyway, I am finally starting to forgive myself for those sick choices. I am not ready to go into a relationship yet; my healing process is too new and I am afraid a "good" man won't be exciting enough or real enough. But, for the first time, it feels okay to be without a man, to not be part of a couple, and I don't feel in a hurry.

It's so validating to read your book and see myself in each chapter and know that I am not the only one who reacted in those self-hurting ways. What is really validating is reading about the recovery process and realizing that I am doing all of those things. I am in a group with other women (and men) who were hurt that same way I was and became really dysfunctional from it. I'm also, for the first time ever, learning to see men as people, just like me—hurting like me, lonely like me, using sexuality as their only human contact just like I did, and healing like me. I am well on my way in this recovery process and I know that soon I may even be ready for a healthy relationship. I am starting with healthy friendships, learning to love and be with people without sex. I've never been close to anyone and it's like being a baby and starting over. I hope someday to be ready for the intimacy (eeek!) of a real relationship.

My daughter is healing, too, through Daughters and Sons United and through my becoming a healthy parent who doesn't keep secrets and doesn't withhold affection and doesn't put conditions on loving her. It's scary, but it's real, and that's worth it!

Sandra S.

Sandra's history in childhood and adulthood is so much more common than most of us realize. We see people who behave in the ways she has and we wonder why. Her letter contains some of the most common reasons. Sandra's compulsion to pick up strangers in bars and have anonymous sex with them is a common feature of sexual addiction in women, and its roots are often exactly what she describes. Having been used sexually as a child, in adulthood she continued the pattern of depersonalization of herself and of sex. Like Sandra, many, many women who abuse alcohol or other drugs have an underlying traumatization from childhood that includes both sex and violence. While their drinking anesthetizes their pain, it also creates for them the opportunity to act out the drama of dangerous, impersonal sex between people who are really only objects to each other. But instead of bringing relief, such activity only intensifies the feelings of anomie, shame and worthlessness that triggered the behavior in the first place. By telling herself she wouldn't have behaved as she did if she hadn't been drinking, the woman effectively avoids taking responsibility for her choice and exploring its meaning in her life. And so the cycle continues.

I think Sandra's letter again exemplifies why recovery is so rare. In order to heal she needed the courage to face not only the painful, buried memories of abuse from childhood but the extent of her own sick choices and behaviors in adulthood. Sandra could never have so significantly changed her behavior without looking at her own disease just as honestly as she has examined her parents' and her husband's affliction.

The next letter is included to demonstrate how subtly the presence of violence and sexual inappropriateness may be alluded to by someone struggling with either of these issues. "Incest," "sexual abuse" and "violence" are all terms that people often have great difficulty even saying out loud, much less using to describe the conditions of their family life. Sexual and/or physical abuse so commonly occur in alcoholic families that any therapist consulted by someone whose family system is or has been alcoholic must be able to probe for the occurrence of such behavior effectively—which means kindly, gently and slowly.

> *Dear Robin Norwood,*
> *I have been in a very sick relationship for nine years. Your book has helped me to see things in a new way. I am now going for counseling sessions and am trying to decide what to do about my relationship. The man I am involved with is an alcoholic. A very successful alcoholic. He got sick, we got sick and all of us came really close to going down the tubes together. We were never*

*married but have two daughters together. My girls and I
are recovering but he is still sick. I keep wishing and
hoping he will change but I am beginning to realize he is
only going to change if and when he wants to. It is a
dream, a fantasy of mine that I will ever see him healthy.
He is financially very independent and getting richer by
the moment so his power is more important than his
mental health. The biggest thing that keeps me from
breaking away is fear. Fear of what? I don't know. I am
just scared. Partly because of my girls. I don't want him
around them if I can't be there with them but if I break
the relationship with him I know he will want to see them
and I won't be able to stop him.*

*I am also very scared of another relationship. I have
tried to have relationships with healthy men but I get
scared and run. I keep on reading your book over and
over and it is slowly but surely helping. Thank you very
much for listening.*

Jane S.

Dear Jane,

I want to focus on your fear of what might happen
to your daughters if you are not there to protect them.
I'm assuming you are afraid that their father will be
verbally or physically abusive toward them or sexually
inappropriate with them or all of these. I'm also assuming that up to now you have been "running interference"
between this man and his daughters, preventing him from
being alone with them in an effort to keep them safe from
him.

First of all, Jane, you need to face *what you already
know,* to stop keeping secret *from yourself* this man's
propensities. It is common for co-dependents to remain
deliberately vague regarding the behaviors and inclina-
tions of their partners or former partners. However, such
vagueness is dangerous.

It is true that if you separate from him he will
possibly have visitation rights that would exclude you.
But many actively drinking alcoholics are much more
interested in *struggling* over custody, visitation rights,

etc., than in actually being with their children. They need the drama and excitement of the battle with their "ex" to provide a problem on which they can focus, as such a problem provides welcome distraction from their alcoholism and its consequences. Ironically, the more you fight the girls' father on the visitation issue or anything else, the more distraction from his alcoholism you provide for him.

Violence and incest happen most frequently between alcoholics and their co-dependents. You need to talk with your daughters about your concerns, which means you need to learn to talk *objectively* (without blaming) about the disease of alcoholism and about the inappropriate ways some alcoholics behave toward others, including their children. You need to discuss your concerns about their safety with the girls in the same clear, dispassionate way you would talk to them if their father experienced, for instance, epileptic seizures. They need to be told what behaviors to expect and how to take care of themselves under difficult circumstances.

When you can do so *objectively,* you may also want to tell their father about the discussion you have had with the girls. But do not do this until you can say what you have to say without becoming angry, argumentative or defensive. Needless to say, to be able to talk with him in this way requires a great deal of recovery. In my opinion, the best place for you to develop a healthy detachment from his behaviors and problems is in Al-Anon.

The secrets we keep make us sicker.

The secrets we keep make us sicker. When you are no longer keeping this man's secrets for him you and the girls will be healthier, as long as your motives for telling your daughters are the right ones. You must not tell them in order to disparage him or bind them more closely to you. And if you eventually also tell him about what you and the girls have discussed, your motive must not be to try to get him to change. That would just be another attempt to control him. In any case, when the secret of their drinking is out, most alcoholics tend to avoid the people who "know."

However, if this man is sexually inappropriate as well as alcoholic (these conditions frequently coexist), he may not easily give up access to his daughters. If this is the case, please do everything you can to find professionals to talk with who are thoroughly knowledgeable regarding sexual abuse of children and who can help you in your efforts to protect your daughters. Many communities now have Sexual Abuse Response Teams that can be contacted through your district attorney's office. You can call anonymously for this information if that is easier for you.

In any case, in order to arrange your separation you will want to find an attorney who understands the disease of alcoholism. If your daughters' father is potentially or actively violent or sexually inappropriate, your attorney must be willing to deal with those issues, too. (Not all attorneys are willing to do so.) Yours is obviously not a situation where joint custody, which is so popular today, is appropriate, if only because of the presence of active alcoholism. You need an attorney who recognizes this fact.

I hope you will become actively involved in Al-Anon and, if sexual abuse is an issue, S-Anon as well. These two support groups will provide you with the wisdom and guidance you need in order to deal with your situation.

Try to remember that you did not accidentally become so deeply involved with a man whom you find untrustworthy. My strong hunch is that the issue of sexual abuse was part of your own childhood history. We tend to choose, in adulthood, the kinds of people and situations with which we have already struggled as children. Women who as children were molested or otherwise abused tend as adults either to aggress against their own children or to choose partners who will. Please address healing this most important area of your own life. Doing so will help you not to repeat the pattern again, with yet another inappropriate man. As you become healthier you will also be helping to prevent this pattern in your daughters' lives, in terms of both the partners they choose and the children they may raise.

———

Many people wonder how, in the aftermath of the feminist movement of the sixties and seventies, women today can be so obsessed with men and with relationships. The next letter very candidly and in great detail describes how a woman with a strongly feminist stance and a politically revolutionary viewpoint could nevertheless live a life made unmanageable by relationship addiction and sexual addiction. Terri's letter strongly suggests that perhaps for those women who are dedicated feminists and yet also "man junkies," the roots for both their politics and their addiction may, ironically, be found in the same childhood experiences: their exposure and subjection in their families of origin to male anger, aggression and dominance as well as female resentment, docility and martyrdom. Throughout Terri's childhood the presence of alcoholism in both her parents exaggerated these stereotyped male-female dynamics. In adulthood, her own chemical dependency combined with her partners' to intensify unhealthy relationship dynamics all over again.

Dear Robin,
When I read your book I saw myself on every page. I'm a forty-three-year-old career woman, presently a middle-level manager in charge of an office of twenty-five people. I've been married twice and have raised two daughters. I've been active in feminist causes and am looked up to as a strong, assertive, articulate woman. My two marriages were certainly not the traditional, chauvinistic variety. But I know now that if you make a man the center of your life it doesn't matter if you bring him coffee and his slippers. Refusing to play the traditional female role in marriage didn't protect me from being a woman who loves too much; it just helped to hide the problem from myself.
I'm the oldest of a family of twelve children. Both

*of my parents are alcoholics. My mother is a woman
who loves too much. She really doesn't see her children
as they are. She's too entangled in her stormy relationship with my father. I never wanted to be like her so I
have always supported myself and have avoided men
who were, like my father, materially successful. I never
intended to have children because I was determined not
to trap myself the way she had trapped herself. Nevertheless, she taught me to be a woman who loves too
much and to use alcohol as a coping mechanism. I
developed a different life-style from hers but we still
ended up with the same addictions.*

*My father's alcoholism has never affected his ca-
reer, only his family. He has achieved fabulous success
financially and has become well-known. He insists his
drinking is under control and in some ways I guess it is.
He's finally learned to control some of his temper in
these past few years but he and I had an extremely
stormy relationship when I was growing up. I vowed
never to become involved with a man like my father, a
vow I'd thought I'd kept. Now I realize that I fought him
and I've fought every man since him. How much money
they had, their politics or what race they were hasn't
really made much difference after all.*

*In childhood I railed against my parents and de-
fended my brothers and sisters from their anger and
criticism. I read books about freedom fighters and mar-
tyrs and wanted to be one. I was unpopular with boys
though I desperately wanted their attention. I discovered
sex at seventeen and ignored my religious upbringing in
order to hold on to this wonderful new experience that
made me feel connected to other people.*

*In college I found Black men and popularity. I had
a baby out-of-wedlock who I gave up for adoption. That
trauma didn't even slow me down. I left home at nineteen to move east, become self-supporting and join a
Black man I had met and fallen in love with while I was
pregnant back there. My father was out of control over
this, threatening to commit me to a mental institution to
stop me. So Dex and I married.*

I was soon pregnant again and became a mother six weeks before my twenty-first birthday.

I was still very needy emotionally and as the excitement of my marriage waned I started having an affair. Then I went back to college and became a political revolutionary. I had more affairs but was discreet because I didn't want to hurt Dex. He was incapable of confronting me because of his inhibited nature, and the marriage deteriorated.

Eugene was a revolutionary like myself and a military deserter due to his political views. He and I had a weekend-long affair and then he left for Canada. When he returned to the States I immediately ended my marriage and we moved in together.

After a year and a half of total togetherness Eugene moved out, saying he needed to find himself. We had been lovers and comrades in arms in our revolutionary pursuits. I had supported him financially because he was hiding underground due to his deserter status.

Eugene's moving out left me in terrible pain. I found the pain-killer I needed in scotch and began what became fifteen years of daily drinking. Eugene launched into daily drinking as well. I drank alone, he with others but that was the only difference. I hadn't found out about the other women yet. He lied to me and I believed him because I needed to.

After about three months of being separated but seeing each other two or three times a week I decided that moving away was the answer. I found a new apartment in a different city. Eugene couldn't let me go so he followed and moved into my new apartment with me.

He had met another woman during the months in his own place and he started staying out, telling me he was at all-night revolutionary organization meetings. It didn't ring true and I kept demanding to be included, but he pulled it off because there were problems with my being white and this being a Black group. Finally the strain got too great and he moved out again. This time he supposedly moved in with a male friend. Ten days after he moved I went over to his new place. When I knocked on the door a woman called out asking who it was. I knew then.

The hell of the next few months is indescribable. He held on to me with protestations of love while he lived with her. He had always wanted me to get pregnant but I never would. Finally, he talked me into trying to get pregnant, promising he would come back if I did. I quit taking the pill. I changed my mind and started taking it again but thanks to fertility equal to my mother's I was already pregnant. But Eugene didn't immediately move back in. I had recognized that possibility even when I agreed to get pregnant but I had decided that even if he didn't come back I already had one child I was raising as a single parent so what difference did it make if I had two? I felt that with a child I would always have some-thing left of our relationship. I also knew I could hurt him if he didn't come back by having his child and not giving it to him.

I spent my pregnancy drinking when I wasn't work-ing, and sleeping. Why I don't have a child with fetal alcohol syndrome (something never heard of or talked of then) I don't know. I slept with a gun under my pillow, wishing I could kill myself.

One more near fatal effect of my pain and rage . . . I nearly killed the "other woman" on New Year's Eve while Eugene was in Canada. I had decided to go to her house and shoot her at midnight on New Year's Eve when perhaps the "accident" would be interpreted as New Year's revelry that got out of hand. I didn't care if I got caught. I didn't care about anything. I just had to do something to resolve matters, no matter what the consequences. I'll never know if I could have gone through with it. She wasn't home. She had gone to Canada to see Eugene for Christmas. But my addiction to love had taken me to the point of nearly committing murder.

In the summer when Eugene came back from Can-ada, I showed up at the house where the other woman lived. When she found out I was pregnant, Eugene was forced into a choice. He chose me. I had won.

After he moved back in with me, thoughts of her tormented me daily. My daughter was born in July. In January Eugene and I married. I don't know why he married me. I married him to prove to everyone that he loved me, to restore my pride since I'd hung in there through so much hell. I told myself that now I could always get a divorce and that a divorce would be my way of knowing it was over. (I had figured out the meaning of rituals like funerals and divorces. They were to let the living know when it was over.) Maybe some part of me married for love but only a very small part.

Eugene finally got caught for his desertion five years after it happened. Naturally I stood by him because whatever problems we had, we were always political comrades and I would never turn my back on him at a time like that.

He came out of the brig ten weeks later a changed man, a man truly in love again.

It was nice while it lasted but it didn't last long. We moved again—and again. I worked. He didn't. Four years into our marriage he told me he wanted us both to have other sexual partners. I agreed to some swinging which I didn't like but I wanted to please him. I allowed him to completely control me sexually and yet told myself I was very liberated to be able to do this.

Eventually he started an affair with a friend of his. This violated our agreement that casual sex was okay but a meaningful affair wasn't. (Insane how we think and act, isn't it?) This situation put him back in the old bind of not knowing what he wanted. When combined with our other problems, it eventually led to the divorce.

After the breakup I was terrified I wouldn't find anyone else. In spite of my strong feminist conscious-ness, men had been my total focus. Without a man I didn't know who I was. But I was so grateful for the peace after all the fighting with Eugene that I waited for a few months before looking for his replacement.

When I did get into my next relationship, Eugene went crazy and repeatedly threatened his own life and mine. Later he admitted that he almost killed us all—

*himself, me and the new man in my life. As for the new
man, he was married. I was entranced by him at first but
when the truth began coming out, I pulled away. He
beat me up badly and yet I only managed to stay away
from him by becoming involved with still another man.
The next man was totally closed emotionally, twice divorced and unwilling to make any sort of commitment to
me. When I fell in love with him he pulled away. We
went back and forth in a seesaw relationship that drove
me crazy. Then he lied to me about fidelity and I finally
broke up with him.*

*I ran at top speed into my next relationship, this
time with a man ten years younger than I, a sweet man
who reminded me somewhat of my first husband. We
immediately began living together and I discovered his
addiction to freebased cocaine. I had always used drugs
carefully because I didn't want to be an addict. I'd tried
just about everything in the sixties and had smoked a
fair amount of grass but had quit in the mid-seventies
because I preferred drinking. But with all this cocaine
around I was off and running.*

*Last year I read your book. It was the final straw. It
helped me put my life in perspective. I saw that my
problem had a name, that other people had it too, and
that it was curable. I made an appointment with a
therapist who specialized in treating adult children of
alcoholics and I was told that in order to get well I had
to deal with myself as an alcoholic first. Well, I was able
to quit drinking but found I couldn't quit the cocaine.
The live-in boyfriend was still using it, which made
quitting twice as hard. I finally got clean as well as sober
but since I was still a woman who loved too much it took
me four more months to get him out of the house. It also
took becoming reinvolved with the "closed" man who
had been my lover before the cocaine addict. This man,
I now realize, is also an alcoholic. In Alcoholics Anonymous they tell us, "No serious relationships for a year."
I can see why but I don't know if I can do it. I create all
kinds of rationalizations for continuing to be involved
with this man. I'm clean and sober but I'm still a woman*

who loves too much—the very thing I always promised myself I'd never be. So much for my politically enlightened feminist consciousness.

Thanks for listening, Robin.

Terri D.

Dear Terri,

From reading your letter I strongly suspect that, along with being an alcoholic, a cocaine addict and a relationship addict, you are also sexually addictive. Your sexual behavior in your teen years and as an adult, the sexual compulsivity of many of the partners you have chosen, and your feelings of rage and desire for revenge all very strongly suggest the presence of this addiction. Another clue is your father's domination, violence and alcoholism and your mother's alcoholism and extreme passivity. These, too, are factors that are frequently present when sexual abuse occurs in childhood.

Being exploited sexually as a child provides the typical impetus behind most compulsive sexual relating in adulthood. However, violence alone, when it is highly sexualized, is also a sufficient cause for the development of sexual compulsivity. Similarly, exposure to a parent who compulsively indulges in secret affairs is also a sufficient cause for later development of this addiction. Although in your letter you do not describe a childhood that includes having been exploited sexually, everything in your pattern of relating as an adult indicates that you were either sexually abused as a child or that the violence in your home had a strongly sexual theme. In other words, your story is diagnostic both of sexual addiction in the present and sexual trauma in the past, whether or not you are consciously aware of that trauma today.

Some facts:
- One out of four women in this culture has been molested by the age of eighteen.
- The great majority of molesters are known and trusted by their victims. In fact, most are close family members.

- Eighty percent of sexual abuse and eighty percent of domestic violence (two categories that frequently overlap) occur in alcoholic families. The next highest incidence of both incest and battering is in highly religious homes.
- Most victims of sexual abuse "forget" their experience(s) through the unconsciously and automatically operating defense mechanism of denial.
- Victims of sexual abuse tend to either sexually abuse their own children or choose a partner who will do so.

Incest is the ultimate trauma, the ultimate devastation, so impairing to the child that massive defensive efforts to deny and to "forget" operate throughout childhood and into adulthood. Typically, the defense mechanism of denial very efficiently and thoroughly buries the painful memories in order to protect the ego from being overwhelmed. Because these memories are not expunged but only covered up they retain all their power to influence, albeit on an unconscious level, daily behaviors, feelings and choices. They produce high levels of anxiety, distrust, fear and a kind of free-floating shame, all of which effectively prevent the adult survivor of incest from living a comfortable, reasonably happy and secure life. Further, while buried they remain impervious to all efforts at healing the anxiety, distrust, fear, insecurity and shame, not to mention the commonly resulting sexual addiction that has its roots in this trauma.

The problem of sexual trauma is so difficult to address not only because of the victim's natural aversion to admitting to the experience and her automatically operating defense mechanism, which serves to block the event(s) out of conscious memory, but also because it is so difficult to define what exactly constitutes sexual exploitation. As with so many other kinds of damaging experiences from childhood, each of us wants and needs to believe that whatever happened to us wasn't really that bad. The dependency on our parents that we experienced as children naturally develops into a loyalty that compounds the difficulty of assessing the degree of trauma we've experienced. If memories begin to surface, we try to convince ourselves that we are imagining it all, that we've dreamed it or that we are exaggerating it. We remain deliberately vague and decide our feelings are baseless and our reactions are all out of proportion. Almost always the case is exactly the opposite. We so underrate what happened and its effect on us that we are left distraught with anger, shame and despair but without anything to which our agony can reasonably be attributed. Our wholesale, albeit unconscious denial or our consciously deliberate concealment of our past keeps us wedded to its effects in the present.

Terri, let me help you identify some of the less easily recognized forms of sexual exploitation along with those that are more readily acknowledged as damaging. But remember, these are not legal concepts but psychological ones, to be evaluated in terms of the effect on the victim rather than from the standpoint of whether or not what happened constitutes a prosecutable offense in a court of law.

Each of us wants to believe that whatever happened to us wasn't really that bad.

Sexual exploitation, on the one hand, may be overtly physical, involving inappropriate viewing, examining, touching, fondling, stimulation and/or penetration of the child's body. It can be a single event, an occasional one or one repeated again and again over many years. On the other hand, sexual exploitation can be covert and primarily psychological. The use of inappropriate sexual words, descriptions, nicknames or name-calling, sexual suggestions, questions and topics of conversation, lewd story-telling or jokes or the presence or display of patently sexual and/or pornographic materials all constitute sexual exploitation of children who are exposed to these activities. Another factor to keep in mind is that physical violence can be a highly sexualized form of aggression.

Many girls, besides being beaten, have had their clothing ripped, their hair cut off and their possessions destroyed by sexually jealous mothers or sexually possessive fathers.

Covert incest also includes the severe and repeated violation of a child's emotional boundaries. When a parent makes a companion and confidant of a child, reporting in detail troubles in the marriage (including sexual problems), elevating the child to the level of an adult in terms of responsibility, burdening the child with the parent's emotional distress and depending on the child for relief from and solutions to that distress, and otherwise leaning on the child for validation and comfort, a violation of that child's vitally essential separateness and independence has occurred. If the parent further elevates the child to the position of being his or her primary emotional partner, that in itself can be strongly conducive to the development of sexual compulsivity in adulthood because such treatment amounts to seduction of the child. As such it generates much of the same sense of having been overwhelmed, of free-floating shame, of impotent rage and a drive for redress and revenge that overt incest does. Nor are overt and covert incest mutually exclusive. A father, for instance, may exploit his daughter physically while at the same time her mother exploits her emotionally.

Many women deny, in adulthood, that they were ever victims of incest because they were not involved in physical sexual relations as children. But the degree of trauma is not necessarily greater for a child who has endured physical exploitation than for one who has been psychologically abused. A woman whose childhood experiences included being repeatedly required to be present in the room to serve drinks to her father and his male friends while they told crude jokes and stories may well grow up just as impaired in her capacity to trust and to experience healthy intimacy as another woman whose childhood experience included her father secretly visiting her in bed at night in order to have sexual relations with her. The violation of trust, the enforcement of secrecy, the denial of protection, the invasion of boundaries whether physical, psychological or both—all these constitute the trauma of incest. And this trauma is what drives the victim, in adulthood, compulsively to re-create sexual encounters that again contain these elements of distrust, secrecy, danger and psychological and/or physical abuse.

As a society we tend to explain away compulsive sexual behavior (as long as it occurs between a man and a woman of appropriate ages) as the expression of a "strong sex drive." This is as inaccurate as explaining an alcoholic's inability to control his drinking as the expression of a "strong thirst." Sexual compulsivity, like all addictions, is the pursuit of relief from the effects of that which is also seen as the source of relief. It is the alcoholic's drinking that creates the need to drink again. It is the compulsive spender's debting that creates the need to spend again. It is the sexual addict's experience of seduction that fuels the need for the next sexual encounter.

If we remember that sexual compulsivity is an unconscious effort both to deny and to overcome the feelings of powerlessness, shame and rage that stem from childhood exploitation, it becomes easier to recognize that most women who pursue sex obsessively do not do so because they like men so much but because they feel tremendous fear and rage toward them. Again, these feelings operate unconsciously, producing unbearable anxiety and goading the traumatized woman to re-create the sexual encounter again and again. She is impelled to try to restore an inner balance by subjugating rather than being subjugated and dominating rather than being dominated. But she is also playing with fire. Each compulsively pursued sexual encounter sows the seeds for the need to repeat the act again, possibly to "win" again. The most deliberately seductive women tend also to be the most deeply traumatized and the most filled with buried rage and anguish. Compulsive seduction is a desperate and hostile act, the point of which is to prevail over another human being.

Terri, you were extremely fortunate to have had a therapist who recognized that your first order of business was achieving chemical sobriety. I would suggest that your next order of business, in conjunction with ongoing sobriety, is experiencing a period of sexual abstinence during which you focus on the original source and current function of this addiction in your life. You will not recover from relationship addiction until this more primary addiction is addressed.

———————

Dear Ms. Norwood:

Reading WWL2M *was part of an earnest search for the underlying problems which contributed to two divorces and several failed relationships, my inability to let go of impossible men and my feelings of worthlessness, inadequacy, etc.*

My history of relationships is basically that of attracting men younger than I (the youngest being nine years my junior) or men who are my same age but never men who are older. Because I am a small, slim woman, I am also young looking. My most recent relationship, however, was my first experience with an older man. I'm thirty-six and he's forty-four. We both admitted to being very much in love with each other after being together for nine months. A year later, he claimed that it was ". . . too much, too fast," and he wanted space. I now know that my expectations because he was an "older man" led me to love this man even before I had a chance to get to know him and understand the underlying reasons why he has been divorced once, will not sign the divorce papers for his second marriage and is a womanizer in the worst way (including having ONLY female friends).

While reading your book, I was desperately looking for stories that related specifically to incest but there were only two and only one of them touched remotely on what I have been through. You see I was not the victim of incest but am the fifth child of nine children, six being girls. I was very sickly as a child so my father could not bother me, but I could always hear him in the next room with my sister who is sixteen months younger than I. He molested each of his daughters except me. In fact he seemed to loathe my presence and we fought most of my life. When I was sixteen I threatened to kill him if he hit me as he threatened to do. He told my mother I was a financial burden because of my illness and he wished I hadn't been born. But somehow being the only sister who was not involved in my father's incestuous behavior has left me with a feeling of "not being able to be loved or accepted by a man."

This inner pain has affected many of my relationships—if a man said he loved me, I never believed him and went about disproving his love for me, while at the same time asking for more affection and not being willing to wait until he was willing to express it. Then I would turn around and shower him with love and affection to the point of smothering him. He would inevitably tell me I was pushing him and leave me. The majority of our fights would be over my accusations that he wasn't showing his love for me. Sounds confusing and mixed up, I know. Well, as far as this part of my life goes, I am!

In your research, did you find the incidence of loving too much to be more related to parents with problems of alcoholism and drug abuse than to unloving fathers and incest? I have heard that incest and alcoholism are usually within the same family. Is this true? There was no alcoholism in my family, though my father had an ulcer.

I alluded to a childhood of illness earlier in this letter—I have a skin disorder called atopic dermatitis which is a combination of multiple allergies to many different foods, pollens and chemicals in the air, etc., and a severe case of eczema. I have been marked outwardly on my skin by medication doctors have prescribed incorrectly. So this has added to my feelings of inadequacy.

I'm slowly getting over these feelings because God has blessed me with two beautiful boys, ages six and thirteen, and they have no allergies or skin disorders.

They are very healthy, very bright and very loving. I have been very stern and controlling toward them and not able to give them much loving. I want so much to be able to just relax and enjoy them but am hard pressed as to how to go about it. So I've begun to do some inner searching and am working on loving them truly and being less critical and less controlling but more attentive, teaching them responsibility and whatever else they need. I long to be a friend to both my children, especially my thirteen-year-old. It will take time, but I'm willing to try.

Lana Z.

Dear Lana,

You say in your letter that you were not the victim of incest, but you were. The fact that your father had physical relations with your sisters but not with you does not exclude you from the damage that was done. None of you knew your father as a trusted adult who cherished your well-being and used his resources as an adult to protect you from harm. Instead, he was a source of constant threat and danger, violating and abusing his children out of his own disease.

That you have been attracted to men younger than yourself makes sense if you recognize the need for control that is often operating in women who team up with younger men. There is that sense of being more experienced and sophisticated, stronger, wiser, less vulnerable. (It doesn't always work out this way, especially in terms of vulnerability, but it *seems* at first as though it would.)

The fact that the older man with whom you've become involved has very obvious problems with relating to women honestly, especially in the sexual area, is no surprise either, given our natural predilection for choosing people with whom we can repeat our childhood patterns of relating. Inappropriateness, distrust and threat in the area of sexuality are old themes for you.

Yes, incest happens most frequently in alcoholic homes, but it also has a high incidence in extremely religious homes and in homes where there is very harsh discipline. Incest is a generational disease; that is, the perpetrator or aggressor usually was a victim of sexual exploitation as a child and then, in adulthood, sexually abuses his or her own children or others. The female victim of incest often marries someone who is an aggressor or a potential aggressor and who eventually molests her children. In addition, we are just beginning to recognize the frequency with which women act in the role of aggressor/molester themselves. Thus, the damage is done to generation after generation as the secret is kept and the cycle is repeated.

We can learn to love and cherish the child we were as well as the adult we have become.

All of us who have been traumatized as children have a powerful drive to prevail over what once overwhelmed us. The more overwhelming the experience(s), the greater the need to re-create the conditions and prevail over them. This is what draws those who have been molested either to continue to allow themselves to be abused sexually or to become molesters themselves or to team up with molesters and then try to control them. All of these patterns of relating and compulsive acting out lose their mystery when we can view them as a driven need to control in the present what was uncontrollable in our past.

Your relationship with your sons also carries themes of harshness and control. How could it be otherwise? All each of us knows about parenting is what we experienced as children from our own parents, so in spite of our promises to ourselves to do it differently we find ourselves helpless to do other than what was done to us. This is why I always urge people to work on healing themselves in whatever areas they have been damaged. We can, as adults, learn to love and cherish that child we were as well as the adult we have become. We can, if we are willing to do so, begin to give ourselves unconditional love. It often takes lots of prayer and lots of work, but we can do it. Of course, our own recovery is the greatest gift we can give our children. And it is *never* too late for them—or for us. We *can* change our children's inheritance from one of disease to one of recovery, through our *own* healing.

All physical diseases are stress-related, in that they are either precipitated or exacerbated by stress. This seems to be especially so with skin disorders. The phrase "getting under my skin" is an apt one. In my opinion, you need to join a self-help group made up of people who have had experiences similar to yours. This is where your primary healing will take place. You may need individual therapy as well, but in choosing a therapist make sure you find one who truly understands incest and its effects as well as what recovery entails. Look for a therapist who will support your involvement in a self-help group as well. Those who are most qualified to work with victims of incest are those who are recovering from it themselves.

I want to caution you that your recovery will take time. The damage was done over many years and these patterns have had a life of their own for many more. Try to have courage and not be impatient, because recovery will eventually improve every area of your life: your health, your parenting, your other relationships and your spiritual life.

Dear Ms. Norwood,

I am a twenty-one-year-old senior majoring in psychology. For the past year I have been struggling with painful flashbacks from a childhood in which my father sexually abused me. Up until last year, I had completely blocked this period from my consciousness. But then I began to seriously examine my relationships with men. Unfortunately, it took several of these bad relationships and painful mistakes to realize that there was indeed a pattern. That is what prompted me to read your book. There I saw my problems, feelings and beliefs put into words. I saw the pattern and the reason for it—my childhood experience with my father. I guess I had never wanted to link him to my unhealthy relationships. I didn't want to blame him, so I blamed myself.

In reading your book I realized that this pattern of debilitating relationships is rooted in a much more serious problem, one that needed to be dealt with. I finally admitted to myself what had really happened to me and that it was still causing problems in my life. Fortunately, I have a good friend who works as a graduate assistant in the university counseling center. He recommended a therapist and I went to her and unlocked this secret that I had been carrying alone for nearly thirteen years.

During a month's time we explored my feelings, which progressed from an attitude toward my father of total exoneration to the awakening of an unparalleled anger at him. I saw how he has contributed to making me into a woman who loves too much. The reasons for my need to control, my desire to change and fix, my being in love with a dream and my avoidance of my own feelings were suddenly clear to me. For the first time in my life I felt real because I experienced the pain and anger that had always been there. I knew I could no longer pretend, especially at home.

Christmas vacation came along about a month after I had been in therapy, and I had to return home with these tremendous feelings boiling inside of me. I found it impossible to relate to my father in a normal manner. We had always had a seemingly good relationship, although I remember feeling uncomfortable around him at times while growing up. He definitely noticed a change in me.

My oldest sister came into town, and at my therapist's suggestion I talked to her about our father, only to find that the same abuse had happened to her. I had thought I was the only one, and she had had similar feelings. Finding this out increased my anger, and I felt driven by it. I knew then that he had to be confronted. There were the others to think about in the family as well: my mother, brother, and two other sisters besides the one who shared this secret with me.

My mother's and father's relationship has been rocky all along, but these past few years have been an especially hard time for them. My father is afraid to emotionally share himself with my mother, and she is definitely a woman who loves too much. (I passed the book on to her.) Dad remains distant from her, yet he does not hold back from showing his attraction to other women, always talking about them and occasionally becoming involved with them. Even so, Mom has stuck with him. She's a very intelligent, compassionate, and strongly driven woman, and she has taken great pains to make her marriage work, yet she has put up with way too much.

Now my mother has returned to school to pursue her degree in social work and she and I have become very close. We often have lengthy discussions about my father, his idiosyncrasies, and her relationship with him. Through these discussions I learned just how unhappy she has been.

As we talked Mom became well aware of the anger that I was feeling for my father, and she understood that it needed to be expressed. However, she thought it was due to the fact that his emotional unavailability and obsessive-compulsive behaviors had finally gotten to me. Many times, we children (and my mother) had experienced his irrational anger, his drastic mood swings, not to mention his peculiar habits. Returning home for visits was not always as pleasurable as it should have been. It's no wonder that we all have anger inside; we were never supposed to talk back or be angry with our father because we never knew how he would handle it. My mother has told me of times when he has banged on walls with his head or his fists. She, too, has been frightened by him since the early days of their marriage. The times when he was calm and relaxed can only be likened to the quiet before the storm.

The catch in all this, as I'm sure it is in similar cases, is that many people think my father is perfect; they think our family is perfect. We, as a family, have even held on to this view as we have grown up. Dad is a minister, now retired. His father was a minister, as are two of his three brothers. My friends have often bragged about what a "cool" dad I have. My mother's friends have told her how lucky she is to be married to such a wonderful man. His congregations have practically worshipped him more than their gods. And many women have tried to seduce him. Yet none of these people had to live with him as we did.

As I look back on each of our lives, I now recognize none of it was as great as I'd always liked others to believe. I had several siblings, we all seemed fairly well-adjusted, and we had parents who stayed together rather than following the trend of the rising divorce rate. I grew up as the model child—high-achieving student, well-behaved, attractive, good disposition, and mature for my age. Just about perfect on the outside. My mother even recently admitted that of the five children she thought I was the one who had no big problems. But as we became closer, she got to know me better.

During recent years, even before acknowledging the incest, everyone but my father has gradually become aware of our crumbling image. Now, with our new awareness, my oldest sister and I faced a dilemma. Should we tell our mother what our father did to us so many years ago? Was it worth bringing out? What would happen to the family that really hasn't been a family in the healthy sense of the word? Would our mother's guilt be too painful for us to stand? How would the other family members react to us? And what would become of this superficially great man who no one really knows, least of all, himself?

We decided that yes, something had to be said. My oldest sister was experiencing the same fear of confronting him that I had at the beginning of my therapy, but my anger was so strong that it carried me through the fear somehow. As this confrontation drew near, my mother put two and two together. From hints my sister and I had made and through reading about my father's peculiar behaviors (mood swings, depression, obsessive-compulsive actions, sexual preoccupation, etc.), she caught on. She asked me if he'd ever sexually abused me. I said "yes," and I saw on her countenance all that

I'd dreaded and expected. But I also saw her strength and determination begin to take over. She agreed that I should talk to Dad about it before anything else was done. She had her piece to speak also, and she was anxious to do so.

The next day I took him aside, and we had a long talk. I can honestly say that talking to him—having to open up and be emotionally honest—was the hardest thing I've ever had to do in my life. He had known something was on my mind, and he'd been extremely worried about our relationship. He had also guessed that my anger and distant behavior toward him concerned the abuse. He had obviously not blocked out or denied what had happened.

There were so many tears and so much sadness in our talk. Even though I blame him for what happened and am appalled at it all, I am still saddened by the fact that it ever had to happen and that it still happens so often in this world. To watch the image you've carried of your life and family shatter is truly heartbreaking. Seeing your father dissolve into a helpless, lost soul is tormenting. The strangest thing is that through expressing my anger to him at that time, I was able to still love him. However, that was the last time I've ever felt that love. Now I alternate between feelings of anger, disgust, and pity. Sometimes I feel nothing at all for him and wouldn't care if he simply vanished from this world. I wonder if we'll ever be able to have any kind of meaningful relationship again.

Currently, my mother and father are both in therapy and are separating, soon to be divorced. My oldest sister and I are each continuing with our therapy, and I would someday like to work with children or adult women who have been sexually abused. My other sisters and brother understand the situation, and we talk about it often. In fact, talking to my brother revealed that he, himself, had been subjected to a sexual episode with our father. Actually, I feel that we are a family for the first time, each getting to listen to and understand the others. I finally feel real *and can better pay attention to my needs and wants. This helps me hold my own with my family members and in other situations. I enjoy being with my mother, sisters and brother more than ever. There is a very close bond now. We are all looking out for one another, with empathy and true caring. We are growing.*

We are all shaken but not surprised about the divorce. It is for the best, but it is hard to get used to since they've been married for thirty-five years. What hurts me so is that my mother feels that most of those years were wasted on trying to make this man into what she wanted and needed. Yet, she is ready to move on and realizes that at age fifty-four, she is still young enough to make another go of it. Dad is not so strong, and I can only pity his weakness. Maybe through his therapy he will obtain some strength and gain back some of our respect.

As for me, I sometimes tend to avoid dealing with all of this, and at other times I am overwhelmed with the intensity of my feelings. The main thing I am doing is getting to know myself. It's kind of fun, very challenging, and a little scary. I've stood my ground and done a lot of things I never would have done before I acknowledged this part of my experience. I've actually surprised myself on several occasions. I am slowly but surely becoming in tune with my needs and wants, and I'm learning to recognize what is good and bad for me. I'm tired of making the same mistakes. But what is harder is actually doing the good stuff. I'm not used to it, and sometimes I feel uncomfortable even thinking about being in a stable, healthy environment.

Relationships are hardest. Trying to actively find someone to trust is a job! I don't even trust my own feelings about whom to trust. And I tend to see relationships in a negative light after observing my parents and remembering all the guys who've let me down. I'm trying not to generalize though, and want to keep the faith. It's slow going, but I really believe somewhere down the line I'll be at the right point for the right person. I'm just so grateful that I haven't ended up married to one of those losers with whom I've been involved. The best feeling is knowing that I'll get through, and I'll be okay.

Amy M.

Dear Amy,

Your letter describes poignantly the quandary that many families face when sexual abuse has occurred. As long as the abuse remains unacknowledged the family, though living a lie, can nevertheless remain intact and enjoy the approval and acceptance that society confers on those who appear normal. But when the abuse is uncovered the family is usually so shattered that it cannot survive as a unit. In other words, at least at some levels, the family is rewarded for keeping the secret and punished for admitting it. Rather than healing the family, this acknowledgment of incest can inflict further pain on each of its members. I do not point this out in order to imply that the answer is in keeping the secret of incest buried but rather to affirm that acknowledging this problem is not, in itself, tantamount to healing it. It *is,* however, the first necessary step toward the possibility of healing ever taking place. Obviously you as an individual may be able to heal whether or not, for instance, your father does. But, as you are learning, there is much more to remedying the damage that incest causes than a confrontation with the perpetrator.

In my opinion all the members of your family belong not in individual therapy with separate therapists but together in family therapy with professionals who understand sexual addiction. This approach deals with each of you as an individual but also recognizes that the family system in which incest occurred must be treated as well. I think it is appropriate to diagnose your father as sexually addicted. This means that, like an alcoholic, he has a disease. Having that condition does not exonerate him from responsibility for his acts but it does *in my opinion* relieve him from blame. Your father is like someone who, for instance, has the disease of tuberculosis. While not to blame for having the disease, he must take full responsibility for acknowledging his condition, must employ every precaution against infecting others and must seek appropriate treatment both for his own sake and the sake of those with whom he has contact. His disease is his responsibility but not his fault. I would venture that your father's addiction has its roots in his own history of having been exploited sexually and that, in some ways, the healing of his disease involves facing a trauma similar to that which you have endured. It is in working with the entire family unit in which incest has occurred that the highest levels of honesty, personal responsibility, understanding and forgiveness are reached. It is the ideal treatment approach.

Also, it should be pointed out that the polarizing of your parents into opposing roles—your father as bad, deceitful and the victimizer and your mother as good, honest and long-suffering—may be convenient and even comforting but can never be wholly accurate. For the sexual abuse that happened in your family to have been kept secret required that each of you, including your mother, be less than honest. Questions were left unasked, perceptions distorted, observations denied, feelings stifled. In the treatment of families where incest has occurred it often becomes evident that the non-acting out parent (in your case, your mother) is usually as much in need of help—indeed, is as damaged—as the perpetrator. Your father's disease will not automatically go away just because it has been uncovered; nor will your mother's co-dependency be erased when she divorces your father.

By the way, in-patient treatment of sexual addiction as a family disease is offered at a few hospitals in various areas of the country. Most of these programs incorporate a Twelve-Step approach and have evolved because during the in-patient treatment of chemical dependency the presence of sexual addiction in alcoholic families was found to be so prevalent. To treat the alcoholism and ignore the sexual addiction simply didn't make sense. On the other hand, sexual addiction and co-addiction are amenable to the same family systems approach that is such an effective in-patient approach to treating chemical dependency. This approach gets family members talking *to* instead of *about* each other and bares the family secrets so that they can be openly acknowledged and healed.

Amy, all the members of your family may not be willing to be involved in a single, family-system-focused approach to treating incest (whether in a hospital or not), but it is my belief that such an approach offers the greatest possibility of healing and that the more of you who become involved, the deeper the level of healing will be.

Dear Robin Norwood:

I am a recovering person, involved in Alcoholics Anonymous, Narcotics Anonymous, Overeaters Anonymous and Al-Anon. Recently I came to terms with my sexual addiction also and I am now in recovery for that too in Sexaholics Anonymous. I also see a therapist, and a substance abuse counselor. I am an Adult Child of Alcoholics as well and I am just beginning to try to work through some of these issues. My main problem is I have so much repressed (I think even some incest issues) and I'm not sure the best way to get in touch with this stuff. I am in a relationship with somebody to whom I've been married for eight years. We have five kids. We haven't lived together for two years and he's still drinking. I keep wishing and hoping he'll change. I act out my pain through choosing losers and having sexual relationships over and over again; all these men are alcoholic or drug addicted. With each one I think I'm in love and can't stop the DANCE. I have two months of abstinence from the last of these sexual involvements, excluding my husband.

I am in school and want to someday be a therapist. This is my long-term plan but I want to have a direction now as to where I am going. I once wrote to author Patrick Carnes, he wrote back and that was the beginning of work in this area. I am very interested in the possibility of hearing back from you.

Felice D.

Dear Felice,

I would like to share with you some of what I know about compulsive sexuality. First, it usually stems from having been abused sexually in childhood. While aversion to sexual activity is one result of such abuse, another is sexual compulsivity, which, in my experience, is even more common. Sexual compulsivity is a learned behavior, as is violence. People who are violent themselves or are with partners who are violent (or both) come from violent backgrounds. People who are sexually compulsive themselves or are drawn to people who are sexually compulsive (or both) come from backgrounds where there was sexual compulsivity and, most often, where they as children were sexually abused.

---

*If you suspect that you were an incest
victim it is likely that you were.*

If you suspect that you were an incest victim it is extremely likely that you were, for three reasons. One is that you suspect it. Many victims of incest are unable to remember specifics but have a vague and very unwelcome sense that "something was wrong in that area." The memories are buried because to know, to remember, to face the conflicted emotions is too overwhelming. The second reason is your sexual compulsivity. Your behavior has not been generated in a vacuum. You learned to identify yourself as a sexual object and to relate primarily sexually because in all likelihood that is the way you were treated and traumatized in childhood. Trauma of any kind can lead to compulsive reenacting of the event in an effort to dispel the resulting feelings of emotional shock and pain. When the event was sexual its replay leads to further trauma. Compulsive sexual relating in adulthood for women is virtually diagnostic of their having been sexually abused in childhood. It is both a learned behavior and an urgently repetitive reenactment of the overwhelming event(s) of the past. The fact that you come from an alcoholic home is a third reason why incest is likely to have been a part of your background. Though incest is by no means universally present in alcoholic homes, alcoholism is very frequently present in homes where incest occurs.

In order to recover you must recognize that you are not "acting out your pain by choosing losers and having sexual relations with them." Rather, you must realize that by now you are acting out your disease of addiction and that the present pain both issues from your sexual addiction and serves to rationalize your next episode of "acting out."

You probably wonder why you ended up with so many different addictions yourself. Perhaps the following concept will help you understand. Many diseases of addiction are what we in the treatment field call "over-determined." This simply means that there is more than one perfectly adequate reason for the disease to occur. In your case, your alcoholism and other drug addiction could be attributed solely to the fact that you probably inherited a physiological predisposition to chemical dependency from your alcoholic parents since today we know that there is a definite genetic aspect to alcoholism. Or your alcoholism could be seen solely as either a learned behavior or a coping mechanism, which you adopted through growing up in a family system in which people coped by drinking. Finally, your chemical dependency could be seen as an attempt at self-medicating away the emotional trauma of incest that, through over-use of habituating drugs, turned into addiction. Any and all are probably true for you, and each of these explanations probably applies in some measure to your compulsive eating as well. Compulsive eating is commonly present in women who have been sexually abused.

Try to remember that, even with all the problems your alcohol-drug-food addictions have caused, you may have needed to abuse these substances in order to survive the trauma of your past. Now, with the tools from the Anonymous programs and other appropriate support, you can begin to address what is probably for you your primary addiction, the one with the longest history and the deepest roots—your sexual compulsivity.

You wanted to know "the best way to get in touch with this stuff." Rather than recommend one specific therapeutic technique or another I want to suggest that the most important step for you right now is to work on becoming *willing* to face whatever there is in your past. As you pray for the willingness to face these issues and the courage to deal with them honestly, the rest will take care of itself. You will find the program and the people you need to support you, and your memories will begin unfolding in your awareness as quickly as you are able to handle them.

I salute your courage both in your pursuit of recovery and your desire to become a therapist. No one, in my opinion, makes a better therapist than a person who has personally struggled with addiction and has achieved some years of good, solid recovery. In a way, the more addictions we have personally encountered in ourselves and dealt with the more we understand about how people get sick and how they can also get well. Many, many people who are attracted to the helping professions have backgrounds similar to yours—backgrounds that have also resulted in many of the same addictions, obsessions and compulsions. The question then becomes, are we, as members of the helping professions, in denial regarding our own disease(s) or are we in recovery? In my opinion denial makes us dangerous in every area of our lives. Recovery, on the other hand, requires such a tremendous surrender of pride (the need to look good) and self-will ("I can handle this alone") that most helping professionals choose to carefully guard their own secrets. But when life blesses us by making it impossible for us to go on as before—when we ourselves must either recover or die—the humility we develop by facing our own secrets will serve us very well as we seek to understand our clients' struggles. With all the years of schooling ahead of you, your own ongoing recoveries will be your greatest educational experience.

But when you finally have your degree and license I would urge you always to remember that you are a recovering person first and a professional second. If you reverse these two identities you may find yourself needing to feign recovery in areas that still need healing in order to justify your status as a therapist. There is also the tendency to use our profession as a distraction from our own disease. Since life has a way of continuing to deal us challenges whether or not we have a degree and a license, the personal problems you encounter when you are a professional will either help to keep you humbly working your programs or will make you feel defensive and secretive and will feed the natural human tendency toward denial. If that happens you will inevitably become less effective as a counselor and your own recoveries will be threatened. Fortunately, the same qualities that are necessary to good recovery will enhance your therapeutic skills with others. That's just one of the great bonuses of recovery.

Five

. . . HAVE OTHER ADDICTIONS

Today most experts in the field of addiction accept that the disease model best describes and explains addiction and its treatment. It is generally agreed that addiction is a condition with identifiable behavioral, emotional and physical symptoms that become more serious as the disease progresses. The disease model for addiction includes a treatment approach that advocates involvement in peer support groups to achieve abstinence. When adhered to, this is the most effective approach in that it promotes recovery from what is otherwise a progressively terminal condition.

Once we who are addictive understand what addiction is, how it progresses and the appropriate way to treat it, we then have (depending on our particular frame of reference) a diagnosis, a construct or a metaphor that can explain our feelings and our behavior. This understanding may be the key to providing relief for more than one problem area, because we who are addictive often suffer from more than one addiction. Our various addictions may differ in the degree to which they make life unmanageable for us. For instance, we may have one addiction that covers up another, as when a compulsion to exercise helps disguise the effects of a compulsion to eat. Or we may have one addiction that prevents the treatment of another that is more primary, as when an active addiction to alcohol makes the treatment of a more severe and more primary sexual addiction impossible until the alcoholism is addressed.

There are those persons who will never be able to accept relationship addiction as a *disease process,* just as there are those who for their own reasons are unable to see how the disease concept applies to alcoholism. However, many of us in the treatment field have long regarded recovering addicts of all kinds as the true "experts" on their addiction. Recovering addicts are the ones from whom all professionals who treat that

particular addiction can learn the most. When addicts recognize
their condition as a disease, treat it as such and then recover,
that alone, in my opinion, makes a convincing case for applying
the disease concept to addiction.

The following letter presents a persuasive case for the
parallels between alcoholism and relationship addiction in their
active phases and in the way recovery from each must be
approached. The woman who wrote it has known each of these
varieties of addiction personally. She has also known the frustration of trying to communicate about addiction with someone
who, though deeply concerned and very well-meaning, simply
did not understand.

Dear Ms. Norwood:

*I'll omit the details of my story as I know it is not
noticeably different from others you've encountered
through your research. But I do want to tell you about
the profound effect* **WWL2M** *has had on the understanding between my former sister-in-law and myself. She's
been my friend for thirty years. For twenty-five years,
she was married to my brother and in a traditional
housewife role while I went through two marriages and
was single most of that time. Since her divorce several
years ago, she has chosen very different types of relationships than I always have. Hers seem more stable and
rewarding, while I've been slung hither and yon by the
monsters of romance. Throughout these many years,
she's listened for countless hours to my pain, trying to
help and comfort me. I've spent those same untold hours
trying to make her understand how I could want to
remain in such stressful relationships. No matter how
much we each tried, I could never explain myself adequately and she was never able to understand.*

*I am a recovering alcoholic. Because I believe that
alcoholism is a disease, I attend Alcoholics Anonymous,
get counseling when I need it, and (by the grace of God)
have been sober seven and a half years. I fully believe
that my disease is progressive, whether I am actively
practicing it or not.*

Understanding that alcoholism is a disease has helped me understand my problems with men. Apparently, my romances have become progressively more unhealthy, too. In June of this year, I ended two years of celibacy and non-dating, finally feeling stable enough to take a chance on dating again after the romantic disaster of '83–'84. But even I could finally see there is something wrong with me *as the agony immediately began again!*

I followed the same negative patterns with the new man I started dating in June, and was soon a thousand times more miserable than before.

By August, I was once more almost incapacitated by stress. Within four days, three people in three different locations told me to read your book. I'm a library hound, and seldom buy any books, but I figured (Alcoholics Anonymous person that I am) that God must be trying to tell me something so I bought your book and read it.

Just as I had had a spiritual awakening concerning my need for sobriety, reading your book was the awakening I needed to really assess who I am in relationships. I have felt like such an odd person throughout the years because those I shared my pain with didn't happen to have addictive natures or suffer from addictive relationships. Of course, I therefore received advice that I found impossible to comprehend, much less follow. I didn't know what was wrong, but it was nameless and all-pervasive. I believed I was a misfit.

I was much like a person who is color-blind but neither I nor others were aware of it. When people tried to "explain colors" to me, neither side could understand the communication difficulty. Now, besides finally knowing I had been speaking in a foreign language to my friends and advisors most of my life, I've also discovered I'm not alone. I have a serious problem, yes—but I sure ain't by myself! Just as I became more self-accepting when I confronted my alcoholism and found that millions suffered from the same disease, I saw myself as more "normal" when I confronted my love addiction. The timing of the latest boyfriend, the reading of WWL2M *and my consequent awakening have made it an interest-*

ing August and September, believe me! I was left with three choices about relationships:

1. Make no personal changes, and never have any kind of positive relationship—in which case I couldn't see much reason for living.

2. Give up on having natural, healthy closeness with a special man; remain alone the rest of my life—in which case I couldn't see much reason for living.

3. Face the fact that I'm a relationship addict and do whatever I have to in order to change myself, so I can live in some mental comfort.

I'm glad to tell you I ended the "romance" and chose option number three! Once I could understand that for me loving is really no different than drinking, and since I have learned tools through the years in Alcoholics Anonymous to assist me with overcoming addiction, I felt some confidence in starting on the right path. I spent September in actual physical withdrawal from the relationship (or was I withdrawing from all the past romances?). It was certainly more terrible than quitting alcohol. But I was determined to do it as a matter of physical and mental survival. I went into counseling, participated in an addictive relationships group conducted especially for co-alcoholics, studied myself, examined past ill-fated liaisons and read as much as I could on this and related subjects.

Almost by magic I was "cured" of the latest painful relationship by the end of September. And through that time, as always, I had the firm support of my sister-in-law. But because I insisted that she also read WWL2M, she was able to be there for me in a more constructive way. Now she understands us love addicts!

Oh, I know it's not over, and that this immediate "cure" is only temporary. But I am a recovering alcoholic and I know generally what is ahead of me, and something about how to go forward. I'm still toddling around in my new outlook, but I feel the same principles I've used in Alcoholics Anonymous will help me get through this addiction and on to a better way of life and living. I expect success and I'm willing to work for it.

You have mentioned that you feel the best help for

relationship addiction is to be found in groups similar to Alcoholics Anonymous. I had thought I would start such a group but I haven't done it yet. I think such sharing is necessary though, to help others with this "love-addiction" problem. After I get a little steadier and solve a couple more of my mundane, practical living problems, I'll make the effort to reach out to others of "us."

Rhonda D.

Dear Rhonda,

I agree with you completely that relationship addiction, like alcoholism, is a progressive disease. It is one of the enigmas of addiction that while an alcoholic or drug addict is drug-free the disease is arrested but if the use of mind-altering chemicals is resumed that person is soon just as ill as before abstinence. Physically and emotionally it is as if there had never been a sober period, indeed, as if the person had been using the drug(s) throughout the entire period of sobriety, even if sobriety had been of many years' duration. We don't know why this is true; we just know that it is the case.

When lecturing I've been asked if I believe that relationship addiction is progressive in the same way that chemical dependency is, in that even after a period of abstinence or "sobriety" can a person quickly become sicker than ever by resuming addictive relating? My answer from my own experience and from observation is yes. Your experience with your "August romance" is typical of what I've seen occur. That is, the time period between launching an addictive relationship and finding life completely unmanageable speeds up dramatically as the years go by. Further, the negative consequences to physical and emotional health tend not only to be evident more quickly but to be more severe with each "slip," just as is the case with alcoholism.

Let me tell you just one story to illustrate this. A young woman I'll call Gail had, through dedicated attendance at Al-Anon meetings, finally gained enough sense of self-worth to extricate herself from a live-in situation with an unemployed (except for his drug dealing), physically abusive addict. Through continued attendance at meetings and close contact with supportive friends in her program, she managed to stay away from him in the early months of their separation in spite of his many attempts to reengage her. Finally, he stopped calling.

After four years she had her life in good order. One day, by accident, she met her former lover on the street. They talked for a while and he told her he'd like to take her to lunch. Certain that she was healthy enough to handle seeing him again, especially under such innocuous conditions, she agreed. They made a date for two days later and in the interim she found herself thinking about him more and more, increasingly eager to prove to him how much she had changed, how ''well'' she had become. She even thought, now that she was so healthy, she might be able to help him.

When he failed to show up for their date she endured the mounting tension she felt for two hours, then found herself calling his mother (the only phone number she still had by which she might reach him) to find out where he was. She and his mother had had many other phone conversations like the one they had that afternoon, both women discussing ways to pin down the elusive addict. Soon Gail was calling a new phone number his mother had given her and, when that failed to bring results, driving by the house where he now lived. She was, throughout the next four days, completely obsessed with locating him so that she could get him to see how sick *he* was and how much *he* needed help. There were more phone calls that involved begging his mother to stop giving him money, so that he could ''hit bottom,'' and trying to persuade this woman to attend Al-Anon, a step his mother was not ready to take. Although throughout these four days Gail never did locate her former lover, she nevertheless in every way available to her practiced her disease.

When I saw Gail on the fourth day of this marathon, she looked ten years older, blue-gray and hollow-eyed with exhaustion (she hadn't been sleeping) and deeply shaken by what she had found herself capable of, even after years of good, solid recovery. Agreeing to have contact with this man had exactly the same effect on Gail that taking a drink would have had on a sober alcoholic. Years of recovery were immediately wiped out and the obsession was off and running, stronger than ever.

The good news is that Gail regularly attended Al-Anon meetings and on the fourth day of her binge she was at one of her regular meetings, talking about her "slip" and gaining the strength and the support she needed not to call, not to drive by, not to obsess about her ex-boyfriend. Today she has a deeper appreciation of the power of her disease.

Although the alcoholic can "put the plug in the jug," few of us would want to live without meaningful relationships.

In some ways a comparison between compulsive eating and relationship addiction is more appropriate than a comparison between relationship addiction and alcoholism. Although the alcoholic can "put the plug in the jug" and never take another drink, the relationship addict, like the compulsive eater, must somehow come to terms with the source of addiction. We cannot live without food, and few of us can or would want to live without meaningful relationships. The key, if we are compulsive eaters, is in learning how to eat sanely and abstain from those foods which act as drugs in our body. Correspondingly, if we are relationship addicts, we need to learn to relate sanely and avoid those people who are for us the drug that propels us headlong into our disease. The following letter makes this point nicely.

Dear Robin,
I must tell you of a recent incident in my life, which came about because of your book. After reading

WWL2M, *I decided to try to get my life back in order after my second divorce and to reestablish contact with a group of old friends, all couples, with whom I had been friendly during my first marriage. My second husband had not liked these people and the feeling was mutual on their part. I, of course, chose to "stand by my man" at the expense of a ten-year, close relationship with these people. Having recently reestablished these old friendships, I was invited to play in a golf tournament with the ladies of the group. The men at the club also had a match at the same time. There were two new single men in the match and my friends were dying for me to meet them. All the wagers were placed on Hal, thrice divorced, wealthy, handsome and to quote the men, "a real wild man." (My friends know me so well!) The other man, Greg, is an attorney from Phoenix and was described as "pleasant" and a "nice guy." Two months ago, I would have been like a moth to the flame with Hal, but with my new awareness I avoided Hal like the plague and spent most of the Saturday evening dinner and dance getting to know Greg. Yes, he is nice and he is pleasant. Two months ago, perhaps, I would have thought him boring but now I've found him to be interesting and interested. I think Weight-Watchers has certain foods they term, "safe." After your book, I have decided to term certain men as "safe." Greg is definitely safe. No bells, no skyrockets, just calm, friendly interacting. We're getting to know each other slowly.*

Millie D.

Dear Millie,

Once when I was lecturing on compulsive eating a woman in the audience asked how she could tell which foods were her "binge" foods and which ones were "safe." Another woman called out, "Well, let's face it. We don't get up in the middle of the night and drive all over town looking for broccoli!"

I've been using her words ever since to illustrate this point. I'm not advising that the answer lies in limiting ourselves to men who are as dull as a restrictive diet. I am simply suggesting that some men are like broccoli, not too exciting but wholesome and good for us—and some men are like chocolate cake: incredibly appealing but, for those of us who are addictive, definitely very dangerous.

Dear Ms. Norwood,

I was so struck by your book that I needed to write to you. I saw myself in every story, recognizing my habitual attraction to the "love 'em and leave 'em" type. I had thought my pattern unique. What a relief to know I'm not the only one blinded by the need to be with someone whether that person is healthy or not.

Although I had recognized the trend in my relationships, I felt helpless to control my need. I would fight the feelings which grew stronger and stronger the more I fought. Then I would simply give in.

It would usually begin when I encountered a man who was having a problem. I would counsel him and he, having been relieved of his burden because I had now taken it on as mine to fix, would hang around for a while, allowing me to try my hand at improving his life. I entered these relationships fully aware that this kind of man would not stick around permanently. But it was so heady, so exciting, so flattering while he was depending on me. I even told myself that I had to take this opportunity now, because I might never have another chance to experience these feelings.

As soon as I began to make my own needs for his time and attention known, he would invariably disappear without so much as a call or note to say goodbye. These men would work hard to break down my defenses which came into play if their problems were particularly alarming or offensive to me. Then there were calls, flowers, dinners, long talks about feelings, and lots of time spent together. But it always seemed that as soon as they thought they had me it was time for them to break away.

I've had one or two semi-healthy relationships. I went out with Phil during college for a year which is the longest any of my relationships has lasted. He was everything these other men weren't: trustworthy, caring, dependable, available. Slowly but surely I lost my "love" for him. I tried talking to him about how my feelings had changed, how I had become bored. Finally I took the only way out I knew. I began having an affair with a married and totally unavailable man. This affair was short-lived but it got the message across to Phil and left me with the familiar crisis and pain to replace the intolerable boredom.

I went through a two-year nearly suicidal depression after college. A friend of mine was in Alcoholics Anonymous so I went to some meetings with her. I quit drinking, because I was desperate to make the pain stop. I've been sober now for sixteen months. Alcoholics Anonymous has provided the support and program I needed to change my old patterns, not just with the drinking but with the thinking.

But the relationship dependency is hard to break. After five months of having only a platonic relationship, I began going out with Al who is also in Alcoholics Anonymous. I knew he cared, but I just wasn't attracted to him. Like Phil, he was loving and trustworthy. In an effort to change my previous behavior, I prayed to my Higher Power that I would love Al as much as he loved me. They say to be careful what you pray for because you might get it. I did. I grew more and more emotionally dependent on him. As friends, we had spent almost every day together, going to meetings or whatever. When we became lovers I didn't see that he needed space. I assumed the time spent would be of the same duration and of even greater intensity than when we had been just friends. I gave my all to him, because I thought it was safe now to do so.

Needless to say I practically crushed him with my intensity. We broke up and I was once again devastated. But here's where Alcoholics Anonymous and your book came in. I'm not over it; I still think about him. But there's some comfort in knowing I can care about some-

one who cares about me. For that I'm grateful. I guess I just need to temper my feelings.

Phil used to say that I don't have layers of defenses like most people do. I just have one thick, brick wall. If you can pass through that, I'm all open and vulnerable like a clam whose shell is cracked.

Funny thing is I counsel drug abusers. You weren't kidding when you said there's an overabundance of our type in the helping professions. At least I have attained better understanding of myself and know the kind of help I need.

Suzi C.

Dear Suzi,

A key sentence in your letter, for me, is, "I guess I just need to temper my feelings." If only it were that easy! Since we're talking about relationship *addiction* that sentence is as optimistically naive as an alcoholic saying, "I guess I just need to temper my drinking." Not practicing an addiction requires more than telling yourself to change. In fact, if doing so worked, there really would be no such thing as addiction. People would simply "temper" their behavior the moment it appeared to be getting out of hand and that would be the end of that. Since such self-willed efforts to control addiction do not work, let's look at what does.

In order not to practice an addiction, you must become willing to take the feelings that impel you into your disease to another source for relief. You will not eliminate one behavior, such as addictive relating, without substituting another. Nor will you be able to eliminate one "solution" to your loneliness and anxiety, such as connecting with a man, without substituting another. Often other people who have experienced the same obsession as well as some recovery can become that alternative source of relief, but we must reach out to them and tell them about the feelings with which we are struggling. Attending meetings and reading books on recovery help tremendously and are a very necessary part of filling the vacuum that is created when we begin to eliminate an old pattern of behavior. And nothing works better than prayer as long as we're asking for God's will, not our own. Unless we do these things, the feelings of anxiety and the compulsion to practice the disease grow stronger and stronger the more we fight them, just as you have discovered. In a relationship addict the desperation to connect with a partner (or even a potential partner) can be fully as strong as a heroin addict's desperation to connect with a supply of that drug. The urgency behind our phone calls, our trips past his house—often in the middle of the night—mimics all too closely the drug addict's quest for relief from intolerable discomfort. Our need to "control our supply"— to know where he is and what he's doing when he's not with us—is another parallel. But since a drug can usually be bought, while a person usually cannot, we find ourselves plagued by the nagging fear that we will not be able to keep this man, who is our source of relief, around and available to us. Our attempts to matter to him, to be attractive, even irresistible, to become as necessary to his well-being as he is to ours, can turn us into clinging, seductive, manipulative, smothering, controlling and sometimes self-abasing women who are eventually despised for all our efforts, despised by our partner as well as ourselves.

In your particular style of practicing relationship addiction you offer an unspoken deal to the man who strikes you as needy. It is simply this: I'll take care of you first and then you'll take care of me.

So you begin by assuming the role of the all-giving, all-accepting, all-nurturing parent to his needy, naughty child. As long as you are able to remain boundlessly nurturing toward him the relationship seems to work. But since your posture with him increasingly depletes your own very limited emotional resources, you must eventually turn to him to resupply yourself with all the care and attention you have been giving out. When you do so, you are resented for making demands that, in spite of all your ministrations, this man is unable and unwilling to meet. He agreed to the first part of the contract (that you would take care of him), but not the second part (that in turn he would take care of you). So when you make your demand, no matter how subtly, the deal falls through and the relationship ends.

When we turn to a drug, a behavior or another person to take care of our uncomfortable feelings, especially our fear, we risk developing an unhealthy dependence that can turn into full-scale addiction. There is an old Chinese saying that describes the progression of alcoholism but that, in essence, describes the progression of every other kind of addiction as well:

> The man takes the drink.
> The drink takes the drink.
> The drink takes the man.

The potential for addiction begins when we make a choice to do something that we expect will bring us some relief from a mildly to a severely uncomfortable emotional state. ("The man takes the drink.") We feel bad. We want to feel better. We take a drink, use a drug, eat an ice cream cone, spend some money, meet a new man—and we feel better . . . for a while. But because we've used a shortcut to avoid our discomfort, its source hasn't been addressed or relieved. The discomfort has only been temporarily postponed. Our process of coping hasn't been practiced or strengthened, and so when our discomfort returns we are less able or willing to face it. We've become a little lazy. We've found an apparently easy way to avoid uncomfortable feelings and now we are beginning to rely on this "habit" of avoidance.

But our "fix" always costs us something in return for the relief it brings. Aside from resulting in our inability to develop a healthy coping process, these various habits leave a residue of their own—namely, a "hangover," either physically or emotionally or both. Soon we're turning to our fix to deal with the discomfort that the very use of it produces. For instance, most relationship addicts experience painful anxiety when the man leaves the bed or the room or the house. There is an immediate fear of abandonment that can only be assuaged by his promise to return. Thus, ultimately, being

with him has not reduced our anxiety but rather increased it. Having been with him, we need to be with
him again. ("The drink takes the drink.")

Finally, through repeated use of and growing dependency on our fix, the resultant hangover becomes so
intolerably painful that most of our efforts are directed
at just keeping this hangover pain at bay. ("The drink
takes the man.") Our shortcut remedy—the drink, the
drug, the food, the spending, the person—has become
an addiction and our addiction is controlling us. Not only
does it not bring relief, but we actually feel worse than
ever.

When a man or a relationship has become our fix
we're especially vulnerable, because when we most need
him he may be preoccupied, busy, uninterested or perhaps unkind or even abusive. He is supposed to be taking
our pain away but he isn't; he's adding to it. We're
lonelier, more unhappy and less satisfied than ever.
Because he has come to represent potential relief from
these feelings, we turn to him with greater need, stronger
demands and more desperation. It isn't working but we
can't stop. What once seemed to be an easy solution has
become our biggest problem. This is the nature of addiction.

---

*As recovering relationship addicts, our
sobriety cannot be measured except by
the serenity we achieve.*

Suzi, your relationship dependency may be a more
primary disease than your alcoholism. Of course you
must be sober first in order to address it and you must
stay sober in order to heal from it. But it may present a
more difficult recovery for you.

Respect it. Use all the tools of Alcoholics Anonymous to address it, perhaps in a Twelve-Step program
specifically structured to address relationship addiction.
Know that with this disease "slips" are inevitable and,
at first, discouragingly frequent. As recovering relation-

ship addicts we cannot count the "sober days," because sobriety in relationships, while very real, is also very subtle and cannot be measured except by the eventual degree of serenity we achieve in our lives.

Dear Ms. Norwood:

My history with men has been one of dating guys I knew I couldn't be close to because I didn't really like them. I guess I chose them because I was afraid of getting close. Then, during my college years I dated a very nice, very sweet, very loving man. But I was so afraid. I just couldn't be an equal partner since he seemed so much more mature and naturally more loving than I was. I felt inferior, and even though I cared about him, I felt I didn't deserve the love. He wanted us to marry when I was only twenty-three, but I knew I was too young. So we broke up. I then went through a stage of "sitting still with myself." I spent months not dating anyone at all, just spending time in reflection, building my self-esteem and trying to learn to feel okay.

But today, even after all this work on myself and even though my career is stupendous, my relationship with my present boyfriend hasn't been too great. He's very caught up in finding himself and finding out what he wants to do with his life. Recently, we almost broke up over some actions he took to settle some issues. I was shocked by what he had done and hurt, and I considered ending our relationship. My sister pointed out if I broke up with him I'd lose him and be hurt, too. It wouldn't just be him losing me and hurting. So he and I talked very honestly and I set some limits in terms of what I would tolerate and I cried and cried—and I feel now that through anger, understanding, honesty and forgiveness I grew up a little bit more and learned something about relationships. I realize I still have patterns from childhood that affect me with my boyfriend, especially the way I related to my older brother, always needing to stand my ground and be defensive.

My boyfriend and I also have a food addiction. We both deal with it as best we can. I don't have a weight problem because I exercise every day. My boyfriend is overweight. Having this in common is more a blessing than a curse. At least we can talk about it—no potato chips allowed!! I acknowledge the urge to eat is always there—whether I actually run to food or not. I don't smoke, have never used drugs and I drink alcohol usually only on special occasions. I have no attraction to alcohol even when I'm feeling blue or upset. I can remember only one time thinking, "I'm going to have a drink," but I didn't because the thought of wanting it scared me.

Oh well, can't analyze everything. Life is for living, with hurts, through sad times—to find my daily rainbows.
Mikki K.

Dear Mikki,

Okay, we won't analyze *everything,* but some of what you've written warrants our attention.

First, let's look at what is going on between you and your boyfriend. Your letter poses a way of dealing with a partner's unacceptable behavior that is very common but, in my opinion, not very productive. You state that your boyfriend, in trying to "settle some issues," behaved in a way that shocked and hurt you. You said you finally dealt with that by setting some limits regarding what you feel would be acceptable behavior for him. In other words, you told him what you would and would not put up with and now you expect him to tailor his behavior accordingly.

If his behavior shocked you it is because it violated your value system. You are twenty-six. I'm assuming he is approximately your age. That means that you are both adults, each with your value systems well developed and operating in your lives. What your boyfriend did violated *your* value system but not *his.* Otherwise *you* wouldn't be putting limits on what *he* is allowed to do. He would be setting his own limits in light of his own values.

This is not nit-picking on my part, Mikki. You need to recognize that this man is telling you something important about who he is and how he approaches life. It is both naive and presumptuous for you to think that you belong up at the blackboard instructing him that if he wants a relationship with you he should do A and not do B. He is being himself and he will inevitably continue to be himself. Your job is not to teach him to be different than he is for the sake of the relationship. Your job is to decide if you can comfortably accept who he is and the way he approaches the problem of living. We are happiest being with the people we can accept exactly as they are. When we expect them to change for our sake we are not respecting them nor are we taking care of ourselves. Chances are high that he will shock and hurt you again through his behavior, except that you will have less right to be shocked or even surprised because you already know that the capacity for this behavior exists in him.

I've worked with women who expected their partners to stop seeing other women, or being sexually attracted to men, or using drugs, or drinking, or gambling, or using pornography, or hitting them, or criticizing them or avoiding them through work—on and on. These men were not able to stop in order to please these women, not over time. They might change their behavior for a while in order to keep peace, but they were not able to do so permanently. People are not really able to permanently change for the sake of another person. They can put the brakes on for a while or they can allow that other person to put the brakes on for them for a while, but all this is only temporary. The behavior will eventually resume because the person who makes changes in order to please or placate someone else is unchanged underneath.

I hope you can say to yourself, "This man is capable of doing this thing which shocks me. Can I face that fact and live comfortably with it? Because although I have a right to tell him how his behavior makes me feel, I have no right to expect or demand that he change for my sake. In fact, even to tell him more than once how I feel about his behavior becomes an implicit demand that he change. My job, after communicating my feelings once, is to decide how *I* will handle my feelings concerning what he does. I may tell him of my decision but again, only to inform him, not to bring pressure on him to change. Otherwise, I will probably end up making threats I'm not prepared to carry out." All this is not easy to do, Mikki, but it is a way of handling your situation that can possibly save you many years of anger, pain and recriminations.

The factor that would keep you from viewing your situation with him in this way is self-will. There are strong indications in your letter of self-will operating, particularly in the area of food. This is the second area I'd like to look at with you.

If each of you has an addiction to food you really have no business talking about it together. It is a common practice for people with addictions to marry or team up with others with addictions. Then each person tends to try to control the other's problem. When they both share the same addiction, as is the case with you and your boyfriend, often one person takes charge of trying to manage the disease for both people. This attempt to control the eating, as much as the actual abuse of food, is an aspect of the food addiction disease process. It precludes a willingness to admit one's *lack* of control, which is a necessary initial step in recovery. Besides, trying to manage the eating issue for your partner will not ultimately generate feelings of gratitude in him. Instead your behavior will sooner or later engender in him feelings of resentment, of being overcontrolled. Consequently, he will have the desire to rebel, to get away with something. He will play the "naughty child" to your role of "controlling mother."

If you are going to address your problem with food, begin by ignoring what your boyfriend is eating and focus instead on yourself. This is the only place your attention belongs. His eating behavior and his weight are his business, not yours. Again, it is a lack of respect for others' rights to be who they are that allows us to try to "help" them manage their lives, *even when they appear to invite us or allow us to do so.* This constitutes a trap for both people, an evasion of responsibility for self.

Finally, Mikki, I'd like to look at what may be a clue to some of your struggles with men. Your childhood interactions with your older brother may have left you with a lingering desire to "win," to prevail over him or over any man with whom you become involved, because they each eventually come to represent him. If that need to triumph is still operating, you will find yourself drawn to men and situations that do not really suit you, and you will then try to manage and control them in the way you longed to be able to manage and control your brother. (In fact, I have a hunch that your present boyfriend's "shocking" behavior is in some way similar to your brother's.) This need will keep you locked in a struggle with men who will always at some level represent the troublesome aspects of your brother and your struggle with him. Until you hold still, admit your powerlessness over him and everyone else and become willing to let that part of you that was hurt and frustrated by him heal, you will not be able to surrender your need to control a man enough to love and be loved.

Dear Ms. Norwood,

I, too, am the child of an alcoholic father; I've had a lifelong problem with binge eating and I've been hospitalized with major depression. My family was dysfunctional in the reverse sense in that I was smothered with love and overprotection from my father. By the time I reached adolescence and discovered boys, I naturally needed approval from a world beyond my family. However, I wasn't received with the same unquestioning warmth as I was from my father. I interpreted this as proof of my inadequacy and I tried harder to become lovable. Thus began the vicious cycle.

I believe that I fall into a category of women addicted to love that was somewhat overlooked in your book, namely, those of us who have always been single and who haven't even maintained an unhealthy relationship for long. I know there are many of us who are so terrified of our unlovability to men, yet addicted and tortured with the longing for a satisfying relationship.

*In the few days since I've read your book, I feel a
burgeoning self-love. I've also felt the "knot called love"
in my stomach and the "wind blowing through my empty
soul." I know I will continue to grow.*

Marcie G.

Dear Marcie,

When we have been the object of a parent's smothering overprotectiveness and possessiveness it is very
threatening to begin to redefine that flattering attention
and instead of calling it "love" to recognize it as the
inappropriate, covertly sexualized interaction it really
was. Many alcoholic men pay far more attention to their
daughters than they do to their wives or any other
appropriate adult female partner. This occurs because
having a genuinely honest and loving relationship with a
peer is virtually impossible when alcoholism is present.
For one thing, sexual dysfunction is very common in
alcoholic men because of alcohol's anesthetic quality
and its inhibiting effect on male hormone production.
Also, there is the inevitable attrition of self-esteem in the
alcoholic and the corresponding heightened self-loathing.
Under these conditions it is obviously easier to choose
one's uncritical, adoring daughter as one's love object
than an adult female peer who is likely to be angry,
disapproving and all too aware of one's shortcomings.

When a daughter is thus elevated to peer status with
her father, whether or not anything overtly sexual occurs
between them, there is a sexual undertone to all their
relating *because he has appropriated his daughter as his
own.*

Added to this dynamic is another, interrelated to it
and increasing its pressure exponentially. It is this: Even
though to all appearances the parent is overdoing the
caretaking of the child, in actual fact the child is carrying
the burden of responsibility for the parent's welfare.
Normally, adults meet their needs for love, support,
understanding and companionship primarily with other
adults. To try to meet these needs through a child is
inappropriate because the child is not equipped with a

strong enough sense of self and separateness to survive such a demand from an adult. The child is taken over to serve the adult's need.

For a daughter in your position, Marcie, these two interrelated dynamics can continue to cast their shadow over all later interactions with men. No wonder you are as desperately afraid of a deep relationship with an adult peer as you are of being alone. Either way, the effects of your father's appropriation of you as his partner are operating. With a partner you are betraying your father by deserting him for another man. Alone, you remain trapped in the overwhelming responsibility you feel for him and to him as both his daughter and his (unsuitable) primary partner.

The key to recovery is to stop practicing the addiction first and then start talking about it, not the other way around.

Of course your binge eating and depression are in all probability intimately linked to both your childhood circumstances and your heredity. Many, many binge eaters come from alcoholic families where they not only inherited a biochemical predisposition to carbohydrate metabolic failure but where the parent-child boundaries were seriously violated in one way or another. Your compulsive eating needs to be addressed as the *primary* disease of addiction that it is in Overeaters Anonymous. It is a primary disease because it must be treated directly, not as a symptom of something else. Compulsive eating, like alcoholism, does not diminish as a result of talking about the problems that "cause" the addiction. By the time it *is* an addiction it is a disease process in and of itself and must be arrested. That is the first order of business in recovery. The alcoholic who wants to remain sober or the compulsive eater who wants to remain abstinent can find it very helpful (though not absolutely necessary) to understand the emotional as well as physical factors that have contributed to the addiction. Indeed, the emotional factors often begin to surface soon after abstinence commences. But without abstinence, the emotional component of the disease is not amenable to healing even if it is discussed at length, because the altered state produced by the food addiction, just like the altered state produced by alcohol or other drugs, precludes that healing. The key to recovery from addiction is to stop practicing the addiction first and then start talking about it, not the other way around.

In order for you to address your feelings and condition in relation to your father (and your mother) you need to stop practicing the addiction that serves to prevent those feelings from emerging. Without the use of food as a drug to numb, smother or otherwise disguise and distort them, those very uncomfortable feelings will begin to emerge and serve their purpose in increasing your understanding and promoting your healing.

Looking at all this, talking about it with others who have similar backgrounds, learning that you are not alone with your experiences and reactions to them, all will ease the pressure of your secret struggle. But I would predict that your loyalty to your father will be the greatest stumbling block to your healing. I hope you nevertheless choose to show up in meetings where this healing can happen for you.

Dear Ms. Norwood:

Your book has been of great help to me. When I first spotted the ad for it I said to myself, "That used to be me." I was sure I had recovered. Was I wrong!—and that is why I am presently writing to you. I would like to find appropriate therapy in my area and I am unsure just what that is. I am hoping that you will be able to provide me with a suggestion. I wish it were possible to see you for counseling.

I am a thirty-nine-year-old artist. I've never married. I am quite successful in all aspects of my life except the romantic ones. I have many friends and I usually have a zest for life. However, when I get involved in a romantic relationship all stability flies out the window. The only thing capable of upsetting or ruffling me is my love life. Again and again I've become so depressed over a romance that I don't recognize myself. It frightens me. I don't want that to happen again.

Ten years ago I was in Freudian therapy for a few years. (My mother was dying at the time and I was involved in a disastrous affair.) When I realized last month that I was in serious emotional trouble, I went back to the same therapist. He is now retired but sees a few patients at his home. I have been seeing him since. I am, however, not convinced that Freudian therapy is the answer for me, a woman who loves too much. I would appreciate your advice.

Karla J.
P.S. My father is an alcoholic and I can be a binge eater. I'm not anorexic, nor do I suffer from bulimia.

Dear Karla,

I'm so grateful for your letter because it gives me the opportunity to address several very important issues. I want to begin with your amazing postscript . . . amazing because it should be the heart of your letter since it contains, most definitely, the heart of your problem and the key to its solution. If you become willing to address specifically the issues mentioned in your postscript, you will be healing the lifelong physical and emotional factors that have contributed to your history of troubled love relationships.

You are a compulsive eater and a co-alcoholic. These are your primary disease processes, your diagnoses, if you will. They are interrelated both behaviorally and genetically. Daughters of alcoholics frequently inherit a genetic predisposition to developing food allergy-addictions that comprise the physical component of compulsive eating. Compulsive eating is also a stress-related disorder, which means it can be brought on and/or worsened by exposure to severe stress. Growing up with alcoholism certainly contributes ample stress throughout childhood to produce or exacerbate an eating disorder. But a family history of alcoholism also affects the present, because the learned, unhealthy patterns of co-alcoholic relating continue to be practiced and to create problems in adulthood. The stress these patterns of relating invariably produce can aggravate the eating disorder, and, of course, the eating disorder can seriously undermine the emotional stability and physical well-being that contribute to healthy relationships.

Depression is a nearly universal component in compulsive eating, due not only to problems with appearance and self-image but also to less than optimal metabolic processes that adversely affect the nervous system. Remember, our emotions generate from a physical system of nerve cells requiring a complex diet of chemicals that the body either provides in proper measure or doesn't. The body's ability to nourish and sustain these cells is a metabolic process that, in most compulsive eaters is impaired.

The foods you binge on are acting as drugs in your system, probably due at least in part to some impairment in your ability to metabolize them effectively. You are dependent both physically and emotionally on the food-drug experience to produce in you an altered state. In this, your thoughts, feelings and behaviors closely parallel those of any other addict. Your recovery process, too, parallels the recovery from any other addiction. That is why Overeaters Anonymous, based on the same principles of recovery as Alcoholics Anonymous, is so effective in addressing compulsive eating.

If either a disease of addiction or co-addiction is present, that *must* be the focus of any therapeutic approach. If both addiction and co-addiction are present, they must be addressed as interrelated disease processes. Treatment begins with abstinence from the addictive chemicals or foods, because without abstinence the person is in an altered state and impervious to the recovery process.

People with diseases of chemical and behavioral addictions need to see people who understand thoroughly both addiction to and recovery from their particular problem. It is most helpful if the professional is also a person recovering from that particular addiction. When the issue is co-addiction (in your case, co-alcoholism), the same applies. The therapist should understand co-addiction and recovery and hopefully is a recovering co-addictive person as well. Karla, you need to see someone who is, preferably, all of the above. Looking for a therapist with this combination of experience and knowledge probably sounds like an impossible quest. But remember, most compulsive eaters are also co-alcoholics from their families of origin, and therapists who truly understand compulsive eating as an addiction very similar to alcoholism usually have a good comprehension of co-alcoholism as well. The numbers of therapists who are treating diseases of addiction and co-addiction and who also have the paramount qualification that they are recovering from these diseases themselves are, thankfully, growing.

For you to see a therapist who doesn't have specific expertise in addiction and recovery is, in my opinion, as much a waste of time and money as if you were making appointments to see a heart specialist when you were having problems with your vision and needed to be fitted for prescription lenses. In keeping those appointments with the heart specialist there would be all sorts of attention paid to your cardiovascular system, which might be very interesting, but you wouldn't be able to see any better. People with diseases of addiction and co-addiction need to see someone who recognizes, understands and is capable of effectively treating these problems as *primary* diseases, *not symptoms of something else*. Diseases of addiction and co-addiction produce many psychological symptoms that send people into therapy. It is unfortunate, however, that therapists treating addictive clients so rarely identify the addiction(s) and therefore fail to refer the person to the appropriate program(s) that can support the necessary first step of recovery: refraining from practicing the addiction. Only when that condition is met can even the most appropriate therapy benefit the client.

In my experience, no real progress can be made in

therapy while a client is actively practicing a disease of either behavioral or chemical addiction. Your first step, therefore, is to address your compulsive eating (which is both a behavioral and a chemical addiction). If you were my client I would insist that you become very active in Overeaters Anonymous as a condition of continuing therapy. I would recommend a meeting a day for at least the first thirty days, and three meetings a week thereafter. Once your recovery in Overeaters Anonymous had begun, you would also need to attend Al-Anon on a regular basis, two to three times a week. If you balk at this degree of commitment to recovery, try to remember that these diseases are both progressive; that is, they get worse over time and they are both potentially fatal. If you had cancer you would probably be more than willing to go to whatever lengths were necessary in order to recover. You would find the time and the means to show up for any process that could heal you. Try to bring the same degree of commitment to recovery from these life-threatening diseases as well.

If you balk at commitment to recovery, remember that if you had cancer you would go to whatever lengths were necessary in order to heal.

In your letter you also state that you wish it were possible to see me for counseling. Karla, I am not the source for recovery from your diseases of addiction and co-addiction. The appropriate Twelve-Step programs are. You belong in Overeaters Anonymous and Al-Anon. You *can* recover with only the support of a Twelve-Step program, but you will not, in my opinion, recover with just the help of therapy alone, no matter how wonderful or how qualified the therapist. Indeed, in my opinion, if the therapist were really wonderful and truly qualified she would *insist* that you work your Twelve-Step programs. Most of your recovery will happen in the company of other people who are struggling with the same issues you are.

Dear Ms. Norwood,

Your book comes at a crucial time in my life. My husband of only three years left four months ago and wants nothing to do with me. He hasn't filed for divorce yet but won't accept help to rebuild our relationship. Now I find what I've called love for him may be obsession that has me paralyzed and unable to go forward.

I'm a recovering alcoholic and my husband is as well. We met while drinking, went into recovery at the same time but in different hospitals. We both belong to and work the Alcoholics Anonymous program and I am also in therapy and in Al-Anon. I feel as though I'm not understanding what I need to, or else I haven't heard what I need to in order to understand. That is why I'm writing you. I feel you have some knowledge that I need to know. I sincerely hope to hear from you.

Gloria J.

P.S. By the way, I'm forty-one years old, have a son twenty-five and a daughter twenty-two, have been married six times for short periods of time, raised both children who are college graduates. I look very successful to others and yet feel totally unsuccessful as a human being . . .

Dear Gloria,

You've probably heard the saying around your program of Alcoholics Anonymous, "If you haven't done it clean and sober you haven't done it." Most people who become addicted to alcohol and other drugs began to use those drugs to avoid dealing with reality early on, most typically by the age of fourteen. I don't know when you started abusing alcohol, but in answering your letter, I'm going to assume that like so many people who develop the disease you began fairly early to rely on the drug to carry you through awkward situations. If this is true in your case, then the very difficult task of forging a separate identity, which is normally tackled during the teen years and early twenties and is often referred to as an "identity crisis," has been postponed until sobriety. Many people who have been chemically dependent have *never* danced in public, made a date or showed up for one, or had a sexual experience while sober. Whenever life has been uncomfortable or challenging there has always been recourse to the drug to take the edge off the discomfort or to numb the fear. Since we grow stronger and more mature by facing and living through these awkward, painful times, when they are avoided our natural emotional maturation is stifled.

Obviously, there is so much more to being sober than not drinking or using. In sobriety, it becomes necessary to, in essence, go back to being whatever age you were when you began to depend on chemicals, and then work your way through the lessons and the growth you've missed by being chemically altered. This isn't easy when you are forty-one and the mother of grown children. It requires tremendous humility and courage to pick up where you left off maturing so many years ago. But there is also some comfort in knowing that the problem is not that you are somehow fatally flawed—you just have some growing up to do. What fourteen-year-old is ready for a healthy, mature, committed relationship with a member of the opposite sex? Enough self-knowledge and self-acceptance have not yet developed for a strong, healthy partnership to be possible.

If you can consider that everything I've written applies to both you and your present husband, perhaps you can appreciate why getting sober wasn't enough to make the marriage work. Sobriety doesn't solve problems in relationships; all it does is remove an enormous impediment to confronting those problems. It's as though you are trying to build a road through mountainous terrain. If there is an enormous boulder blocking the way, it must be removed in order to begin the task of building the road. Building a relationship is much the same. Until addressed, alcohol addiction creates an insurmountable barrier to progress.

You and your husband chose each other while drinking. The dynamics that were operating in your relationship then have got to be very different than the ones that are in effect now. I daresay neither of you knows a thing about relating to a marriage partner sober, and that's a very painful truth to confront. It is often easier to say "This other person is my problem" than to admit to the inevitable awkwardness and fear engendered by simply being consistently present with another person when we have never been before.

Very few relationships either between two chemically dependent people or between an alcoholic or addict and a co-alcoholic survive sobriety, for the reasons stated above. Whenever people believe that sobriety is the "answer" to their problems they are bound to be disappointed. Sobriety only creates the conditions under which the answers may be sought and possibly found, through patience, courage, humility and persistence.

A final word: Having seen many people achieve sobriety over many years of working in the field of addiction, I have observed that if they maintain sobriety and courageously face each "next recovery" that sobriety makes possible, their lives get better and better. However, sometimes in recovery people leave or conditions change or things are removed that we, in our own shortsighted assessment of what we believe is our greatest good, would never willingly surrender. When this occurs it is important to remember that we cannot ever lose what is truly ours. Thus, it becomes our task to release that which is being taken from us in order to make way for the greater good that is trying to manifest in our lives.

Dear Robin,

I found it disgustingly easy to relate to your book.

My mother died of alcoholism at age fifty-five, twenty years from the time I started trying to make her well. My father is in a wheelchair, paralyzed on one side,

unable to communicate and still drinking. I am divorced
after twenty-two years of marriage to a man who drinks
like his father and grandfather before him.

I have been in and out of Alcoholics Anonymous—
successful sometimes for years at a time. I believe in it!
I am drinking now and running to and from an unhealthy
relationship.

My question is: Do you know a therapist in Balti-
more who has read your book, takes it to heart, and
might be able to help me?

Looking forward to hearing from you.
Connie V.

Dear Connie,

Many women alcoholics who slip do so over co-
dependency issues. Said another way, alcoholic women
who are sober most often get drunk over their problems
with men. One of the rather obvious reasons for this is
that most women (and men) who are alcoholic came, as
you did, from alcoholic homes. They were thus *co-
alcoholic* long before they developed the disease of alcoholism. Sober, these alcoholics are still untreated co-
alcoholics, with all their early unhealthy patterns of
relating still operating.

For most sober alcoholic women, their co-alcoholism is the greatest cause of problems in sobriety. They
express their co-alcoholism either as tremendously controlling behavior or tremendously dependent behavior
or, most commonly, as both in turn. This seesaw pattern
of relating expresses the simultaneous existence of their
underlying fear of closeness and their even greater fear
of abandonment. Women (and men) who have grown up
in alcoholic homes have often been subjected to various
degrees of emotional, physical and sexual abuse, and
histories of this kind compound exponentially the relationship problems people will face in adulthood. Their
tendency is to choose partners who will provide them
with the opportunity to face again the familiar conditions
and struggles from their past—this time with the hope of
triumphing over those struggles.

All this is by way of explaining what I want to say
next. Your addiction to alcohol makes it easier for you

to practice your relationship addiction. Your relationship addiction gives you every excuse to drink. You can use either addiction in the service of the other. If you want to break this cycle you must get sober again, hopefully this time with a strong emphasis on women's stag meetings. In these "women only" meetings you will be at least safe for that hour from practicing your relationship addiction (mixed Alcoholics Anonymous meetings can be very slippery places for relationship addicts!) and free to discuss your issues concerning men and how these relate to your drinking. Eventually, you will probably want to go to Al-Anon, too, where there is so much wisdom about relationship issues and so much recovery from sick co-dependence.

There is no "easier, softer way" in therapy; getting sober is the necessary first step.

As to your request for a referral, I must tell you that I have for years now made it a practice only to refer to the Anonymous programs, never to individual therapists. I believe more in the power of peer support groups to facilitate positive change than I do in the power of individual therapy to bring about that change. Any therapist who "took my theories to heart" would know that her primary responsibility to you would be to support your attendance at Alcoholics Anonymous and to help you understand and work your program. A good A.A. sponsor would do the same for you without charging you a fee.

If you decide to go back to Alcoholics Anonymous and you still want a therapist, you will probably hear from others in your area who are also in the program of professionals who truly understand addiction and recovery. But remember, there is no "easier, softer way" in therapy, and getting sober is still the necessary first step in your recovery. Good luck to you.

Dear Robin,

Your book came to me through a woman I sponsor in Overeaters Anonymous, she herself having been led to Overeaters Anonymous via reading it.

I still can't see how it happens that I relate so completely to the people in Overeaters Anonymous and Al-Anon, or how I happened to marry a former addict-alcoholic who was schizophrenic and who committed suicide twenty-two days ago, eight weeks after I left him.

Neither of my parents drank. Right now the reasons for my diseases don't matter to me as much as the fact that I'm getting a boost in awareness regarding the devastating nature of my destructive patterns with food, family and men, in that order.

In February I began to recover from a thirteen-year-long eating disorder that encompassed three anorexic periods, two periods of obesity and four and a half years of near-fatal bulimia at the end. (At least I hope it is the end.)

No one has yet explained to me the strange set of physical adjustments and sensitivities characteristic of my recovery. I'm describing them to you, below, in the hope that you might have access to sources of medical information to help me.

I'm twenty-six, weigh about one hundred ten pounds and stand five feet three and three quarters inches. My weight is stable and my diet consists of thirteen hundred calories' worth of a nutritionist's best advice.

Still, for the first four months there was the inexplicable appearance of epilepsy, gone after that time period equally as inexplicably, according to the chief neurologist at the hospital where I am treated. I stopped menstruating when I stopped binge-purging, while at eighty-nine pounds and bulimic I had menstruated like clockwork. I know of three cases of bulimia where serious heart problems have been present. One of these women died two months into recovery; one died an active bulimic. The third, another woman I sponsor in Overeaters Anonymous, experienced both heart and lung failure eight days ago and is lucky to be alive right now. She is also in the first few months of recovery.

Just as your book (for me) heralds the breaking of new ground in the relationship department, someone needs to break ground regarding bulimic recovery (as opposed to illness). I'm no doctor. I don't know what's going on, but obviously there is some kind of incredible shock sustained in withdrawal from binge-purging, a shock perhaps more traumatic and long-term than anyone knows.

The only thing I've come up with so far, is that purging is a convulsion of sorts. Speaking for myself, I induced such convulsions thirty to forty times a night for four and a half years. Was my seizure threshold seriously affected? Was my nervous system damaged temporarily or permanently? This effect stands apart, distinct from the consequences of long-term malnutrition and lack of sleep. Some other bulimics in Overeaters Anonymous often have much longer illness histories than mine. How can we best help each other just to stay alive, physically, in order to explore the emotional issues addressed in our groups and in your book?

If you know of anyone or anything to help us with our physical recuperation, please let me know. Today I want to live. I'd like to know better exactly what's going on and how to serve the healing process, starting with my body.

Pat M.

Dear Pat,

I am writing back to you so long after your letter of December because it has been buried under other work on my desk and has only recently been excavated. Ironically, it was in a pile of letters I very much wanted to answer in greater detail than I'm usually able to.

You ask me many questions about eating disorders to which you are more likely to have the answers than I; you are the *expert* because you have the disease. You and others in Overeaters Anonymous who are recovering and are talking about your disease have a great deal to learn from each other and to teach the medical and counseling professions.

I want to ask you a great favor. Would you write me again and tell me what answers you've discovered in your recovery? Because, again, you are the expert, Pat—I'm not. Nearly everything I've ever learned about various addictions I've learned not from school or from books but from the people who have these diseases and are recovering from them.

I am writing a second book, based on the letters I've received in response to *WWL2M*. I'd like to use both your first letter to me and the second one I'm requesting. Of course, you need not agree—but it is a good way of reaching others like yourself who have questions and perhaps the answers, too, if they only can learn to trust themselves.

No matter what, thanks for writing and my very best wishes to you in your continuing recovery.

Dear Robin,

I can't explain the phenomenon of recovery in my eating pattern. I no more made a conscious decision to recover than I did to become anorexic, obese and bulimic. One day, about two weeks after Patti, my bulimic friend, died of heart failure in her sleep, I lost my "magic," my power to binge and purge at will.

Withdrawal, abstinence and widowhood have devastated me beyond belief. Your letter has caught me at a terrible moment. My husband hanged himself at this time last year, during the holidays. This year my mom has asked me to remove myself from her home where I stay, while my sister visits for the holidays. I feel doubly devastated somehow. . . .

Twenty-seven years old now, physically I am at a stable weight for going on two years, stable for the first time since puberty. I am also anxiety-prone and menopausal and periodically pseudo-epileptic, i.e., my EEG reads both positive and negative for temporal lobe spike abnormality.

Emotionally, I never know what's next. Suicidal despair, controlled tension, quiet fun, or the gentle calm of acceptance.

Mentally, my mind gives me fantasies in symphonic sound and technicolor. Sometimes it shows me scenes of my late husband or of my childhood. Both kinds of visions are usually filled with pain and feelings of powerlessness.

I work full-time as an executive secretary to the chairman of a major department in one of the country's top medical schools. I talk six days a week to my two recovery partners who are both formerly practicing anorexics/bulimics. I attend at least a meeting a day, sometimes two. I also give and receive a minimum of three hugs per meeting and share three phone calls or more daily. I read literature from Alcoholics Anonymous, Overeaters Anonymous, Al-Anon and Alateen daily and write every morning and night about how I'm feeling and what is happening to me. Somehow a good breakfast, lunch and dinner get eaten every day. I never weigh myself. I weigh the food.

When I'm writing about my program and recovery I do so with my left hand as I'm doing now. I don't know why. I'm right-handed.

It's still difficult for me to believe I'm ill and in pain in the area of relationships as well as food. But I can say what just now threatens me most: emotional suppression. It hurts to be with people playing "Are we having fun yet?" And that's exactly the game most Americans my age seem to want to play. Now that I'm in recovery, it scares me to think of giving love in a sexually intimate manner. I take time to try people out slowly to see how we fit together emotionally and I withdraw when I feel upset, whether I understand why or not. I've become aggressively self-protective when it comes to others' personalities. If another's personality and mine don't mix too well, no thanks.

I'm taking steps now to be back in school in January working toward a technical writing certificate in the medical field.

That's the news from my end, Robin. Publish whatever works with my best wishes.

Pat M.

Dear Pat,

Although I do not know the answers to your questions about the body's sometimes catastrophic response to the cessation of the binge/purge syndrome, I feel certain that when those answers are found you will learn of them, given your strong desire to know, your affiliation with others with the same disease, your obvious intelligence and your access to medical research through your work. One possible resource for you regarding the medical aspects of your disease is ANRED* which maintains an information and referral service and attempts to answer questions such as yours.

Probably because I am a therapist rather than a physician your letters cause me to reflect on matters that have less to do with the physical aspects and consequences of addiction and more to do with matters of the heart and soul. As your letters make so clear, Pat, diseases of addiction kill. It is the natural state of the addict to be practicing the disease and it is the nature of every addiction to be progressive and ultimately fatal. The medical details of why and how someone dies of addiction are undeniably important but they do not, in my opinion, contribute as much to our understanding of the whole picture as we would sometimes like to believe. For one thing, the medical details do not *exist* that can reveal why a given person such as yourself, once having contracted a disease of addiction, *doesn't* die of it but recovers instead. Diseases of addiction, unlike other diseases, lay siege to every dimension of the person afflicted; the emotional and spiritual dimensions of the addict deteriorate as well as the physical body. Usually the emotional aspects sicken first, followed by the spiritual, with the body not showing the effects until the addiction is in its late stages. When any form of addiction has brought on an acute medical crisis and life is endangered, all the appropriate medical interventions must be used to try and stabilize the patient's physical condition.

---

*Anorexia Nervosa and Related Eating Disorders (see List of Resources).

But after this is done, one of the great ironies of addiction becomes apparent. No matter how ill the addict was or how severely his or her life was threatened, should the medical approach be the only course of treatment, that patient will in time almost inevitably resume practicing the addiction. Learning the facts about the damage done to one's physical condition because of addiction is not enough to bring about recovery. Information alone, no matter how alarming, is simply not enough to stop addiction.

Information alone, no matter how alarming, is simply not enough to stop addiction.

The following is a case in point. Years ago I was acquainted with a presentable, employed, middle-class man, who was married and the father of four children. In his late fifties he was admitted to a hospital because of serious physical complications due to his alcoholism. Two days later he was discovered by a nurse to have expired. Through the hospital staff's timely and energetic ministrations he was revived.

Having received careful monitoring, conscientious care and precise lectures on the deadly consequences for him unless he abstained from alcohol, he nevertheless resumed his drinking within four weeks of his discharge from the hospital. Eventually he lost his family, no longer worked, was prosecuted for molesting a young child and served time in jail. Finally, after being on welfare for a couple of years, he died, a last time, of his alcoholism.

I recite this story not to be morbid and certainly not because it is particularly unique, but rather to point up the fact that, although diseases of addiction require that their physical manifestations be treated medically, they are not permanently arrested by medical treatment alone, no matter how fine or appropriate that medical treatment is. This is because the medical field cannot properly address the emotional and spiritual dimensions of the addict, which must be continually healing in order for recovery to continue.

Sometimes addicts are blessed with a sudden and profound insight into themselves and their disease—a "moment of clarity" that is often felt to be a deeply spiritual experience—and they are thus able to stop practicing the disease and begin recovery. More frequently the change is subtler and the disease process simply "stops working" for the addict. This was what happened to you when two weeks following your friend's death you found you'd lost the "magic" of being able to binge and purge for relief. It often happens that alcoholics, too, find that drinking simply doesn't work anymore. When that occurs, no matter how much or how often they drink, there is no more "magic" in alcohol.

But whether it begins with the great gift of a brilliant moment of clarity or whether the addiction simply stops "working," recovery must still be pursued on a daily basis. Even those who are brought to their knees with streams of tears running down their faces as they see a way out of addiction that wasn't there before—even these blessed people must nevertheless work with all their hearts at hanging on to recovery one day at a time.

I know you don't need to be told this, Pat. Your letters make clear how great a priority your recovery is. I know that you know you are a miracle.

And your recovery doesn't end with a stable weight and a sane relationship with food. Even in the few words you use to refer to your family, it is clear there is a great deal of anguish for you in that area.

There are many characteristics which female compulsive eaters tend to have in common. Compulsive talking (to maintain control of what will be said) is one. Extremely perfectionistic attitudes regarding their own accomplishments and goals is another. One of the chief ones in my experience is that they are often inordinately tied to their mothers in a relationship fraught with mutual hostility and dependence. Each frequently comes to the other's rescue with advice and aid for various problems, which nevertheless persist unabated. Both mother and daughter behave as if they are in a constant battle to get the other to be their caretaker. Each is so needy and yet each wants so badly to be in control that they switch back and forth from giver to receiver. Food often plays a key role in this exchange as a token of or substitute for love. The more time they spend together the sicker they both become, because neither has adequate emotional resources even for herself, much less for the other. They "borrow" their emotional supply from each other, constantly blurring their individual boundaries. For all their "support" of each other they each feel progressively more needy and consequently hang on to each other all the more tightly.

You have displayed so much courage and determination in your recovery, Pat. My strong hunch is that for you your mother's house is a "slippery place." Please remember, she is not your supply. God is. Use your program for support both to bless your mother and to let go of her.

The letters in this chapter demonstrate so well that addictions aren't discrete entities. They very often overlap in their physical and emotional roots. The recovery from one addiction may either cause another addiction to accelerate or allow the possibility of another recovery. Healing from every addiction requires the application of the same principles of surrender, honesty, humility and willingness, but the details of how one's behavior must change in recovery may differ drastically. For instance, in order to stay sober most alcoholics need to become less self-centered and more concerned with helping others. However, most relationship addicts, and particularly those of the co-alcoholic variety, need to progress in exactly the opposite direction; that is, they must become more selfish (self-loving and self-nurturing) and less concerned with others' welfare. Further, I've known alcoholics and addicts who could not achieve a full year's sobriety until they addressed their co-dependency issues and stopped completely exhausting themselves with trying to save everybody else. And I've known relationship addicts who could not stop their addictive pursuit of men until they stopped drinking and using drugs.

Sometimes it can feel overwhelming to face all the addictions that seem to be running our lives. But, as many of the women whose letters have appeared in this chapter have stated, once we know how to recover from one addiction we can use the same tools we've already learned to address the next one that becomes apparent.

Six

. . . ARE INVOLVED IN THERAPY

Aside from wanting to share the letters I have received with others who have had the same experiences or concerns, I had another motive for assembling this book. It is my hope that these letters will educate some of those who are leading groups supposedly based on *WWL2M* in the basic concepts of addiction and recovery. I have found it very difficult to watch the great numbers of therapist-led groups springing up that advertise adherence to the principles of *WWL2M* and yet are obviously run by persons who have yet to understand what relationship addiction is, what it has in common with every other addiction and how it is best treated.

For instance, I was told a story by a newspaper reporter who, in her research for an article on the topic of "women who love too much" had talked to some members of therapist-led groups that dealt with the subject. This reporter, who had made it known that she would be interviewing me, was asked by the members of one such group to tell me that what they really needed was another book, a sort of *WWL2M II*. Since *WWL2M (I)* had been out barely a year at the time, and since my own recovery of more than six years still had such a long way to go, I asked her if these women actually felt they had already accomplished everything *WWL2M* recommended. She answered that they had told her that they had completed a six-week course on the subject, had all "dumped" their bad relationships and consequently they and the therapist felt it was time to find some "good" men. Frankly, I was appalled that such a process could somehow evolve out of what I had written. In six weeks these women could not possibly have assimilated all the lessons they needed to learn from having been with those previous partners, nor could they have adequately mourned those relationships. It seemed to me that they could only be "looking for a new man" to provide relief from their anxiety over being alone and facing themselves. In other words, with the support of a therapist they were using the quest for a new relationship *as a drug*. And all this was being done in the name of recovery!

In trying to make the point that therapists are often the *most* relationship addicted category of professionals (besides nurses) and that we are often leading groups on this subject without knowing what recovery is, much less achieving it ourselves, I told this story in a seminar. A member of the audience shouted out angrily, "You are so *hostile* toward therapists!" Several audience members applauded in support of her statement. It was a difficult moment, but as with many difficult moments it was also a gift. It caused me to consciously examine my own experiences both as a therapist and as a client in therapy, as well as my own experience of recovery.

Doing so has made me aware that I do indeed have deep reservations about therapy being the panacea to so many ills that it is generally thought today to be. The belief that if one could only find the right therapist life's problems would be solved is nearly as widely held in some parts of this country as is the belief that finding the right relationship would bring about the same result. There was a time in my life when I, too, firmly believed that counseling with a skilled, compassionate therapist offered the answers to most of the emotional difficulties with which individuals and families struggled. That belief played a large part in my own very strong desire to become a therapist. I yearned to be able to make a difference for the better in other people's lives.

It took several years of my working with alcohol- and drug-addicted clients and *not once* being able to make that difference before a dent was made in my staunch faith in therapy's potential to change lives, at least in those cases where addiction is present. After about five years of sincerely trying to help addicted people refrain from using their drug(s) and always, sooner or later, failing, I was invited by some sober members of

Alcoholics Anonymous to attend open (to the public) Alcoholics Anonymous meetings with them. Without a trace of condemnation for my many years of ineffectual efforts, they said to me, "Robin, if you're going to work with us alcoholics, maybe you'd like to come along and see how we get well."

My first exposure to Alcoholics Anonymous brought me in contact with a roomful of hundreds of sober, happy people. What I had been unable to help anyone do for more than one or two weeks at the most, many of these people had been doing for years, even decades. They were staying clean and sober, off alcohol and other drugs, and were living lives of dignity and worth.

Through continued attendance at open meetings I heard sober alcoholics talk freely, and often with humor, about their harrowing past experiences as addicts and then describe how they were now recovering, one day at a time, with the help of the Alcoholics Anonymous fellowship and a Higher Power. Hearing their stories changed the way I practiced therapy, because for the first time I truly began to *understand* addiction. I began to understand, too, what a miracle recovery from addiction was—a miracle that I, as a therapist, could not bring about.

With this new awareness I began to insist that my addictive clients attend Alcoholics Anonymous as a condition of continuing in therapy with me. Since many of my clients in those days were required by the court to see me because of alcohol and other drug-related offenses, I was able to exert considerable pressure on them to attend meetings. Through their exposure to Alcoholics Anonymous some of these clients did indeed begin to recover, and their success eventually rubbed off on me. My reputation as a skilled counselor in the field of alcohol and drug abuse grew.

It took me five more years as a counselor in the addiction field (during which I worked primarily with the chemically dependent person's family members) to realize that attendance at Al-Anon was as necessary to these co-dependent's recoveries as attendance at Alcoholics Anonymous was to the alcoholic's. Seeing co-dependents become sicker and sicker and even die of stress-related disorders brought on by their many years' obsession with the alcoholic finally made clear to me that co-addiction, as well as addiction, was a progressive and ultimately fatal disease. I saw that recovery from co-addiction was just as great a miracle as recovery from any addiction—and that again it was a miracle I, even with my years of experience and my dedication as a therapist, could not bring about. So attendance at Al-Anon became a requirement for every co-alcoholic I saw in therapy, and after a while many of these clients, too, began to change their lives and recover.

The greatest lesson of my fifteen years as a therapist has been learning what I cannot *do for the addictive client.*

The greatest lesson of my fifteen years as a therapist in the field of addiction and co-addiction has been learning what I *cannot* do for the addictive or co-addictive client. I cannot bring about their recovery, but the Anonymous programs with their loving fellowship and their basis in spiritual principles *can,* if the client is willing to be healed. Letting go of my own need to save my clients single-handedly has, thankfully, resulted in sobriety and serenity for many of them through the magic of the Anonymous programs working in their lives.

While all this was going on at the career level in my life, a few changes were occurring at the personal level as well . . .

When I began my career in counseling I had no real belief in a Higher Power. But, at the same time, I felt that if God did exist He wasn't doing a very good job of taking care of things. I was sure I could do better. With this level of self-will operating I consider it a minor miracle that I ever learned to take a back seat, even to God. However, life often has a way of bringing us very self-willed people to our knees. Due to increasingly un-happy and chaotic personal circumstances that ultimately cost me a job, the custody of my children and my health, I finally had to admit that I could not manage even my own life. A career in which I assumed the role of an authority on the subject of successful living finally struck even me as a bit presumptuous.

I had heard in the stories of many alcoholics how unman-ageable life becomes due to addiction but that it could change for the better if certain principles were followed. Although I was not abusing alcohol or other drugs, my life was beginning to mimic theirs during the active phases of their addiction. This was because I, too, was in the active phase of addiction. I was not addicted to a chemical, but to relationships with men, which I had always used to gain relief from unbearable anxiety. In other words, I had used these relationships as a drug on which I had eventually become completely dependent.

Only from hearing all those recovering alcoholics in Alco-holics Anonymous did I finally realize that I, too, was an addict. Even more important, I realized that I, too, could recover if I followed their example.

So finally I turned to God for help, and when I did so my life began to change in the same miraculous ways I had heard about from other recovering addicts.

That was nearly seven years ago, and with each passing year I am more deeply convinced, based on my own admittedly very subjective experience, that the basic premise of all thera-peutic endeavor, whether addiction is involved or not, must be this: to initiate a search for and support an ongoing contact with the healing and guiding spiritual principle within the person who suffers. However, it has been my observation that many of us who become therapists, in addition to having in common per-sonal histories of pain and trauma, also share a basic anger both at our parents and at God. The urge to take over from a nonexistent, indifferent or capriciously cruel God the reins which guide the lives of our clients is, I believe, a fairly common one among us. It frequently results in a tendency to guide clients toward becoming more self-willed rather than less so. Clients are encouraged to rely on their own intelligence and on that of the therapist rather than on seeking and finding their own personal and unique guiding spiritual principle within. Naturally, a therapist who doesn't live by such inner guidance will not see the point of helping a client to do so.

Since I've done all this both ways, personally and professionally, let me say just two things. First, in my experience seeking an inner spiritual principle and surrendering to its guidance is very hard work. Nearly everything in life—people, circumstances, material objects, ambitions, desires and fears— all seem to pull in another, outer direction. It requires my *constant* attention and surrender in order to remember that I am not running the show and that a Higher Principle will guide me if sought.

Second, although this constant and repeated surrender is difficult and challenging, living any other way is just about impossible for me today. I would not want to go back to the way my life was before I gave up having to have all the answers myself. Today I know that all healing, whether of a broken leg or a broken mind or a broken heart, comes about through the operation of spiritual principle. Those of us who want to help facilitate any kind of healing do so best when we are able to acknowledge that spiritual principle with both humility and gratitude.

Today I no longer work as a therapist. One of the reasons for this is that my own recovery did not come about either through all the academic and experiential training for my career nor through being in therapy myself, though I certainly looked in both those directions for a long time for the answers. In my search I tried many, many approaches along the way, some of which were harmful, some ineffective and some, in a limited way, helpful. But my recovery happened, and continues to happen, in a support group of peers conducted along spiritual guidelines. There no one is the expert; all are equals and each of us is responsible for finding our own way with the acceptance, the love and the understanding of one another. No money is required, no advice is given and there is no pressure to be other than who and what we are. It is the closest thing to unconditional love I have ever known, and its healing power continues to astound me.

Another reason that I have chosen to leave my practice as a therapist is that I've come to a point in my life where I can no longer charge a fee for sharing with others the tools that saved my life and yet were given to me free. Those tools are really all I have to give another person today—and then only if that other person really wants them. They comprise the only approach I have seen work in the face of addiction, and are a gift that comes from a Power greater than ourselves—to us and through us but never *from* us. One of the greatest privileges of having been given these tools is sharing them with others.

None of this is intended as a prescription for others who are therapists nor as a rebuke. There is no way of living or working that applies to all of us. This is simply what has evolved for me.

Perhaps some of my reservations about therapy also have to do with the reasons why I sought it. I think most of us seek therapy for some of the same reasons we develop and practice addictions—to avoid embracing the pain that is beginning to erupt at intolerable levels in our lives. We hope that by seeing a therapist this pain can be stopped, headed off, relieved, fixed or at least considerably lessened. In fact, we are very blessed when a therapist, or anyone else for that matter, helps us recognize that our pain provides us with an invaluable lesson and then guides us in finding the courage to face that pain. This is done best, in my opinion, from personal experience on the therapist's part and through personal example.

Emotional pain exists because we have not been able to acknowledge honestly something about ourselves or our condition that, at some level, *we already know*. Whatever our secret, we perceive it as too threatening, too overwhelming, too shameful or unbearable to be faced. This feeling drives us to try to keep our secret from surfacing—and the pain continues and deepens until, perhaps because we have no other choice, we finally become willing to look at it.

True change and growth demand a surrender to that pain and all its lessons that is virtually tantamount to a crucifixion. Often we must give up our most cherished beliefs about our identity, our family history, our present circumstances, the very essence of who we believe ourselves to be if we are to regain the precious self that has gotten buried beneath the external images and the internal lies. Few of us welcome such an excruciating experience, no matter how potentially transforming it might be. We look for a way out of the pain when what we really need to seek is a way *through* it.

None of us has invented a new variety of horrible secret.

Emotional pain is to the psyche what physical pain is to the body: a signal that something is sick or damaged. It is an urgent invitation to address the necessary healing. If we want to heal, we need to welcome the pain as we would the wisest teacher knocking at our door; we need to become willing to learn the lessons it is trying to impart. Life is, after all, about waking up and growing up, and those are often even more agonizing processes than they need to be *because we don't welcome them*.

No one, thank God, can save us from our own soul's work. Our worst problems come from trying to avoid or postpone that work. We need finally to accept that work, explore it, learn from it, bless it and go on, grateful for the gift of deeper understanding of ourselves as individuals and of all humanity as well. Because our pain is not unique. None of us has invented a new variety of horrible secret or terrible loss. What is true for us has been and continues to be true for many, many others. What helps us to heal may be helpful to others' healing as well. What we have faced in ourselves we can help others face, too, if they are willing. This is true whether or not we are therapists by profession. To the degree that we have recovered and are honest and humble and willing to be used for a higher purpose—to that degree even while we are peers we are also therapists, ministers, healers of the highest order.

On the other hand, perhaps because it is *not* a peer relationship but one that inevitably implies superiority in one person and inferiority in the other, choosing a therapist, being in therapy, can be a very risky business. This is especially true because no one is more vulnerable than the client seeking help for emotional problems. At the time of this writing, three therapists (two of whom are also ordained ministers) are being prosecuted in the city in which I live for alleged inappropriate sexual conduct toward their clients. Sexual misconduct is only one of the more obvious ways therapists can violate their clients' credulity and trust. Someone who is a professional with required degrees and licenses is not automatically healthy enough or skilled enough to be capable of helping clients. In fact, in many cases therapists may actually do psychological harm to their clients either through simple lack of skill or because of very serious and unaddressed character defects. So many of us who choose the professions that involve helping others do so because we are damaged ourselves. We often inherit the biochemical and behavioral legacies of our own dysfunctional families of origin and thus have our own unacknowledged and untreated problems of addiction and co-addiction. These conditions inevitably negatively affect both our personal and our professional lives until they are acknowledged and treated. Until then, we continue to defend ourselves against our own pain and secrets by hiding behind the role of "expert" and using our work as a way of focusing on other people's lives and problems in order to avoid facing our own.

None of this is to imply that therapy can't be helpful and that therapists can't be wise, gifted guides for those who seek their services. But therapists are human, too, with lives that are often moving and changing in directions other than they themselves would wish or want anyone else to know. The question then is: What does a therapist do when his or her professional credibility is tied to a personal life that, for one reason or another, is becoming progressively more unmanageable?

My personal struggles with this dilemma have been some of the most difficult of my life. They have also been the most rewarding and transforming experiences I have known. I now recognize that these lessons were my soul's reason for choosing this career.

In addition to wanting to help others I was drawn to the field of therapy because I had always been in deep emotional pain myself and wanted answers and relief. But the longer I worked in the field of counseling the more difficult it became for me to acknowledge honestly that I still didn't have those answers I had always been seeking and that the pain was getting worse. Too often, needing to appear as a competent professional overrode being totally honest regarding my own condition. For me, being a therapist ultimately made it more difficult for me to get well. My pride and my fear of losing professional credibility both got in the way, and I continued to get sicker. I had to reach a point where I was willing to surrender it *all* before my own healing could take place.

The pain and agony of that turning point, that surrender, simply cannot be described. I have an acquaintance who has never truly recovered from the fact that the therapist who was so wonderfully helpful to her committed suicide. Indeed, the highest rate of suicide in any profession is among psychiatrists. Every one of us in the field of therapy knows all too well the pressure that begins to build when our own life is becoming increasingly unmanageable. We must become more and more defended, more secretive and more fearful that the truth about us will become known and we will lose our credibility and our career. Or we can acknowledge our own essential vulnerability, face whatever humbling and yet instructive lesson is before us, pick up the pieces and go on. As frightening a step as that may be, it is through seeking our own recovery that our fearful secrets are transformed into our cherished gifts, the means through which we can truly understand both ourselves and those we wish to help. In the course of my healing I found I had lost nothing that was truly for my own highest good and that my life was evolving into something higher and better than I had ever known. Furthermore, I know my experience is not unique. Two of recovery's promises are that life gets *better* and that we are now *more* able than ever to help others.

Those who understand best why people seek therapy (and most people who seek therapy have undiagnosed problems of addiction and/or co-addiction) are those who have personally experienced the conditions leading to such a decision themselves and achieved a significant level of recovery. Those in the helping professions who haven't been adequately trained regarding these diseases and who lack personal experience of recovery are often unaware of the help and support available to their clients through the Anonymous programs, or they may underestimate the necessity of their clients' involvement therein. The following letter illustrates some of the mistakes commonly made by professionals who don't understand these issues.

Dear Robin Norwood,

I briefly looked over your book—positive it would only show me how totally hopeless everything is but you are pretty accurate, at least in my limited knowledge of these problems—my problems.

Anyway, I'm twenty-nine, bulimic, anorexic, addict, alcoholic—I'm not doing very well. I have been in therapy since I was nine. Last year I admitted myself into a private hospital and stayed for three months. While there I started having panic/anxiety attacks. I had one yesterday. My doctor is out of town.

The relationships you describe in your book are precisely what I'm experiencing with my therapist. In the very beginning I begged him to please not allow me to love him so much but he said that it was okay, that he loved me too, that he would never abandon me, mislead me or break commitments that we made to one another. He told me that he would love to have a relationship with me that was an extension of our doctor/patient relationship, that he truly loved me and saw things in me (other than externally) that he thought were terrific.

While I was in the hospital he would see me every day including Sundays. When I was discharged I saw him three times a week and still do. It has been over a year and I live from session to session. If I could die, if I could get up the courage to kill myself, believe me it would be a relief. It wouldn't be my first attempt. I'm not threatening. I'm aware of how selfish and cowardly that would be. I'm truly exhausted and confused. I want to say that originally I would ask my doctor about the possibility of becoming physically intimate. He would tell me that he thought at this point it would destroy me but that nothing was impossible, that as sick as I was that he just couldn't fathom it. During my hospital stay I went on leave and spent $15,000 on clothes just so that I would have something new to wear every day. I couldn't wear the same dress twice. I was totally self-consumed—literally starved. There are two Sallys in this body.

I have made many attempts to see other doctors. I would let him know, and he has such control over me that, of course, I would cancel these appointments—to his satisfaction. My mother's close friend is a powerful and brilliant professor of internal medicine here in the East and has tried to set up appointments for me but finally gave up because I always canceled them.

My childhood goes without saying. Fragments of every case history in your book. As for the men in my life: They have to have at least $300 million in the bank or they are deficient as human beings. In addition to this attitude there is the fact that I ran away from home many years ago to become a stripper, etc., etc., etc.

One of the great issues was/is abandonment. My father left home when I was four. He would say he was coming to visit me and I would make myself pretty and he would never show up. He hated my mother and I was part of her. . . . We made him feel inadequate. I still do that to men.

Anyway, two months ago my therapist left on vacation for Florida. (He tells me his schedules weeks in advance because I get frantic.) When he came back from vacation he told me he was leaving. He will leave for Florida in two months. Abandonment. Everything changed at this point. He says he loves me but (1) that we will never have anything but a doctor/patient relationship; (2) that he is not my mother, father, daughter, son, etc., etc.; (3) the bill which I have always paid is a major issue even though before he said not ever to worry, that it was not important. He grew distant and cold and I felt and knew that he wasn't with me during our sessions. He has already left. I only stay in this area for therapy with him. I despise it here.

Initially, when he told me he was leaving I took out my anger on myself—cutting my wrists—so on and so forth. We decided I would move to Florida as well. I felt really strong. I could run for miles. He was really thrilled. Nothing is consistent. He has taken away everything. In other words, everything that I feared the most has happened.

I love him enough to let him go: I love him enough to continue therapy if that is what this is, to follow him to Florida. My question is: What is going on?

I apologize for the sloppiness of this letter but I'm really having trouble. I hope you can help.

We had this silly agreement—if I would keep my food down then he would take me to this cafeteria for lunch. Never in my wildest dreams would I set foot in a cafeteria. Well, I stopped throwing up and now he's not going to take me. This sounds so silly but that really breaks my heart. He's fully aware of how important that was to me.

Sally V.

My first reaction to Sally's letter was one of anger at her male therapist for interacting so inappropriately and unprofessionally with her. The sexual theme of their encounters especially upset me and I perceived Sally as the victim of an opportunist who used his profession as a way of meeting and seducing vulnerable women such as herself. That such therapists certainly exist has been well documented, and I felt reinforced in my conviction that women in therapy are safest seeing female therapists.

While I feel very strongly that the only appropriate way of handling her case would have been for this man to refer Sally to a competent female therapist with a thorough understanding of addiction and its treatment, on rereading the letter I now see his behavior as more co-alcoholic than it was unethical. This revised view of what went on between them is further informed by a telephone conversation I had with Sally. (After having made it a necessary policy not to respond by phone to the numerous requests I receive, I was so alarmed by the dramatic content of her letter that I made an exception in Sally's case!) That exchange made it clear to me that her first order of business was being free to pursue her various addictions unimpeded by a serious approach to recovery and that the ongoing drama of her own life was her chief form of entertainment. Sally was not the least interested in seeing a female therapist, which I urged her to do along with attending the Anonymous programs that address her several addictions.

The reference in her letter to running away to become a stripper and the provocative "etc., etc., etc." hints that another area of compulsiveness for Sally may be in the sexual realm. Far more often than not women who become stripteasers or prostitutes or otherwise professionally sexual have a history of sexual abuse and a need to reenact the sexual drama, always seeking a feeling of power and ascendancy over men. It is a serious therapeutic issue, but in Sally's case, chemical addiction must be addressed first. Sobriety is required before any other problems can be dealt with in therapy.

My entire interaction with Sally, through the letter and the phone call, has been an important reminder to me of how little any of us—family, friends, or professionals—can do to bring about change in another person when addiction is present. Everything we do naturally in response to addiction is wrong. We try to help or we want to punish. Both reactions are co-alcoholic. Our efforts to help come from a feeling of pity for the addict and a mistaken belief that if we can make things easier for her or help her feel better about herself she will then feel encouraged enough to change. This approach seems logical, but it doesn't work, because people rarely change except through what finally becomes unbearable pain. With our efforts to help we are ameliorating the addict's pain and thus actually prolonging the disease.

When this "helpful" approach doesn't work we become frustrated and angry and want the addict to suffer, hoping that doing so will teach her a lesson and she will then be forced to change. However, the addict's tolerance for pain may be far greater than our tolerance for watching it, partly due to her use of mind-altering substances that work as anesthetics. Out of feelings of pity and guilt we may soon be back trying, again, to help.

What we need to be able to do is to give clear information about what addiction is, how it works, what its consequences are and the best approach to recovery. Then we need to get out of the way and allow the addict to make up her mind about whether she is ready to do what is necessary in order to recover. Perhaps the greatest difference between her therapist and myself is that I could hear Sally's unwillingness to address her addictions and hearing it I could let go. The ability to hear that an addict isn't yet ready to begin to address recovery seriously and then to let that addict go comes easier after many years' experience of trying too hard to help and seeing that it doesn't work.

It is very difficult for professionals to be clear and objective and stick to the principles that work in the treatment of addiction—not to alter the rules or make exceptions or keep on trying to convince the addict to do what we think she should. It is made even more difficult because, after all, we're being *paid* and we're expected to get results. To further complicate things, many of us in the helping professions wouldn't be in the business at all if we didn't have a strong need to rescue others or control them or both. But for the addict's sake we must lay aside our fantasy of being the one who will make the difference in this person's life. We must accept that it is our responsibility to deal privately with the frustration inevitably generated by the fact that we work with people who do not typically recover. Our caring must be as impersonal and detached as it is genuine. The client's recovery must be more important to her than it is to us. Otherwise we are going to be trying to do far more than what is our appropriate share of the work in this client's life, an approach that is not ultimately in our own or the addict's best interest.

It is impossible to know clearly what motives were behind the actions of Sally's therapist. Perhaps he was a womanizer of the worst sort, preying on his vulnerable clients. Perhaps he was operating with the best of intentions, believing that if he could convince Sally that she was lovable and provide her with a stable, caring relationship that validated her self-worth she would begin to get well. Perhaps his motives were mixed, as are those of most of us who enter the helping professions. Without a sufficient understanding of and respect for the self-willed determination that fuels the manipulations of an addict of Sally's caliber, his misguided and/or self-serving efforts with her turned their interactions into a duel that she ultimately won. She is still practicing every addiction she started with and yet she now views the therapist who was supposed to help her as her main problem—rather than her alcohol and drug abuse, her life-threatening eating disorder and her compulsive spending.

This case provides important warnings for us all. Clients need to be wary of therapists who think they can "love" someone into changing. As appealing as the idea of a therapist's love and wisdom being the magical catalyst for change may be, recovery does not work that way. It is the client's job to change. The therapist can merely serve as a guide.

And therapists need to be alert to clients who want the professional to be the paid solution to their problems. No professional can be that to a client, any more than anyone else can, whether husband or wife, parent or child or friend. Change and recovery are between each person and a much higher Power than any one of us professionals can ever be, no matter how much we, or our clients, would like us to try.

In the next letter the writer's problem is not chemical addiction but relationship addiction, specifically co-alcoholism. Again, because the therapist is unable to diagnose and treat it appropriately as a primary disease process, there is little progress in spite of both the therapist's and the client's sincere efforts.

It is my observation that going to a therapist when one has an addiction is actually likely to delay recovery unless the therapist has a thorough understanding of the approach taken in the Twelve-Step programs and can fully support that approach. If the therapist believes that therapy by itself can provide the basis for recovery, the addictive client is being done a serious disservice that can cost a great deal of money and time and allow the addiction, in spite of the effort spent, to progress. It is the observation of many of those who work in the field of addiction that therapy by itself has a miserable success rate in the treatment of addiction. Even when the therapist recognizes that addiction is causing the client's problems and then helps the client become aware of her destructive behavior patterns and the roots of her addiction, the client is most often still unable to *stop practicing* the addiction. Information, identification, understanding and insight regarding addiction are simply not sufficient to bring about recovery. Nor will the therapist's best efforts to help the client control the behavior work, because, in the long run, no matter how sophisticated, these efforts are always part of the disease itself. Through such efforts to control any addict, the therapist becomes, in essence, a co-dependent to the client, trying to control that over which both client and therapist are, of themselves, powerless. This generates frustration and anger in the therapist and guilt and resentment in the client.

To be of help to addictive clients a therapist must thoroughly understand the disease concept of addiction, as well as the concepts of powerlessness and surrender as they apply to recovery. The therapist must unstintingly support involvement in the Anonymous program that is appropriate for the client's particular addiction. When the therapist does not understand the principles of the Twelve-Step approach and sets forth disparate goals for therapy, these goals may confuse the client and collide with those found to work so well in the Anonymous programs.

For instance, the therapist may not be willing to support the client's reliance on a Higher Power, interpreting this as an expression of immature dependency. Or the therapist may not realize that in order for recovery to begin the addictive behavior must *stop*. The therapist might subtly or actively encourage the client to blame others for the addictive condition (blaming produces resentment, and resentment *feeds* addiction). Or the therapist may suggest confrontation of others rather than an inner healing and forgiveness and then the making of amends to others. In addition, unless the therapist has personally experienced addiction and has achieved significant ongoing recovery, it is difficult for him or her truly to respect both the addictive client and the power of addiction, much less acknowledge the time involved in recovery. It is especially this personal experience that allows the therapist to be able to help the client by predicting the stages of recovery, the difficulties that must be surmounted at each stage, the issues that must be faced and the ongoing danger of relapse if these issues are avoided. But again, a good program sponsor can do these things as well as a therapist.

On the other hand, one very important facet of recovery that a therapist may be better able to handle than a sponsor is that of helping the client probe more deeply into difficult family background issues. Therapists can be of greatest benefit, in my opinion, in treating the addictive family as a unit, helping members address together the various roles each has developed to cope with addiction and to explore how these roles have actually enabled the addiction to continue. Family therapy helps family members redefine themselves in ways that promote their own individual recovery as well as the family's greater health as a unit. Effective family therapy sessions reduce the habit of blaming and promote self-understanding and the taking of personal responsibility for one's own choices and behavior.

For some years now, many professionals, treatment hospitals and clinics dealing with alcoholics and drug addicts have been using this family systems approach in conjunction with recommending involvement in Twelve-Step programs. This same approach is also being used in treating other addictions such as compulsive eating and now sexual addiction. But relationship addiction is not widely regarded as being an equally serious disease process as yet, perhaps because of the great need in this culture to romanticize addictive relating even in its most destructive varieties.

Aside from either inpatient or outpatient treatment programs that address addiction and co-addiction as equally serious disease processes, relationship addiction is rarely seen as something more serious than simply having made some foolish choices in one's love life. There is such a thing as making one or two foolish choices in love relationships, but there is also such a thing as the very real disease of relationship addiction. Years ago when marijuana and then cocaine first came to be widely used, both these drugs were generally regarded by the medical and counseling professions as nonaddictive. Only after several years had gone by and those dependent on these drugs found they could not stop on their own did the professionals begin to recognize that these substances were, for some people, definitely addicting. Likewise the concept of relationship addiction is a new one for most people, and the term may be rather lightly employed unless there is a deeper understanding of the true nature of addiction.

In my experience people do not truly recover from relationship addiction with therapy alone any more than they recover from any other addiction by that means alone. They may stop *for a while*, but the tendency is not only to resume the addictive behavior but to practice it at a more seriously debilitating level unless there is a surrender of self-will and a spiritual focus in recovery.

Mary Ellen's letter, which follows, clearly illustrates these points. She has sought therapy because of the emotional pain and turmoil brought on by her (as yet undiagnosed) relationship addiction. Because the addictive nature of her own behavior has not yet been acknowledged, much less treated, Mary Ellen's commitment to therapy and her therapist's best efforts to help her have so far failed to improve her condition. In fact, she is getting sicker.

> *Dear Ms. Norwood:*
> *I have been divorced from an alcoholic for almost nine years—for the last three years I have been in therapy with a woman who is a doctor of psychology. I started seeing her after the abrupt ending of a relationship with another man who was an alcoholic.*
> *In both my marriage and this relationship, I felt all the feelings of desperation and the need to make constant phone calls to each of these men just as your first chapter describes.*
> *Over the years I have always felt that I could get in touch with my ex-husband . . . that he was out there somewhere still loving me but unable to pull through for*

me and our kids because of his illness. I never really broke that tie. Whenever I saw him (he lives in California and I live in Oregon), I slept with him and always felt that if I showed him how much I loved him, he would somehow change.

Last May, after not seeing him for almost two years, I set up a "date" with him, as I would be in California on business. I had not been in any type of relationship with a man for several years and seeing him seemed to be the answer to all my prayers. Yes, he was still drinking and had done really nothing to improve his life, but he was still a man who showed me love and attention. To make a long story short, we got very involved and started commuting back and forth all summer. We were talking about him moving back to Oregon and starting all over again when he had a very serious heart attack in August while I was with him.

He was in coronary care for three weeks—very, very sick. His heart is severely damaged and to complicate it he developed a serious case of pneumonia and also suffered three days of severe DT's in the hospital (caused by his sudden withdrawal from alcohol).

I talked to his doctor then and described the situation. The doctor talked to me and his two brothers (both recovered alcoholics) and suggested that Michael had no chance of improvement if he stayed in California working at his old job. He was a doorman at a large hotel, carrying heavy baggage. He also smoked and drank heavily. He ended up coming back to Oregon with me when he was released from the hospital. The doctor warned me that I should really consider what I was taking on, but I wanted to have him with me and felt it was the only way. He stayed for six months.

During the time he stayed with me, I knew in the back of his mind he wanted to go back to California to his old life. But his brothers and I kept warning him that he could not do that because of his health. I tried and tried to make everything okay and I guess when he brought up California I just either ignored it or raised a fuss. He even acted like he was very happy most of the time and got into a cardiac rehabilitation program here.

He ended up just leaving one day, taking my older son's car and most of his clothes. He called me and said he was going down to straighten out his disability insurance which had expired after six months and would be back in a couple of days. After two days, I called his brother and found out that he had started drinking as soon as he hit California and was unwilling to talk to me. After another day of my phone calls he finally spoke with me and acted like I was a scolding parent. He finally showed up with the car a week later, after drinking and driving all night, and immediately told me to take him to the bus—that he was no good and was doing me a favor by getting out of my life. He was unwilling to talk about anything—just very depressed and hostile.

I took him to the bus and that was the last I have seen or heard from him. He has not contacted either of his brothers, but one of them tracked him down and found that he is staying here and there around the city with his drinking buddies and is back in his old life-style.

All of that was background. I know, intellectually, that he is doing what he wants and I am powerless to help or change him. I want to put it all away and just go on with my life, but it is so hard. I keep wanting to pick up the phone and find him and talk to him, even though I know there is nothing to say.

My therapist is very disturbed with me and feels that I am giving up on myself and don't have the will to change my lifetime patterns of destructive behavior. I get angry at her, because I don't think she should give up on me right now when everything is so awful for me.

I know there is no surefire formula that you can give me for letting go of all this. I thought about going to Al-Anon, but I don't want to deal with living with an alcoholic—I don't live with him anymore and I probably will never see him again—until his funeral which probably won't be long.

Incidentally, my childhood was not troubled as you described. But there were some problems with my father dying when I was ten and my mother just being unable to cope in her loneliness with a teenage daughter. I grew up lonely. *My sister and brother were grown and away and when I married Michael I was pregnant. It was against all their wishes. I think they gave up on me then.*

My career is excellent. I have worked very hard in the past eight years in a big company and have finally reached a management position. I am finishing up an MBA and will graduate in May. My kids are wonderful and doing well. Even Michael's leaving didn't affect them too much. They have seen my therapist and she feels they never really believed that he would stay with us as I did. My problem is inside me. I can't let go of him and feel like I just got divorced all over again and my life is over. I don't feel like going to work or school and have to work at being cheerful for my kids.

Have you suggestions? My therapist (who I really love and trust) feels I should see a psychiatrist for a medicine evaluation. I am now on several drugs because of severe hyperthyroidism which popped up in November. She thinks getting a second opinion on my condition is advisable, that maybe someone else can pick up on something with me that she may be missing.

I don't want to give up. Most of all I would love a healthy relationship with a stable man. I've never been able to have this. As WWL2M says, this kind of man has always been "boring" to me.

My kids will be gone in less than five years and I'm terrified of that and also of turning forty this May. How can I be so successful in all aspects of my life but the personal?

Mary Ellen J.

Dear Mary Ellen,

When you say, in your letter—

"I know, intellectually, that he is doing what he wants and I am powerless to help or change him. I want to put it all away and just go on with my life. But it is so hard. I keep wanting to pick up the phone and find him and talk to him, even though I know there is nothing to say."

—you are facing the same struggle an alcoholic faces who knows that drinking is making things worse and yet cannot stop on his own. You are struggling with your own addiction to *him,* which is just as powerful and just as progressive as any addiction to a chemical. Indeed, as with chemical addiction, every area of your life is being affected: your other relationships, your work and your, health.

Your therapist is frustrated with you because you are not able to stop practicing your disease of relationship addiction—in your case, specifically, co-alcoholism. Like any other addict, you cannot stop on your own or with just the help of therapy. You need a program. I personally believe that a therapist who sees an alcoholic who won't go to Alcoholics Anonymous or a co-alcoholic who won't go to Al-Anon vastly underestimates the power of these addictions and overrates the effectiveness of therapy, by itself, in addressing them. Ideally, a therapist would not only be willing to insist the client attend the appropriate program but would also have a thorough understanding of how the program's principles bring about recovery, so that therapy can support those principles.

Keep in mind that most addicts do not recover. Most die.

Mary Ellen, your resistance to going to Al-Anon is exactly like an alcoholic's resistance to Alcoholics Anonymous. I hope you become willing to go to the lengths necessary to achieve your own recovery by beginning to attend Al-Anon several times a week. It is a program for the families and friends of alcoholics. Living with an alcoholic is not a requirement, because the disease of co-alcoholism is present whether the alcoholic is or not, as your letter makes clear.

I also hope that you take your disease seriously enough to make sure that any help you get is from professionals who, themselves, understand the diseases of addiction and co-addiction and *recovery.* I would personally question any therapist's expertise in this area who did not *require* you go to Al-Anon as a condition of therapy. When we professionals understand addiction and co-addiction we learn to deeply respect the healing powers of the Anonymous programs and to accept that these programs can do for our clients what we cannot.

Further, any evaluation of your children must take into consideration much more than whether they believed that your husband would stay in the home. Children of alcoholics (and co-alcoholics) are often able to "look good" while suffering great emotional pain that they are unable to acknowledge to others or even to themselves. Living with a co-alcoholic parent who is obsessed with the alcoholic, depressed and physically unwell (and possibly self-sacrificing and overcontrolling, too, since these are such common characteristics in co-alcoholics) can be fully as damaging as living with a practicing alcoholic. Again, a thorough understanding of the diseases of addiction and co-addiction is necessary to any such evaluation.

It is important for all of us, professionals and lay persons alike, to keep in mind that most addicts do not recover. Most eventually die of their diseases. This is true for chemically addicted people and I believe it is true for relationship-addicted people, too. It would not be an exaggeration to say that, given the present state of your health, like your husband, you are dying of your disease of addiction.

If you spend the next five years working on your own recovery, I daresay your physical problems will heal, as will every other area of your life. Even when it comes time for your children to leave home, you will be less alone than ever before.

Dear Ms. Norwood,

I have been in various forms of therapy almost all my adult life, and it never did anything to change my patterns.

Although I am attractive and look younger, I am in

my fifties, so I don't have all that much time left to develop a healthy relationship. I'm just coming out of a nine-year relationship with a man who treated me badly, was insensitive to my needs, had many other women— and in the course of our relationship married a woman who lived in another city. I even went along with that, until his wife insisted on coming to live with him. He wanted to keep me as a mistress on the side, seeing me about once every three weeks! That was too much (or too little) even for me.

Throughout your book, I wept, remembering how my parents seemed to need each other so much, and paid almost no attention to the children. I know that with this latest love affair I kept having the feeling that if only I could make him love me, all would be right with the world. This man, like my father, seemed able (in a very flawed way) to love someone else—why not me? And I still ask myself that question.

I should add that since the age of twelve, I have had episodes of clinical depression and the only thing that was ever able to help me was my recent discovery of psychiatrists who treat depression with medication. Which is not to say that I feel happy, simply that when I take the medication I can function. Without it, I am truly depressed and begin to fear that I will need to be hospitalized.

Thank you for taking the time to read this and to respond.

Tanya L.

Dear Tanya,

Many, many women who love too much have serious problems with endogenous depression,* often lifetime struggles such as you've faced. I, too, spent most of my life trying to run from it and cope in spite of the

---

Endogenous depression is physically based, the result of chemical imbalance due to a variety of factors. These include heredity and severe and prolonged stress, which eventually alters metabolic processes. It is often linked genetically with alcoholism. *Exogenous* depression is reactive; that is, it occurs in reaction to loss, and therefore is basically grieving. However, for a person with a tendency toward endogenous depression, any stress (including loss and the resultant grieving) can precipitate an episode of endogenous depression.

monstrous dark cloud that would overtake me at increasingly frequent intervals as the years went by.

Endogenous depression is a condition of chemical imbalance, triggered or deepened by stress, whether of a physical or emotional nature. In many ways depression of this sort is similar to being drunk. The brain chemistry is as seriously altered as in a state of severe intoxication. Many of us, when we are in the acute phase of depression, have litanies that we repeat over and over, much like a drunk in a bar repetitiously bemoaning the fact that his wife left him twenty years ago. We may repeatedly express regrets or make apologies or feel a need to make an inappropriate phone call (again, like someone who is drunk).

At one time I led a group for depressives, and together we shared what it was like for us to struggle with this disease. I was struck by how much like alcoholics in Alcoholics Anonymous we were, coming together and talking honestly about how depression had affected our lives. There are many myths held by professionals about depression, but in our meetings we talked about how it *really* was for us. We helped each other get better by learning together to respect the disease's power over us. We helped each other with simple reminders to rest whenever depression struck, rather than employ our usual gambit of coping behaviors and becoming completely overwhelmed. All of us had tremendous guilt about being depressed, as well as a tendency toward perfectionism, which we had developed in order to compensate for our secret disability. Many of us had come from alcoholic or otherwise dysfunctional families and had, in adulthood, chosen incredibly stressful relationships. We were living in constant chaos and yet feared that if we were depressed the men we were involved with would leave and we would become *more* depressed. No wonder most of us were getting sicker.

Some things that helped:

- Many members of the group joined Recovery Inc., a self-help group begun by a psychiatrist, Dr. Abraham Low, for people with nervous disorders. The techniques employed in Recovery can be of great help to anyone who suffers from depression, and it is unfortunate that so few professionals refer their clients to this excellent, *free* resource.

- We called each other when we were becoming anxious or despairing. We learned not to wait until we were so far gone before we called. Often, by not waiting too long, we could effectively forestall a really serious episode, *because we reduced our stress* by calling.

- We stopped being ashamed of our depression and stopped trying to hide it. It was a condition we had to respect before we could expect others to take it seriously.

- We came to regard it as a disease like diabetes. And, as is the case with diabetics who cannot continue to eat sugar and maintain their health, we learned that self-discipline was necessary if we were to keep from being disabled by our diseases. Many of us suffered from severe food allergy-addictions that needed to be addressed. We supported each other in following our strange new diets, which made us feel like social outcasts at first but often brought significant relief from symptoms.

- A few of us required maintenance doses of medication, but for several in the group, *no* medication had ever worked over time. For these individuals each prescribed drug had eventually lost its effectiveness, and some medications had caused serious problems in and of themselves. No one in this group found any medication to be "the answer."

- We all came to realize that complete abstinence from alcohol and other recreational drugs was an absolute must in our efforts to avoid episodes of depression. We had no business hampering our bodies' metabolic efforts to reduce toxicity.

- For all of us, the support that came from talking to others who understood was invaluable. Facing our individual allergy issues and addressing them, as well as developing tools for coping more realistically with the outer environment and with our inner thought processes, were all important aspects of recovery.

What was *not* helpful when we were in the throes of depression was traditional verbal therapy. Talking to a therapist about deep-seated emotional problems usually increased the depression, because of the stress that a typical therapy session produces. Besides, when in the grip of endogenous depression each of us was no more herself than someone who is drunk. The therapist was talking to someone in an *altered state,* a state of chemical imbalance affecting brain function. We realized that the only appropriate role of a therapist at these times was to provide support as we struggled with our disease—and we could do that for each other.

Trying to live a normal life when suffering from endogenous depression is a lot like trying to ski on a broken leg. It is very difficult and very painful. What makes it worse is that because we're not bleeding from open wounds no one, ourselves included, knows the severity of our handicap. Because of our shame, we try with all our might to hide how overwhelmed we feel by the struggle to appear normal. This posture produces more of our enemy, stress.

Once again, as with so many emotional/physical/ spiritual problems, it is trying to keep the secret that makes us sicker and letting it go that helps us to recover. To try to hide the condition, while we are simultaneously growing more distraught with the effort, is desperately difficult. How much easier it is to acknowledge, "I have episodes of depression that occur from time to time due to chemical imbalance. When this happens I'm not myself and need to rest and reduce my stress until I'm all right again."

For most of us in that group, endogenous depression is not a condition from which we hope ever to be completely free. But it can be better managed when we remember that, as in the case with the disease of alcoholism, our recovery has a physical, emotional and spiritual aspect. By changing what we can in each of these areas we create a climate for healing ourselves.

————

Dear Ms. Norwood,

I read your book at the suggestion of my therapist, who I am seeing because of my own potential alcohol problem. My relationships seemed to be falling apart around me and I was starting to fall apart, too. I thought I was doing everything I was supposed to in a relationship, but was just accidentally finding jerks who didn't appreciate me. I can see now that this is not the case, but rather that men have been an obsession.

I have quite a few obsessions other than men: sugar, clothes, smoking, drinking, occasional bouts of over-cleanliness and spending. I was surprised that you did not focus more on the spending. I feel so bad inside sometimes that I want to look good on the outside (denial), and think if I project a certain look and confidence, everyone will like me (control). It doesn't work; the only thing it has done is to leave me "in debt" (another thing to obsess over).

My biggest problem is getting help. Yes, I do see a therapist, but I'm feeling like a cry baby. I spill the hurt out, but I can't get unstuck enough to make any progress. I have been to Alcoholics Anonymous meetings, where I feel out of place because I have not "hit bottom" yet. I've been to meetings for Adult Children of Alcoholics, but again feel out of place. I feel like I'm complaining when I do speak. When I just listen, I do hear some important things, but being there really scares the hell out of me. I don't feel strong enough to start my own group. See what I mean? I feel stuck somehow.

Right now I don't want anyone in my life. I am extremely lonely, but I don't want anyone in my life because it's too difficult for me to take care of myself with someone else around. If I could only think about myself first. Do people from normal homes think about their happiness first?

I grew up thinking that you did all for love, that you sacrificed, that love demanded bending and forgiving and putting up with pain. Now the world has somehow turned around and I missed the turn—because now you are telling me that love requires selfishness (the good kind). Will I ever grow up enough to love in a way that keeps me a separate individual and in touch with myself?

Jeannie C.

Dear Jeannie,

Something in your letter tells me that you are not yet ready to do what you need to do in order to get well. I hope I'm mistaken about this, because there is a lot of very appropriate help for you if you choose to avail yourself of it—help that will truly change your life.

You qualify for several of the Anonymous programs and there, in my opinion, is exactly where you belong. If you really want to grow up, the first thing you need to do is stop drinking. Being in therapy while using any mind-altering drug is a waste of time and money. You need to be clean and sober in order even to begin to get well in the other areas of your life. So go back to Alcoholics Anonymous to get support for leaving alcohol alone. By the way, most of the alcoholics I've worked with throughout my fifteen years in the field of addiction felt just as you do. They didn't think they belonged in Alcoholics Anonymous either. Most are still drinking and their lives are becoming progressively more unmanageable, but they still don't think they're alcoholic.*

When you've been sober awhile—six months to a year—you may find you need help with the other obsessions you've mentioned. Debtors Anonymous has helped many sober alcoholics and others overcome their compulsive spending. Overeaters Anonymous is as important

---

*Alcoholism is not all that difficult to define. If someone's drinking causes problems and that person nevertheless continues to drink—that's alcoholism. In many ways alcoholism is like being pregnant. You either are or you're not. But if you are, at first it doesn't show very much so you may not be aware of the fact and neither may other people. As time goes on, though, it becomes more and more obvious.

to the recovery of a compulsive eater as Alcoholics Anonymous is to the alcoholic. (Most compulsive eaters find that they must abstain from alcohol even if it isn't their primary addiction, because alcohol and sugar react almost the same way in their bodies in that the ingestion of either substance may precipitate a binge.) Many areas of the country now have Relationships Anonymous meetings for those who use relationships as a drug; this, too, may be a place where you belong.

None of these recoveries can take hold if you continue to drink, however, because one of the primary functions of alcohol is that it puts to sleep the part of your brain that says no. And Jeannie, you know how important that part of your brain is when you are trying not to practice an addiction. You can't afford to be putting it to sleep, because you'll find yourself saying yes to the two-hundred-dollar shoes or the chocolate mousse or the married man, or all three.

Loving yourself enough to become free from addiction is a prerequisite to loving another person.

You also qualify for Al-Anon and Adult Children of Alcoholics meetings, and these programs should eventually become an important part of your recovery. In my opinion, these programs should wait until you have a solid year of being clean and sober. When in Al-Anon or Adult Children of Alcoholics meetings, newly sober alcoholics will often identify more with the alcoholic whose drinking is causing so much pain to others than with the co-alcoholics there. The guilt thus generated can be tremendous. Or, conversely, alcoholics without a year's recovery may choose to ignore their recovery from alcoholism and focus strictly on their co-alcoholic issues, perhaps drinking again in the process. So a year's sobriety is appropriate to help all these recoveries.

Finally, let me say that you need to begin the very important work of addressing your addictions and your co-dependency issues in the appropriate programs and in the appropriate order *much* more than you need to see another therapist or read another book. Meetings will take care of the loneliness, the fear and the obsessions. There you will learn firsthand what putting healthy self-ishness to work in your life means—how to find support for your recovery rather than indulging your addictions. Best of all, though, with the unconditional love available there, you will eventually come to the point where you choose only that which serves to support and maintain your well-being and serenity—whether those choices involve food, drink, material possessions, behavior or people. Healthy, loving relationships require healthy, loving people. Loving yourself enough to become free from addiction is a prerequisite to being truly healthy and loving with another person.

Dear Ms. Norwood,

I am in the metaphysical field. I have done counseling work, lectures, workshops and I use a healing technique that deals mostly with the emotional body.

I stayed a week with my son in an alcoholic, drug addiction rehab center and they are using your book. My future daughter-in-law had read it so she was also recommending the book, especially to the families of the patients.

Since it is so helpful, I would like to give a workshop on your material. I would appreciate your viewpoint on this workshop and your feelings.

Ginger J.

Dear Ginger,

First of all, thank you for asking for my viewpoint as I certainly have a very definite one. I am frankly alarmed by the numbers of therapists who are offering workshops on relationship addiction who do not at all understand what addiction actually is and how it is appropriately treated.

Addiction means that a person cannot stop on his or her own. More information or a group experience will not turn the trick and suddenly enable a person to permanently halt a destructive pattern of dependency, whether on food, alcohol, work, sex, drugs or relationships.

I fervently wish that anyone who is going to teach classes on relationship addiction would at least attend several open meetings of various Anonymous programs, particularly Alcoholics Anonymous and Al-Anon. Only in this way can they begin to grasp the tremendous power of addiction and co-addiction. Only *from people who are recovering* can they learn what a slow, difficult process recovery is, and understand it as an unfolding requiring literally years of effort and dedication.

Recovery requires reliance not on a therapist but on a Higher Power, something that is rarely stressed in most of the workshops I've heard about. Instead, these short-term workshops tend to stress greater efforts at self-willed control, an approach that is *not* over the long haul effective in the face of addiction.

Like yourself, Ginger, so many people who want to teach these classes or lead these groups are themselves co-alcoholic. The need to tell others how to get well is so much a part of untreated co-alcoholism. I really believe that if each of us would address our *own* recovery and make it our first priority we would ultimately teach a great deal more to others than all the classes can ever do, because our lives would then be an *example* of what it is to no longer manage and control and advise all in the name of "helping." Talking about, lecturing about, writing about recovery are all far more commonplace than is recovery itself.

Many of us who become counselors or therapists are greatly attracted by the idea of healing others, and some of us are, indeed, gifted healers. But the admonition, "Physician, heal thyself!" applies to those of us who want to help the healing of the psyche as well as to those who would facilitate the healing of the body. We must start with ourselves, and sometimes, especially if we are co-alcoholic or otherwise relationship addicted, our own healing means that we must, for a time, *stop* looking for ways to help others. We need, instead, to learn to hold still and take care of ourselves.

Everything of worth I've ever learned about recovery I've learned from those who were, themselves, recovering. I don't believe any of us can help another reach a point we haven't reached ourselves. That's why our own recovery must always be our first priority if we want to be of help to others. In order to give something we have to have it in the first place.

Recovery cannot be bought. It cannot be obtained by seeing the right therapist or attending the right class (although doing these things may be very helpful). It is not a once-and-for-all proposition. Recovery is an ongoing process that begins minute by minute, grows hour by hour and, finally, continues year after year, but it never proceeds more than one day at a time. It requires, not a prodigious, dramatic, temporary assault on the problem, but rather a daily surrender in the face of the power of the disease and a daily commitment to go to any lengths not to practice it, not to do any of the little or big things that constitute a "slip," not to make any of the moves that come so easily and naturally and insidiously to mind. Only someone who *is* recovering can truly understand this and impart it.

———

Ms. Norwood,

I've just finished reading your book. I thought after the first few pages I would never pick up that book again. I cried because I found out that I had yet another disease. I'm already a recovering addict and alcoholic. I've been in Narcotics Anonymous and Alcoholics Anonymous for over a year, and I have six months' clean time. I've been in therapy for a year and a half and I've also been in two rehabs. I'm an adult child of an alcoholic and I probably qualify for Overeaters Anonymous.

When I first started reading your book I was overwhelmed. There I was in black and white. All of my old ways of thinking started to kick in. I'm working on my fourth step (moral inventory) and I decided I didn't need the added pressure. But as I wrote about my relationships I started to see my patterns with men starting first with my father. I decided maybe I should get up some courage and pick the book up again.

It was painful. It's not fun to see yourself like that. The thing that helped me is that you said it is a disease. I could deal with that because I knew that meant it wasn't my fault, I wasn't to blame. (I just didn't want another disease.)

I've been in a relationship with another recovering addict for almost a year now. I was told in therapy that getting involved with a man was the most dangerous thing I could do besides picking up a drink or a drug, that if I did get involved it would lead me back to my chemical addiction. And it did briefly. Until I read your book I thought maybe something in my mind didn't work right, because for the life of me I couldn't let go of this very unrewarding, unhealthy relationship.

I work my program to the best of my ability and that's helped me a lot. But for me to close the door completely on this relationship is so hard to do. Your book has given me some very basic tools that I can use to help myself with that part of my addictive personality. First, I'm going to be honest with my therapist (she thinks I'm out of the relationship) and get the help I need. I also found out a week ago that some women have formed a support group as a direct result of your book, and I'm going to get involved. I've already been in one support group for relationship addiction. It only lasted six weeks but it helped me a lot.

Roberta J.

Dear Roberta,

Your letter is so important because in it you describe what none of us wants to face, but is unavoidable for most of us—the Next Recovery. Especially for people like yourself with membership in one or more of the Anonymous programs, there comes a point when the feeling is, "There. I've done it. I've given up enough and it's time now for me to be able to sit back, work my program(s) to the best of my ability, of course, but to relax a little bit, too." Yet so very often, recovery in one area simply clears away enough debris so that it becomes possible to see just how unmanageable life still is in another area, and why.

Having dealt with one addiction or one disease process, many people try very hard not to see, much less confront, the next one that is waiting to be addressed. Ironically, the more recovery they have in one area the harder they must work to ignore the next piece of work they need to face. The man sober in Alcoholics Anonymous for several years may nevertheless refuse to acknowledge what his addiction to illicit sex is still doing to his family life. Or a woman with a good solid Al-Anon program may have made peace with her husband's alcoholism but continue to try to ignore her own compulsion to eat certain foods.

Like yourself, most alcoholic women, once sober, need to address their relationship addiction, because most come from alcoholic families where they learned co-dependency early. Many have been victims of physical and sexual abuse, and eventually these areas, too, must be healed in order for sobriety to be truly comfortable. Sober alcoholic women who "slip" most often do so over co-dependency issues. This is why you were warned not to become involved with a man early in your sobriety. No other area is as "slippery" as relationships are for clean and sober women.

Facing that Next Recovery requires great courage and humility, the more so the longer-standing the first recovery is. Some pride begins to build up behind the number of years one has been recovering, and it isn't easy or pleasant to admit that cleaning up one area of life didn't take care of all the pain or all the secrets. But, instead of viewing the Next Recovery as a blow to one's pride or a failure to work a perfect program, it would be more appropriate to welcome it. Remember the relief that came when you fully surrendered before the power of the other addictions you've already faced. And recognize that recovery is never an end in itself; it is not a door to be closed on an old way of living but one that must daily be opened to a new, better, freer, more expanded experience of being alive and whole and well.

• That is what is ahead of you, Roberta. What lies ahead for you is not a diminished life in which you have to give up more and more of your favorite substances and activities in order to barely survive and stay sane. What you have to look forward to is just the opposite: a life in which the way has been cleared and there is a great open free place for all the good that is trying to come to you. With your Next Recovery you're just busily working to remove one more impediment to its arrival.

A final note. I had to laugh, albeit ruefully, when I read your "confession" that you had been deceiving your therapist about still being involved in your present unhealthy relationship. This practice of paying for therapy and then being less than honest with the therapist is *so* common, more common than any therapist likes to admit because we are so helpless in the face of it.

People who enter therapy are usually looking for relief from the pain that is the natural consequence of the way they are presently living. They hope, by paying someone who is an "expert," that they will be able to secure that relief. In other words, they bring to the therapy situation the same consumer attitude it is natural to have when a car is taken to a mechanic. They are willing to pay money to have someone with that particular expertise fix whatever is wrong, but the burden is on the expert to discover what the problem is and to correct it. But, of course, a consumer attitude simply doesn't work in therapy for many reasons. For instance, when the problem is a malfunctioning car our ego is not involved in hiding whatever conditions are contributing to the car's problems; but with an unhappy, unmanageable life our ego is usually tremendously involved in concealing whatever attitudes, behaviors and secrets are creating the pain. This is especially true when any form of addiction is present.

It is the nature of addictive persons to greatly minimize how bad their situation has become.

It is the nature of addictive persons (no matter what their addiction is) to greatly minimize or completely deny how sick they are and how bad their situation has become. If we as counselors are working with an alcoholic, that person will typically either greatly minimize the extent of the drinking or deny drinking altogether. If our client is a relationship addict and we know how to diagnose that particular addiction, we know that most likely the stories of unhealthy involvement will either be cleaned up considerably or never be reported at all.

When we therapists sit with a client we can only work with what the client tells us, coupled with our understanding of the client's situation or disease as it is typically experienced by others who have been through it. When we have personally grappled with it, that adds immeasurably to our understanding of the client's predicament. We try to provide a mirror that reflects back to the client a combination of what we are being told coupled with what we, as professionals and possibly as recovering persons ourselves, know about the condition with which the client struggles. But the client's inevitable denial is why one-to-one therapy with addictive individuals (again, no matter what the addiction is) can never, by itself, be the treatment of choice. The reflection given back by the therapist, which is of necessity based on what the client is reporting, has already been distorted by the client's unconscious need to minimize or omit what are often the most relevant facts. But, when the addictive client is attending meetings with others who have the same addiction, this situation is remedied. Even though each participant may be in denial about particular aspects of his or her disease, when all their stories and all their struggles are combined they cover every facet of the disease and provide a mirror that ultimately reflects for each of them the entire picture they need to face.

Roberta, you need this mirror as much for your relationship addiction as for your chemical addiction. As you've already discovered, meetings on relationship addiction in addition to your therapy will do the most to promote your healing in this area, too.

SEVEN

. . . ARE IN
SUPPORT
GROUPS FOR
RELATIONSHIP
ADDICTION

Many, many groups for relationship addicts have been started all over the country. Some were begun before *WWL2M* ever appeared and many more have been started since its publication. Some of these groups are led by therapists; others follow closely along the guidelines in *WWL2M* for forming a peer support group to address relationship addiction. However, my many years in the field of addiction have taught me that the Twelve-Step programs offer the most effective and appropriate treatment approach to all forms of addiction, including relationship addiction. I am so pleased to see that all over the country groups based on the Twelve Steps from Alcoholics Anonymous are being held to address relationship addiction. These groups have nothing to do with me personally. They are, after all, anonymous. But they, along with any of the other Twelve-Step programs that would be appropriate, are the *only* groups to which I feel comfortable making a referral for a relationship addict. While I believe that the ten steps to recovery set forth in *WWL2M* have significant value for all women who love too much, it is my belief that the best context in which to follow them is in a Twelve-Step program, with its greater emphasis on spiritual development. If relationship *addiction* is present, no other approach is likely to work effectively over time. None of this is to imply specific endorsement of any particular Twelve-Step meeting. That would be both inappropriate and inadvisable, since meetings can vary in how closely they follow the Steps and Traditions developed originally by Alcoholics Anonymous.

It has long been my practice only to refer to the Anonymous programs, never to individual therapists, group practices or treatment centers. And I have never yet encountered a troubled individual who didn't qualify for membership in at least one of the over one hundred varieties of Anonymous programs that exist today.

The following letter reveals what is true for many recovering alcoholic women: that after they become sober there is another disease that must be addressed if they are going to maintain their sobriety. The disease of relationship addiction is present in so many alcoholic women because they so often come from alcoholic homes where they were co-alcoholic long before they developed their own chemical dependency.

When the disease of chemical dependency is arrested, the emotional roller coaster caused by co-alcoholic patterns of relating becomes the greatest threat to continued sobriety. The lengths to which the following woman has gone in order to achieve recovery from relationship addiction fully match her efforts to stay sober, and for good reason. She recognizes that her relationship addiction is at least as serious a threat to her life and well-being as is her alcoholism.

Dear Robin Norwood,

My name is Ramona A. and I'm not only a recovering alcoholic but I'm now also a recovering woman who loves too much.

I got sober three years ago due to the threats of my actively drinking (now ex) husband who insisted that I do something about my drinking. So I went into treatment full of fear that if I didn't do what he asked, I'd lose him.

Sometime down the road I decided I liked being sober and started working my Alcoholics Anonymous program for me. As I worked my program my husband started making remarks that made me realize he didn't like the changes he saw in me. He began staying away from home more and drinking more as well. The fear of losing him was still uppermost in my mind, yet I knew if we stayed together, with the way things were going, I'd drink again and then I'd lose him for sure. So, ten months sober, I left his house hoping he'd miss me enough to do something about his own drinking. Then we could be sober together and both work our Alcoholics

Anonymous programs and live happily ever after. He had been honest enough to tell me when I asked him to go to counseling with me that he wasn't ready or willing to change. But, of course, I thought with time he'd see things differently.

I had been told in treatment, that he, too, was my addiction, not only alcohol. But I just couldn't see it or accept such a farfetched idea. So I started reading everything I got my hands on so I could show him in black and white what was wrong between us and then I could fix him and go on with our marriage together.

I went to Al-Anon, but for me it just gave me the hope that he might get sober, and that kept me tied to him even more. In my mind that is.

And, of course, I kept seeing him and allowed myself to believe his lies and to be treated any way he saw fit. He wasn't physically abusive, but the emotional abuse was unbearable. While he ran around with other women and drank, I'd wait for him, hoping and praying he'd change. And doing anything and everything I could think of to please him, always wanting to believe he'd come back to me for good.

That I didn't drink I know now was only by the grace of God, Who it seems had better things in mind for me. I hit an emotional bottom last year just like I had hit with my drinking. I went to bed at night praying to die and cursing God when I awoke because I was still alive. I went to work, came home and isolated myself, cried and prayed to die. Only one dear friend didn't give up on me. I've since lost her to cancer, but she was the friend who gave me the encouragement and unconditional love to do later on what has changed my life.

Somehow in my emotional hell I found your book and read it. There I was on every page and there was what was wrong with me. Only then could I accept and see that there was hope.

Al-Anon was still confusing for me because all I could hear was that if I did it right he'd stop drinking (that's not what they said, that's just what I heard). I felt my only hope of recovering was to start my own group for women like myself—addicted to men. I was already in therapy but I felt I needed more. So with the love and encouragement of my dear friend Carla and another friend Lois, I started a group based on your book.

I can't begin to tell you how my life has changed since then, how the doors have opened for me, how my self-esteem has grown, how my faith has grown, or how I have grown.

I truly believe had I gone on the way I was before, I wouldn't be around now to write this letter to you. I tried three times while drinking to kill myself—all prompted by my addictive love for my now ex-husband.

Since I formed the women's group, besides working my regular job, I've started working part-time at a halfway house for recovering addicts and alcoholics. I wouldn't have been able to do this without the personal growth I've achieved over the past six months.

I no longer sit and cry, or isolate myself, or pray to die. Nor am I constantly depressed. Nor do I feel that I need a man in my life to be happy or to take care of me.

Today I'm happy most of the time. Today I'm full of gratitude for all God has given me (and for the things he hasn't given me, too). Today I'm leading a full and busy life. If I happen to be dating someone my awarenesses tell me if it's good for me or not. I'm able to enjoy being with a man, but if I'm not, I'm not a basket case waiting for him to call. I'm living my life for me now. If a man happens to come along that's fine, but if one doesn't I'm just fine leading my life for me. I'm never bored and I know I never have to be alone.

Ramona A.

Dear Robin,

I have read and am wowed by your book. We have started a support group (ten ladies) here but have run into a problem. There are men in our area who have read the book and very much want to be in the support group. We are terrified! But they could be suffering just like we are. What do we do?

Rachel R.

Dear Rachel,

I believe that women and men need to have separate support groups when the disease is relationship addiction. Both women and men behave very differently in the presence of the opposite sex. When only with members of their own sex, women are generally more honest and self-revealing, especially when they are discussing problems in their lives that involve men. For men, the opposite is true. They often become more self-disclosing in the presence of women than they would be if only men were present, at least at first. But eventually they, too, are more fully honest when in the presence of only their own sex. If the men you've heard from really want the help of a support group they will start their own. You don't need to provide the opportunity for them to recover.

Long before *WWL2M* was written there were support groups in existence using the Twelve-Step approach to deal with issues of relationship addiction. Many of them are open to men and women, so there is not one "right" way to handle this. What you are getting here is my opinion only. If you do choose to restrict your group to women only, you might decide to cohost a meeting with these men after both your groups and theirs are well-established. That could conceivably lead to an occasional shared meeting for women and men together, which can help reduce the tendency toward an "us against them" feeling. But should you do so, by all means remember when you meet together to work on your own recoveries, not theirs! Perhaps the next two letters will help your group decide what to do.

———————

Dear Robin,

After reading WWL2M, *I tried desperately to find a support group in my area where women were exploring these issues together. After finding, to my great disappointment, that no group existed, I decided to follow your advice and start my own. I am happy to say that we now have a solid, involved and enthusiastic group which has grown from twelve the first week to twenty-five at our last (fifth) meeting. I'd also like to share with you, Robin, that starting this group, and being an active participant in its teachings, has been one of the most positive things I've ever done for myself.*

Although we have worked out several questions as they have come up, we would really like your help with some of our recent concerns. For one thing, do you recommend having men in the group? This issue has already caused some confusion, as a man showed up at one of our meetings recently. I invited him to stay, of course, but since we have been in the process of deciding whether we wanted to include men and weren't sure yet of which way to go, his presence caused some anxiety among our members. Also, we have decided to follow the Twelve-Step approach used by Alcoholics Anonymous and Al-Anon. Do you agree that this is a good format? In addition, we would like to vary our format from time to time by using video tapes and/or speakers, etc. Could you recommend any other effective means of presenting the material? And what general guidelines should the meetings take? Right now, we are just leaving it up to volunteer leaders each week to choose the topics and have open discussions, but is there a better, more effective way?

Also, could you tell me about the group "Relationships Anonymous"? Is that the same as "Women Who Love Too Much" only under a different name?

We would really appreciate any suggestions, feedback and support materials you could give us, Robin, as we are anxious to get the most benefit possible from our group. It has become of primary importance to me, but at times I feel a little bit in the dark as to the "right" way to structure it.

Marti S.

Before addressing the other questions posed in Marti's letter I think it is instructive to include the update on the "men" issue that she noted on the agreement form she sent back giving permission to use her letter in this book.

Dear Robin,

Concerning the issue of men being included in our group: As I mentioned, we weren't sure about including men, and after one brave guy sat in our group one week, I telephoned each member to ask her opinion of how the group had seemed that night. I had polled three or four women and couldn't understand why they were all agreeing to have men in the group, when I had sensed strong discomfort with his presence that night. Then it hit me! I was asking women who were caretakers *of men in the first place, if men should be included. Everyone was saying, "Yes, because he'll have no place else to get help," or something similar. So I changed my question to, "Are you as open and as comfortable with men in the group?" and the overwhelming vote was "No!" This really pointed out to me and to the other members of the group how we place others' (especially men's) needs ahead of our own!*

Marti

Concerning the other questions Marti raises, as stated elsewhere in this book, I do not know of any more effective means of addressing addiction and achieving recovery than the Twelve-Step approach of the Anonymous programs. As far as questions regarding varying the format for a particular meeting, those are best dealt with by the members of that meeting following the guidelines developed in long-standing Anonymous programs for making group decisions.

From its inception Alcoholics Anonymous (which is the original Twelve-Step program) has used the most democratic principles as the means of deciding every issue pertaining to its organization and purpose. Any support group that adapts this Twelve-Step approach to its purpose would do well to study the literature of Alcoholics Anonymous closely and borrow those principles for making decisions. The Anonymous programs have always recognized that no one person, no matter how "expert," should decide matters for the others. Indeed, they have always believed that each person who struggles with the particular addiction being addressed *is* an expert and should have equal say in all decision-making. Every question (including the one about including men) can be decided by any group using the guidelines that have served for over fifty years to keep the decision-making process of Alcoholics Anonymous so democratic. It is tempting to believe that someone else knows what is best for us, thereby underestimating our capacity and abdicating our responsibility for making important decisions. But if each of us is willing to take the time and make the effort to search our own heart for the answer to every question, we can then share what we have discovered with others who have made the same search and together come to a decision that is best for all concerned.

Being willing to learn a new way of living one day at a time is far more productive in the long run than trying too hard to go too fast.

Often when people have begun the process of recovery they want to find a way to speed things up. This attitude is so counterproductive that it must be battled constantly. Being willing to go slowly and learn a new way of living one day at a time is far more productive in the long run than trying too hard to go too fast and soon feeling frustrated, disappointed and discouraged.

Groups dealing with relationship addiction that use the Twelve-Step approach have developed under many names, the most common one being Relationships Anonymous. Other such groups that address this issue include "Love-n-Addiction," "Love and Sex Addicts Anonymous" (which addresses both relationship addiction and sexual addiction), and various "Women Who Love Too Much" groups *that follow a Twelve-*

Step approach, as opposed to groups by that name that are led by professionals. (I must add that one of the best names I've heard for a support group for relationship addiction was suggested by *WWL2M*'s hardcover publisher in jest and yet it states the case very well—"Overlovers Anonymous.")

Dear Robin,

We saw you recently on a television talk show and felt inspired to write. We are a group of women who got together as a result of your book. We have been meeting once a week since early August of this year.

First, a little of our group's history. This area's "Women Who Love Too Much" group had become so large that it was necessary to split it into smaller groups. Ours is composed of women who, for the most part, participate in Twelve-Step programs. One of the members typed an agenda with preamble and obstacles to success borrowed from the Twelve-Step programs and off we went, basically following the format of your book and ending with the Serenity Prayer. We've had a number of women come and go, but five of us have stuck with it and more recently three more joined us as active participants in the group.

Often we feel as though we haven't made any progress but watching your television interview we realized the long strides we have made in the past four months (a relatively short time). We recognized our old denial in the two women on the show with you and we're so relieved and grateful that we're moving along to a new understanding.

It hasn't been easy and we're far from recovered. We work hard, each in our own way and at our individual capacity, often taking scary steps into the unknown thanks to the sincere support of one another in the group and our willingness to share what we feel inside.

It occurred to us that perhaps a lot of feedback that you receive is from women just embarking on recovery and still in stressful states. We wanted to assure you that

there are some of us out here who are getting well and
starting to know and love who we are.
   We often hear people in Alcoholics Anonymous say
that when they first got to Alcoholics Anonymous they
weren't glad to be there, but they sure were glad those
other recovering alcoholics were! We're very glad you're
here.

> *Eight recovering*
> *women*

Applying the Twelve-Step approach to relationship addiction is best done after becoming familiar with how the Anonymous programs work. The best ways to do this are either by
attending many open (to the public) meetings of various Twelve-
Step programs or through active membership in another Twelve-
Step program of recovery.

The following is one format for a Twelve-Step approach to
relationship addiction. I did not compose this format. It was
sent to me by some women who had formed their own group,
borrowing from Alcoholics Anonymous and Al-Anon as they
did so. Many other similar formats have been developed and
perhaps someday all these individual programs will meet together to consolidate their approach to this particular addiction.
However, even now the similarities between the formats I've
seen are far greater than their differences.

I have shared this format, along with others that have been
sent to me, with women who have written asking for more
direction in starting support groups. The important things to
remember when using these formats are:

- Everyone involved must remain anonymous;
- there are no professionals (unless they are involved anonymously and as peers, rather than as professionals);
- there are no required fees;
- leadership is rotated and decisions are made by the group
  as a whole.

The literature of Alcoholics Anonymous and Al-Anon is an
invaluable source of information about addiction and recovery,

suggested guidelines for meetings, the process of decision-making and the working of the Steps and Traditions. However, rather than borrowing other programs' literature wholesale it is best for each individual Twelve-Step program to develop, through its own experience, strength and hope, the literature that describes the illness with which it deals and the recovery process as it has worked for members.

A SAMPLE FORMAT FOR A ONE HOUR MEETING OF RELATIONSHIPS ANONYMOUS

Hi everyone. My name is————and I am your leader for tonight.
Welcome. (Read the preamble)
A moment of silence and then the Serenity Prayer said together
The Twelve Steps
The Twelve Traditions
Guidelines to promote recovery
Introductions: First names only
Discussion: Select a topic of own choosing or one from the *Women Who Love Too Much* index
Seventh Tradition: RA is self-supporting by its own contributions
Choose a volunteer to lead next week's meeting
Read the Promises of Recovery (adapted from *Women Who Love Too Much*)
Read the suggested closing (adapted from *Women Who Love Too Much*)
A Closing Prayer

PREAMBLE

The parallel between the progression of the disease of alcoholism and the disease of loving too much is clear. Addiction,
whether to a mind-altering chemical, or to a relationship, ultimately affects every area of the addict's life in a progressively
disastrous way. We seek recovery from our addiction by practicing the Twelve Steps adapted from Alcoholics Anonymous.

SERENITY PRAYER

God grant me the serenity
To accept the things I cannot change,
The courage to change the things I can
and the wisdom to know the difference.

RA TWELVE STEPS*

1. We admitted we were powerless over relationships—that our lives
   had become unmanageable.
2. Came to believe that a Power greater than ourselves could restore
   us to sanity.
3. Made a decision to turn our will and our lives over to the care of
   God as we understood Him.
4. Made a searching and fearless moral inventory of ourselves.

*Reprinted for adaptation with permission of Alcoholics Anonymous World Ser-
vices, Inc.:

THE TWELVE STEPS AND TWELVE TRADITIONS OF ALCOHOLICS ANONYMOUS**

1. We admitted we were powerless over alcohol—that our lives had become unmanageable.
2. Came to believe that a Power greater than ourselves could restore us to sanity.
3. Made a decision to turn our will and our lives over to the care of God as we understood Him.
4. Made a searching and fearless moral inventory of ourselves.
5. Admitted to God, to ourselves, and to another human being, the exact nature of our wrongs.
6. Were entirely ready to have God remove all these defects of character.
7. Humbly asked Him to remove our shortcomings.
8. Made a list of all persons we had harmed, and became willing to make amends to them all.
9. Made direct amends to such people wherever possible, except when to do so would injure them or others.
10. Continued to take personal inventory and when we were wrong promptly admitted it.
11. Sought through prayer and meditation to improve our conscious contact with God as we understood Him, praying
    only for knowledge of His will for us and the power to carry that out.
12. Having had a spiritual awakening as the result of these steps, we tried to carry this message to alcoholics, and to
    practice these principles in all our affairs.

**Reprinted with permission of Alcoholics Anonymous World Services, Inc.

5. Admitted to God, to ourselves, and to another human being, the exact nature of our wrongs.
6. Were entirely ready to have God remove all these defects of character.
7. Humbly asked Him to remove our shortcomings.
8. Made a list of all persons we had harmed, and became willing to make amends to them all.
9. Made direct amends to such people wherever possible, except when to do so would injure them or others.
10. Continued to take personal inventory and when we were wrong promptly admitted it.
11. Sought through prayer and meditation to improve our conscious contact with God as we understood Him, praying only for knowledge of His will for us and the power to carry that out.
12. Having had a spiritual awakening as a result of these steps, we tried to carry this message to others who love too much, and to practice these principles in all our affairs.

RA TWELVE TRADITIONS*

1. Our common welfare should come first; personal progress for the greatest number depends upon unity.
2. For our group purpose there is but one authority—a loving God as He may express Himself in our group conscience. Our leaders are but trusted servants, they do not govern

*Reprinted for adaptation with permission of Alcoholics Anonymous World Services, Inc.:

3. The only requirement for RA membership is a desire to heal from relationship addiction.

4. Each group should be autonomous, except in matters affecting other RA groups or the Anonymous programs as a whole.

5. Each RA group has but one purpose—to help ourselves and each other recover from relationship addiction. We do this by practicing the Twelve Steps of AA ourselves and by welcoming and giving comfort to other relationship addicts.

6. RA groups ought never endorse, finance or lend our name to any outside enterprise, lest problems of money, property or prestige divert us from our primary spiritual aim. Although separate entities, we should always cooperate with other Anonymous programs.

7. Every RA group ought to be fully self-supporting, declining outside contributions.

8. RA Twelve-Step work should remain forever non-professional, but our service centers may employ special workers.

9. Our groups, as such, ought never be organized, but we may create service boards or committees directly responsible to those they serve.

10. RA groups have no opinion on outside issues, hence our name ought never be drawn into public controversy.

11. Our public relations policy is based on attraction rather than promotion; we need always maintain personal anonymity at the level of press, radio, films and TV. We need guard with special care the anonymity of all those to whom we've been addicted.

12. Anonymity is the spiritual foundation of all our traditions, ever reminding us to place principles above personalities.

TO PROMOTE OUR RECOVERY THE FOLLOWING GUIDELINES ARE SUGGESTED

1. We avoid advice-giving and cross-talk during the meeting. We meet to help ourselves and others by sharing our experience, strength and hope. Each person must have a safe place to talk without comments, questions or advice from others. Things we wish to say to others about what they have shared are best said after the meeting.

2. We avoid talk about "him." We are here to learn to change our focus to ourselves. It is important to talk about our own

lives, not another's. We also avoid indulging in blame, resentment and self-pity as these hinder our recovery.

3. We avoid dominance by any individual through rotation of
leadership and through limiting our sharing so that everyone
has time to speak. While no one should feel pressured to
speak, all are welcome to do so.

Remember: No one is going to solve all her problems in one
meeting—and it is important not to try.

THE PROMISES OF RECOVERY FROM RELATIONSHIP ADDICTION

1. We accept ourselves fully, even while wanting to change
parts of ourselves. There is a basic self-love and self-regard,
which we carefully nurture and purposely expand.

2. We accept others as they are, without trying to change them
to meet our needs.

3. We are in touch with our feelings and attitudes about every
aspect of our lives, including our sexuality.

4. We cherish every aspect of ourselves: our personality, our
appearance, our beliefs and values, our bodies, our interests
and accomplishments. We validate ourselves rather than
searching for a relationship to give us a sense of self-worth.

5. Our self-esteem is great enough that we can enjoy being with
others, especially men, who are fine just as they are. We do
not need to be needed in order to feel worthy.

6. We allow ourselves to be open and trusting with appropriate
people. We are not afraid to be known at a deeply personal
level, but we also do not expose ourselves to the exploitation
of those who are not interested in our well-being.

7. We question, "Is this relationship good for me? Does it
enable me to grow into all I am capable of being?"

8. When a relationship is destructive, we are able to let go of it
without experiencing disabling depression. We have a circle
of supportive friends and healthy interests to see us through
crises.

9. We value our own serenity above all else. All the struggles, drama and chaos of the past have lost their appeal. We are protective of ourselves, our health and well-being.
10. We know that a relationship, in order to work, must be between partners who share similar values, interests and goals, and who each have a capacity for intimacy. We also know that we are worthy of the best that life has to offer.

SUGGESTED CLOSING

The first phase in recovery from loving too much begins when we realize what we are doing and wish we could stop. The second phase comes from our willingness to get help for ourselves, followed by our actual initial attempt to secure help. After that, we enter the phase of recovery that requires our commitment to our own healing and willingness to continue with our recovery program. During this time we begin to change how we act, think and feel. What once felt normal and familiar begins to feel uncomfortable and unhealthy. We enter the next phase of recovery when we start making choices that no longer follow our old patterns, but enhance our lives and promote our well-being instead. Finally, genuine self-love evolves. Once self-acceptance and self-love begin to develop and take hold, we are then ready to consciously practice simply becoming ourselves without trying to please, without performing in certain ways calculated to gain another's approval and love.

Nothing, absolutely nothing happens in God's world by mistake . . . Unless I accept life completely on life's terms I cannot be happy. I need to concentrate not so much on what needs to change in the world as on what needs to be changed in me and in my attitudes.*

---

*Excerpted from p. 449 of the Big Book of *Alcoholics Anonymous*, third edition, used with permission of Alcoholics Anonymous World Services, Inc. See the Recommended Reading list.

Eight

. . . HAVE
QUESTIONS,
SUGGESTIONS,
COMPLAINTS

What can we do about our violated sense of justice when the men who hurt us seem to get along so easily in life while we continue to suffer? How did the men who are so incapable of loving get to be that way? If loving too much isn't really loving at all, then what is the nature of real love? What about mothers who smother their daughters with love and daughters who make their mother's happiness their chief concern? What is the lesbian experience of loving too much? What connection is there between relationship addiction and someone in a stable marriage risking everything by plunging into an impossible affair?

Letters from readers of *WWL2M* that voice specific concerns and yet do not fall within the scope of other chapters of this book are presented here in what amounts to a miscellaneous section.

Dear Robin,

I wanted to write to you because I'm too embarrassed to share my feelings with my friends and family.

With the help from WWL2M *I was able to end a destructive relationship with a real loser. I told him to move out two months ago, after we had been together ten months. I won't bore you with the details. However, I exactly fit the profile of the women in the book and my ex-boyfriend, Burt, is right in there, too, with the drug-addicted, workaholic, self-destructive unavailable men you describe. I'm troubled by the way I still feel about him and the relationship now, even though it's over. He has a visible, somewhat glamorous job, which he had when we split up and it eats me up with jealousy that he appears so outwardly successful when he is really so greedy, money-hungry, self-centered and callous toward other people's feelings.*

It doesn't strike me as fair that he seems to profit from doing bad things (he dabbles in criminal activities) while I always try to do the right thing and yet that doesn't seem to have gotten me very far.

I believe in honesty, loyalty, appreciation and love. My ex-boyfriend believes in money, greed and power. Robin, I think you get the picture.

I want to know why bad people seem to sometimes have it so good while good people aren't appreciated! I wouldn't feel so bad about my ex if he would say to me that maybe I was right about some things. I'd like it if he would at least tell me he is grateful for all I did for him. (I did plenty!) I would love it if he would apologize for all the lies he told me. I won't hold my breath waiting for all this to happen because I know he has no depth of emotion or sense of right and wrong.

Robin, I feel so much pain over that jerk. I never want him back but it would be nice to know that I mattered to him although I know I never did.

Thanks for listening. I was too embarrassed to let anyone know I still give a thought to this man.

Bonnie J.

Dear Bonnie,

I appreciate your very honest description of the feelings you still find in yourself toward this ex-boyfriend. They are feelings commonly experienced after a breakup, the sense of, "He's no good and yet he's doing fine while I, the injured party, am still suffering terribly."

These feelings will fade naturally over time unless you allow yourself to dwell too much on the apparent unfairness of it all (an inaccurate as well as unproductive assessment). If you indulge in such thoughts, you will build a resentment. Resentments are like a Frankenstein's monster in that they take on a life of their own in time unless we work to free ourselves of them. They grow and grow and eventually come to require daily care and feeding. So if you're not careful you'll find you have a pet resentment named Burt who is your constant companion, demanding a larger and larger place in your thoughts, feelings and perhaps eventually in your behavior as well. If we tell the story of our victimization enough times to ourselves, eventually we have to tell it to others as well, dwelling on the injustice of it all and, to use your phrase, letting it "eat us up." An example: I was once in a restaurant where a customer said to the waitress, "How are you today?" and she answered sulkily, "I'd be fine except that today would be my twelfth anniversary if my husband hadn't left me seven years ago for another woman!" Obviously, this woman had a pet resentment she'd been feeding and nurturing for seven years. So, Bonnie, beware! You need to become willing to heal *your* attitude toward this man and this relationship for your own sake.

We do not receive more in life by wishing others less.

Nothing in a relationship happens by accident or in a vacuum. Burt was exactly who he was from the first day the two of you met. Perhaps then you were intrigued by the same questionable activities and difficult personality which you find so distasteful in him today. But in order to learn what this relationship is trying to teach you and receive the blessing—yes, *blessing*—it is trying to bestow on you, it is necessary for you to do some soul-searching of your own. If you can begin by refusing to view yourself as Burt's victim in any way, and acknowledge that you fully participated in whatever games went on between the two of you, and used all your tools for manipulating him to be and do what you wanted, you will be halfway home in your healing. Conversely, as long as you indulge any fantasy that all your motives were pure while all of his were tainted, and refuse to see your own self-will operating both throughout the relationship and since it has ended, you will not only remain stuck but will be very likely to repeat the whole process again, perhaps to a more seriously unhealthy degree.

Become willing to look at what was your part, what were your steps in the dance with Burt.

More than that, become relentless in your pursuit of self-understanding. If you allow it to, this relationship can help you acknowledge where you first learned those steps, how you practiced them with him and with others before him and why you've danced that dance. Of course, learning all this will then give you the full responsibility for your own life and take away the convenience of blaming another for your unhappiness. Admitting that there are no accidents and that we are not victims requires that we grow up and face our own dark side rather than always seeing the problem as outside ourselves and inside someone else.

Finally, to promote your own healing, you need to do one more thing that requires great discipline. Each time you find yourself dwelling on Burt with anger, envy and resentment, you need to bless him, bless him, bless him, affirm his highest good and release him. There is an old verse that embodies this highly practical spiritual advice:

> When confronted by a foe
> Praise him,
> Bless him,
> Let him go.

Praying for the highest good of someone we feel has injured us and has gotten off scot-free isn't easy, I know. I've had to do it, too, while struggling with emotions just like yours. It requires great willingness and tremendous discipline, but it works to free us of our own burden of resentment and self-pity.

When we are envious of another person, we are caught up in the mistaken belief that there isn't enough good in the world for everybody and that their good diminishes our supply. This is a false and counterproductive belief. We do not receive more in life by wishing others less. Quite the opposite. We receive what we send out—so, again, send out blessings!

I hope you can see, Bonnie, that if you work diligently at changing your attitude toward Burt you will eventually receive the gifts the relationship is trying to give you: self-understanding and freedom from self-pity and resentment. Whether Burt is grateful to you will no longer matter. In a healthy, detached way, you will find yourself grateful to him and for him—and more truly released from him than you could ever be otherwise.

Dear Ms. Norwood,

I find your book's information helpful, but do you work only with white women? I seemed to be reading only about them!

Also, when will you (or perhaps someone else) write a book on the subject of "men who love too little"? After reading these women's recollections of their fathers and ex-lovers, I wondered to myself, "Where in the hell did these men learn to be such rotten fathers, lovers and husbands?"

For my own part (though I have no memory of being molested or abused physically by my parents), I am trying out an affirmation for forgiving my own dad: "I forgive my father for his unenlightened behavior toward me."

Marcie K.

Dear Marcie,

In answer to your first question, I no longer "work with" anybody, white or otherwise. It has become very important to me at this point in my life simply to continue to pursue my own recovery in a support group of peers. I do not have a private practice any longer.

The stories in *WWL2M* were primarily derived from the lives of women I've known professionally and personally as well as from my own life. These women are mostly white, like myself; some are Hispanic. I do think that it makes sense if you are seeking a therapist to look for someone whose background is similar to yours and who therefore understands the life you live. In my opinion, cultural factors are important in order for a therapist and client to understand and relate to each other, although many in the field of counseling would disagree.

In answer to your second question, my belief is that any book about why men love too little would best be written by a man who knows that subject personally and possibly professionally as well, and has learned and employed the principles necessary for turning around that pattern of relating. It would never do for me to write a book about men because I do not understand what it is to be a male, just as, in my observation, men do not understand what it is to be a female. We of each sex would all do well to understand ourselves better. Since that is such a demanding undertaking, I daresay we can never really hope to be "experts" about each other.

Your question about why so many men have developed patterns of relating that are unloving, unkind and even abusive toward those closest to them is an important one. I have yet to discover any behavior between human beings that is less than honest, open and caring that doesn't have its root in fear—fear of shame and ridicule and humiliation, fear of punishment, fear of being overwhelmed and smothered, fear of physical or emotional pain, fear of being out of control, fear of weakness, fear of loss, fear of abandonment, fear of death. To a degree, each of these fears is an inevitable consequence of being alive and being human. But when fear is too great, the resulting behavior becomes exaggerated, stereotypical and counterproductive. That is, when we are overcome by fear we tend to regress to a more primitive way of behaving. Rather than calmly and consciously choosing words and actions that are well thought out, objectively honest and fair, and likely to achieve the end we desire, we tend to either cling desperately, attack viciously or retreat blindly.

In relationships, men generally have a greater fear of being overwhelmed and smothered, while women tend to be in greater fear of abandonment. In conflicts between the two sexes men who are feeling threatened tend to emphasize attacking (in order to subdue the threat) and retreating (in order to escape the threat), while women tend to emphasize clinging (because the threat is abandonment) and attacking (in order to produce guilt in the man and thereby control him and the threat of abandonment he represents). Of course, neither of these styles of dealing with the stress of conflict is likely to produce harmonious resolution, and precisely because they don't work they increase the fear and consequently become even more exaggerated.

I have yet to discover any behavior between human beings which is less than open and caring that doesn't have its root in fear.

The physiological, sociological and psychological reasons for this basic difference in male and female styles of relating, especially under stress, would justify an entire volume. Without going into great detail, let me simply acknowledge that the reasons do exist at each of those levels. These styles tend to become even more exaggerated if there was a dysfunctional family of origin. In women from certain kinds of dysfunctional families there develops an excessive need for the reassurance of closeness; this need produces clinging, placating, nagging and pleading, and overly dependent behavior (all motivated by fear of abandonment). In men from similar backgrounds there develops an excessive need for distance that produces emotional aloofness and preoccupation with outside interests (again, motivated by fear of being overwhelmed). Put very simply, the more damaged such a woman is the more she tends to see the man and the family as her "supply," while the more damaged the man is the more he tends to see the woman and the family as threatening his safety and independence.

Men who, to use your phrase, Marcie, "love too little" tend to team up with women who love too much because they share a common emotional background. Each is already familiar with the role the partner plays and thus feels "comfortable" with or attracted to that partner. Then children come along, and they are raised by this pair of equally damaged partners. So a cycle is created and perpetuated in which relationship-handicapped men and women raise relationship-handicapped men and women.

It goes without saying that every child is influenced by his or her father, whether that father is present or absent and whether that influence is positive or negative. Indeed, the influence of fathers and father figures can be enormous for good or otherwise. However, this book is for and about women, and so I want to focus on what part we play in the development of men who are unable to form and maintain loving partnerships.

In this culture most men are raised primarily by women. By focusing on women, I do not want to imply that they are primarily responsible for men "loving too little." But, if many, many men are incapable of loving others it may be in part due to their mothers' overt or covert anger and frustration either with men in general in this still very sexist society or with particular men, usually these women's husbands and/or fathers. This female anger at the male may be expressed toward male children through aggressive dominance and overcontrol, ridicule and shaming or physical abuse, or all of these in turn. Or, a mother who is lonely because she has been emotionally or literally deserted by her adult partner may substitute an available male child for an unavailable adult male in a relationship that is both inappropriately overdependent and often highly sexualized as well.

In our cultural biases, we tend to consider those young male children who are sexually used and/or seduced by older females fortunate rather than exploited. This perception makes it difficult for us to assess or even acknowledge the degree to which covertly seductive mothers damage their very vulnerable sons. Overt incest between mothers and sons is acknowledged by most experts to be the most devastating of all varieties of incest. A friend of mine told me about two single mothers she had known who shared an apartment and had three boys between them whose ages were from seven to ten years. These mothers would give frequent parties, drink heavily along with their guests and then, for entertainment, chase their sons around and "pants" them (that is, pull their pants down in front of everyone there). My friend ended the story with the comment, "I now know where some of our rapists and murderers come from." Indeed, she was describing an especially humiliating form of child abuse with dreadful implications for those boys' adult relationships with women.

While I do not want to imply that women are the primary source of the various impediments to healthy relating from which so many men suffer, I do want to acknowledge that many, many men and women have suffered psychological, physical and sexual abuse at the hands of females. At a time when there is so much attention paid to the various forms of abuse from which children suffer, the role that women play in this abuse is still not fully acknowledged. When we have been damaged and are not healed we tend to be dangerous. Since women have been victims of abuse for so long it only makes sense that some of us have also become victimizers.

And finally, Marcie, I commend your approach to your father's lack of parenting skills. For your own sake it is much more important that you forgive him than that you understand him. Because of the spiritual principles involved in forgiveness, when we really do become willing to forgive another person often we are suddenly given all the understanding of that person's condition that we need.

Dear Ms. Norwood:

A question came to mind several times throughout the reading of your book, for which I found no answer. According to your book, we women who love too much are willing to go through the pain of unsuccessful relationships in order to either have a reason to exist or to distract ourselves from our own lives or to follow our familiar martyrdom patterns. But you never said what

*love truly is. What is real love? How do we distort it so
that we think what we feel is real? I would like to know
what we have to look forward to in recovery in the
"love" department. At the end of your book Trudy was
afraid of experiencing intimacy, yet she was recuperat-
ing. How did she know what she felt finally was love?
What is love?*

*There are several women in my area who are read-
ing this book, and we are planning to get together and
follow your suggestions for a support group. I would
truly appreciate your letting us know the answer to this
question. It is primarily my own question, but I am sure
it has crossed others' minds as well.*

*I really want recovery! Not only for myself but for
my three boys who I am afraid I might mess up as much
or worse than I was ever messed up.*

Barbara M.

Dear Barbara,

A tall order! I cannot claim to have the final answer
to the age-old question, "What is love?" But I have
learned over the years that love is not what I'd always
thought it was, and that it is, paradoxically, many of the
things I'd always believed were too "tame" to be love.

As you know, Barbara, the word "love" is applied
to many highly charged conditions and feelings and experiences that may actually embody the essence of what
love is *not*. For instance, lust, passion, jealousy, suffering, fear, excitement, greed, seduction, subjugation, sub-
mission, relief from boredom or loneliness, humiliation,
vindication, competition, pride and self-will are some of
the states of arousal most commonly dressed up to
masquerade as love. Further, the more compelling one's
experience of any of these states, the more likely we are
to call that sensation love. The consensus tends to be
that the person who is the most stirred up is the person
most in love. Conversely, we tend to believe that the
person most at peace could not possibly be in love at all.

Today I believe that quite the reverse is true. Personal love is not compulsive, it is poised. There is no

desperation to it, nothing driven about it, and only a person who is willing and able and well-practiced at thoroughly loving and accepting herself is even capable of it. The ability to love another person arises from a full heart, not an empty one.

This creates a terrible dilemma for so many of us who emerged from childhood with empty, lonely, longing hearts and who have spent our adult years searching feverishly for the person who could take away our pain. When our search, rather than bringing relief, has brought more pain, we've become increasingly more desperate. Where is "he"? we ask, because "he" is our answer, our hope, our need. Through the intensity and ardor of our quest we make a virtual religion of relationship, laying at its feet the greatest burdens of being human.

We make a virtual religion of relationship, laying at its feet the greatest burdens of being human.

We ask of a relationship that it give us a sense of meaning and identity and purpose, that it take away our feeling of isolation and soothe our fear of abandonment. We expect that if we are with the "right" person we will feel safe in an unsafe world and we will be protected from the threat of loss and separation and death. We expect this perfect relationship to make us a better person and to heal us of our human faults and shortcomings—our dissatisfaction and envy and pride and despair—as well as to make us more tolerant of others' faults and shortcomings. In short, we think a relationship should make us perfectly happy. The man with whom we're involved becomes our Higher Power, the source of healing for our pain and answers to our questions and the provider of all that is missing or undeveloped in us. What a foolish, even dangerous set of expectations!

A relationship with another human being, whether parent, partner or child, was never meant to provide us with all this. A relationship can provide companionship, yes; a degree of understanding, yes; and always, always, the opportunity to learn more about who we are and where we need to stretch and grow. A good relationship with a mate includes tenderness, caring and sexuality. But it is not meant to provide the rest. The struggle with anxiety and fear of the future, the needs for identity and security, the yearning to find meaning and purpose in our lives, the necessity for coming to terms with loss and death without caving in to despair or to bitterness—our struggles with these life issues belong in the realm of a spiritual quest, not in the realm of a relationship quest. We have no business asking of another human being what we need to be asking of God. As long as we persist in doing so we will never find that for which we are searching.

On the other hand, when we develop a willingness to cast these burdens on a Source of Power greater than ourselves and then allow that Power to work in our lives, we become much better able to be present to all other human beings in a less needy and demanding, more loving and accepting way. We also become less attracted to people who are not for our highest good, and more attracted to that which is best for us. We become able to discern more clearly while at the same time being less judgmental. It is paradoxical that as we grow in our ability to accept all people as they are, rather than categorizing them as good or bad, we become more able to choose to be with those people who are good for us, and bless and release those who are not.

And who is good for us? The simplest answer I know is, the person who does not diminish our contact with our Higher Power. As long as we are making our spiritual contact our *first* priority the relationship questions (and answers) will sort themselves out. The moment we begin to make the relationship our Higher Power, those of us who are relationship addicts are back in our disease. Reliance on something larger than ourselves and other than the relationship *must* be present in order to love freely, deeply and well. Otherwise, fear of loss of the relationship grows where we wish love would.

Personal love, then, in my opinion, is an outgrowth of a spiritual foundation. It is a slow-growing plant if you will, requiring the right conditions—the proper soil, climate and care—and many years in order to grow to its fullest development. Essential to its germination is an atmosphere of mutual trust and respect. If these two elements are missing, many of those stirrings that are mistakenly called love but that are more closely related to obsession can take root and grow, but love cannot.

In addition to the basic requirement of mutual trust and mutual respect, in order to flourish love needs to be rooted in common interests, values and goals. Since we can never change our values to please another person, and since interests and goals are impossible to pursue with enthusiasm over the years unless the involvement is genuine, it is virtually impossible for love to grow when we try to feign a rapport with someone. The roots of the relationship will simply be too shallow. The presence of these factors, on the other hand, makes for deep, strong, healthy roots.

Finally, if love is to grow to its greatest dimensions, it requires a climate of intimacy. Those who tend it must together be committed to creating and renewing that climate frequently, even when they would rather avoid the effort. Intimacy requires that we become vulnerable—that we drop our defenses and our need to look good—and allow ourselves to be known as we really are.

Dear Robin Norwood,

I am writing on behalf of my mom, who has a problem with a love relationship with my sister.

I do not know if you could be helpful to my mom, because it's not a husband-wife type relationship, but in a brief few words my sister is thirty-two years old and has had a drug problem for at least fifteen to eighteen years; prescription as well as street drugs. My mom has basically been my sister's support system for all these years. When she doesn't help my sister she feels guilty,

*and all of the attempts at helping my sister have failed.
It hurts me to see my mom give up her life for my sister.
My mom is only fifty-three and I feel she deserves a life
of her own. She has actually said that she feels addicted
to my sister.*

*All I've ever wanted was for my mom to be happy.
Once again, I'm looking for a source of help for her.
Any advice or information would be deeply appreciated.*
Rebecca V.

Dear Rebecca,

Your mother needs to stop looking for help for your
sister and you need to stop looking for help for your
mother. You can see how all your mother's efforts on
your sister's behalf actually serve to support your sister's drug addiction. But you may not be able to see that
all your efforts on your mother's behalf actually enable
her to continue in her sick co-dependency. When we are
dealing with addiction and co-addiction we must realize
that people only decide to change when the pain gets bad

---

*When dealing with addiction, we must
realize that people only change when the
pain gets bad enough.*

---

enough. Because of all your mother's efforts, your sister
is not in sufficient pain to be ready to seek help for
herself. Because of all your efforts, your mother's pain
is still tolerable, too. You need to stop being co-dependent to your mother as much as your mother needs to
stop being co-dependent to your sister. When you face
your own issues around this you will realize just how
difficult recovery from co-dependency is and you will
understand why, for now, your mother needs to continue
to enable your sister. You need to recover for your own
sake; but when you learn to stop suffering, your recovery
may be so appealing that your mother will be interested
in pursuing her own. There's no guarantee of that, of

course, and it must not be your reason for taking care of yourself. But recovery can be as contagious as addiction and co-addiction are.

Find some Al-Anon meetings in your area, as well as Nar-Anon meetings if they are available. Go in order to learn how to help yourself, not your mother. And don't drag anyone with you. Work on *you*. That's what this recovery is all about. With co-dependency everyone is always waiting for the addict to recover—which may never happen—before they can be happy. Learn how to be happy no matter what your mother or your sister are doing. By doing so you actually increase their chances of recovering, too.

Dear Ms. Norwood:

I fit the prototype in your book quite exactly, and if I had known you, I would have been quite upset that you wrote about me and spread my intimate thoughts and feelings on the pages of your book for the world to see.

While my former husband was not an alcoholic, he was a compulsive gambler. I attend Gam-Anon meetings regularly, and find that those of us who are in Gam-Anon are very similar to the women you have described in Al-Anon. In future editions in your book, you might mention the fact that the spouse or significant other person in the life of a compulsive gambler is basically in the same role as those who are co-alcoholics and suggest the Gam-Anon program to them. The Gam-Anon program is essentially the same as the one followed in Al-Anon.

In my neighborhood, a group of women are getting together to form a support group along the lines suggested in your book. I plan on attending this group as well as my Gam-Anon group for the support that I need.

As you can see by the stationery, I am an attorney. I am successful in my professional life, and enjoy it very much. I was formerly a high school teacher for twelve years, went to law school at night, four nights a week for four years, and during the course of my attending law school and working full time, I had my three children. Thus, functioning in a professional capacity has never been difficult for me.

I am now a single mother, having gotten divorced three years ago, and am raising my three sons on my own. I feel that I am very successful as a mother and my friends and family wholeheartedly concur in this opinion.

I have, throughout my life, however, had difficulty in my relationships with men. In reading your book, I realized that the problem stems from my family background. While neither of my parents fit the classic mold of compulsive drinkers or compulsive gamblers, my mother nevertheless is a very compulsive person. Her compulsivity showed up in her housekeeping and mothering.

Last year, after having read WWL2M, I went to a party for single parents. My attitude and whole approach was different at this party than it had been previously. Given the awareness that I had as to the kinds of problems I had encountered before with men, I decided not to try to select anyone in particular to speak to, but to speak casually to whomever I happened to be near. Four men took my number at the party, and all four of them subsequently asked me out. Two of them called the day after the party and one called two days later. I have been seeing one of the men for the past ten months and while I do not know yet the ultimate outcome, so far the relationship has been vastly different than any I have previously had.

My friend is very different both in appearance and in personality from the previous men I have been involved with. Yet the temptation to fall back into my old patterns of behaving and reacting is still strong and I am constantly fighting against it. The knowledge that I've gained from my program of Gam-Anon and from your book has enabled me to have strength in this ongoing struggle. I expect I will continue to grapple with it for a long time to come.

While I still have a long way to go, I have made tremendous progress. I am constantly on the lookout for my old patterns of giving too much or mothering the man with whom I am in a relationship. I have also promised myself that I will not get involved ever again with anyone who fits the personality type of my former husband, who was a compulsive gambler.

Gina R.

Dear Gina,

I agree with you that the personalities of women who marry compulsive gamblers are very similar to those who marry compulsive drinkers, as are the dynamics of their relationships. In many respects addiction is addiction and co-addiction is co-addiction, no matter what the particular variety. That is why the same basic treatment approach works equally well with each form.

You describe your mother as compulsive in her parenting and then go on to say that you, in turn, are struggling not to mother a man with whom you are involved. Many of us who are co-addictive promised ourselves that we would never parent the way we were parented and never behave toward a spouse the way our parents behaved toward each other. Yet we find that as adults we cannot seem to do otherwise. This is because in many respects parenting and, if I may coin a word, "partnering," are imprinted behaviors rather than intellectually chosen approaches to these tasks. We automatically learn how to be a parent and how to be a partner from what our own family members did with us, to us and around us. The influence of their actions, healthy or otherwise, has been inexorably absorbed by us into the very fiber of our being. So we find ourselves speaking their words and acting out their ways of behaving, often in spite of our most determined resolutions to do otherwise.

These learned patterns of behavior have some elements in common with the phenomenon of imprinting in the animal kingdom. An example of imprinting is a newly hatched duckling following the first moving object it sees, instinctively identifying that object as its mother. Due to circumstances (sometimes contrived by those who study the imprinting phenomenon), the first moving object the duckling sees may not be a mother duck but, say, a rolling basketball instead. The duckling is irresistibly drawn to follow the basketball no matter how impractical such behavior may be to the little bird's ultimate best interests for survival.

Another example of imprinting, which is much more relevant here both because it involves primates and because of the cogency of its implications to human behavior, is Harry Harlow's experiment with rhesus monkeys. Most of us who have ever taken a course in psychology have seen the film of this experiment in which the baby monkeys, deprived of their natural mothers, chose to cling, when not actually eating, to a padded frame rather than the wire one that held their food supply.* The theory Harlow evolved from observing the baby monkeys' behavior was that the (scant) comfort offered by the softly padded frame created more of a bonding effect than did the unpadded frame that provided food, indicating how very important a source of comforting is in relation to a source of food.

What is perhaps even more noteworthy in terms of its implications for human behavior is the next step in these experiments.** As the baby monkeys who had been raised in this deprived environment grew toward adulthood, they developed no normal social skills for interacting with others of their kind. They either cowered in fear of each other or struck out with inappropriate aggression. Having had their nutritional needs met but having been denied their needs for affectionate interaction with others of their own kind (particularly their own parents, who would in the natural order of things have cuddled, fed and protected them), these monkeys were incapable, in adulthood, of carrying out normal mating and parenting activities. When the females were either forcibly or artificially impregnated they gave birth to infants they would not feed or nurture. In fact, they

---

*"Mother Love," produced by Columbia Broadcasting System, 51 West 52nd Street, New York, NY 10019. Distributed by Carousel Films, Inc., 241 East 34th Street, New York, NY 10016.

**"Love Among the Monkeys," *Science News,* December 20, 1975, pp. 389–390.

either ignored their infants or actively abused them or both in turn. Having not received the nurturing that would normally have been necessary for their own survival, they could not, as adults, nurture their own offspring.

We humans bear the weight of guilt when we violate our own value systems by our behaviors or even our thoughts. Often we struggle desperately and blindly against our own variety of imprinting, the inexorable acting out upon others what was acted out upon us and around us as we grew up. If we were overcontrolled as children, we tend in adulthood to overcontrol our mates, our children, perhaps even our coworkers as well. If we were physically abused in childhood we tend to abuse our children or marry someone who threatens us as our parent(s) did and abuses us or our children. If we were the object of an adult's inappropriate sexual advances we become inappropriately seductive ourselves or team up with someone who is out of control in the sexual area so that we can indulge our own obsession with sex by trying to control him.

It is not difficult to imagine generation after generation of rhesus monkeys, fed adequately enough to insure their physical survival but, because of their own lack of appropriate parenting, unable in turn to parent their offspring—generation after generation of unloved and unloving monkeys.

Like Harlow's monkeys it is nearly impossible for us to give what we haven't been given. It is also nearly impossible for us to allow what wasn't allowed us. If we were smothered, overprotected and stifled in our efforts to reach out, grow up and become independent, we will find ourselves having the same unhealthy responses to independence in our own children. This principle creates the generational aspect of diseases of behavioral addiction and contributes, along with genetic factors, to the generational aspect of diseases of chemical addiction.

Overcoming the force of these deeply embedded behaviors is not a matter of simply making a decision. A promise to oneself or to others not to behave that way again is not enough. It requires the approach you're taking, Gina, a one-day-at-a-time commitment to a program of recovery.

————

In *WWL2M* I wrote for and about heterosexual women who were addicted to their relationships with men because that was (and is) the variety of relationship addiction I know and understand best. While I acknowledged in the foreword to that book that men, too, could love addictively, unfortunately I seem to have inadvertently implied that I thought all relationship addicts were heterosexual. I know better than that. Some of the most addictive relationships are between same-sex lovers.

Phyllis and many other lesbian women wrote (sometimes gently, sometimes not so gently) to point out my negligence.

Dear Robin Norwood,
Thank you very much for writing WWL2M.
I've been in Al-Anon for two years and many of the concepts were familiar and many were further clarified—how denial actually happens, and how good sex doesn't necessarily mean that the people involved are connecting in a healthy way. I winced through the first few chapters, but by the end of the book I felt much hope.
If the book is reprinted, which I'm sure it will be, I was wondering if you could add a clause to your introduction to include me and others like me. I am a lesbian and had a hard time with the constant implication that my obsession is with men. Since the ten to twenty percent of the population who are gay or bisexual could benefit greatly from your concepts, that revision would make a lot of sense. My Al-Anon program has taught me to take what I like and leave the rest, but the feeling I had of being invisible to you was difficult to get past. Your book is very helpful and I ask that somewhere in it you acknowledge my existence. Thank you very much!
Phyllis R.

After writing back to apologize for my oversight and to explain that I had written only about relationship addiction as it applies to heterosexual women because I only trust my expertise in that area, I received a second letter from Phyllis in which she described her own experience of relationship addiction.

Dear Robin,
I was thrilled to get your response and to find you so receptive to my letter. Of course, I spent an hour going over in my head exactly what the letter said, but I do remember the theme.
A little about my story: I lived with a very sweet, passive, addict/alcoholic man for seven years. I finally left, swearing to myself that I would never take care of a full-grown adult again.
Three years passed, and not only was I taking care of a full-grown, flipped-out woman, but also her two children.
In many ways, this relationship was very different and very fulfilling for me because it was with a woman. Yet, in many ways, it was very much the same because I have a progressive disease. No one was more surprised than I to see the similarities between these two relationships.
Very vital information I have gained: 1) the awareness that I always thought my "love" could "fix" everything; 2) the awareness that those who are being "loved too much" feel resentment rather than gratitude; 3) learning that I really can see how this dance begins in the first few meetings, if I dare to not be in denial; 4) the fact that one hundred percent recovery is possible for me and I do not have to relive my childhood in my adult relationships and 5) the validation for the incredible pain that leaving these relationships and ceasing this behavior pattern creates.
I am using the Al-Anon program in new ways to change my life. Thank you for your support, love and information!
Phyllis R.

Phyllis's letter brings up another related point that is important. It is essential that a person who is pursuing recovery be specific rather than generic in her choice of treatment. For instance, Phyllis has been with at least one alcoholic/addict. That means that she is co-alcoholic and belongs in Al-Anon. Should she choose to be in a support group for her relationship addiction, it should be in addition to the more specific program of Al-Anon but not instead of it. Another example: If a woman is married to a compulsive gambler her primary program of recovery should be Gam-Anon, though she might benefit from attendance at a support group that focuses on relationship addiction in addition to her Gam-Anon program. Often people want to be involved in a more general treatment approach rather than a specific one, due usually to embarrassment at too closely identifying the conditions in which they have lived or are living. But the most help is to be had from the most focused approach, so it's important to summon sufficient courage to show up in a room with those who share our condition: that is, with other co-alcoholics, or others who have endured incest, or others who have been battered, or others who have married gamblers, and so on. If you are a lesbian and a co-alcoholic it's wonderful to be able to attend gay and lesbian Al-Anon meetings (designated as such in a given area's schedule of meetings) where the special issues with which you deal can be freely discussed. There is something so healing and so affirming in being with people who are truly our own kind, who share so many of our same thoughts and feelings and experiences and struggles—and who can deeply appreciate and applaud our victories.

Dear Robin Norwood,
I run the whole gamut of case histories from your book. I lived in a children's home during part of my childhood. I had a stepfather who was a full-blown alcoholic. In the middle of a second marriage of thirty-three years that produced five children, now grown, I

decided to "go for it" and became involved with my high school sweetheart (married). I moved to his area where he was the pillar of the community, and yes, we danced! *I worked at my career (as a nurse, of course!) and waited for him to divorce. Every month there was a different excuse until finally I told his wife what was going on. From then on my true-life story became one no playwright would touch. Too bizarre!*

I've returned to my husband and yes, it's boring but it looks like it may have a happy ending. I am fifty-seven years old which no one believes, saying I look not a day over forty. This has never been a consolation to me as I had no self-confidence, just a blind desire to right the wrongs around me. In nursing I felt if I made one patient smile or feel comfortable I had earned the right to another day in my life. Also the man with whom I had the affair told me he was so unhappy at home and said he had not loved his wife for years. I was sure that the two of us would be ecstatic together for the rest of our lives. I know now he was the same remote, unavailable person my mother was. What a shock to realize this!

What I want to know is this: Are there other reasons for my "fling" that you can see from reading this letter? I figure the more I understand about myself the better chances I have of not repeating my mistakes.

Regarding the exercise you suggest—looking in the mirror for three minutes each day and saying my name and "I love you and accept you exactly the way you are"—it was so difficult for me. At first I just looked in the mirror and cried, unable to speak. I am finally managing to conquer this and it is beginning to work. Thanks.

Helena J.

Dear Helena,

Many women who have grown up in chaotic, unhappy situations in which emotional abandonment was a theme do what you did. If, in spite of their backgrounds, they are able to join with a partner who is stable, they eventually feel a restless discontent because the element of excitement that was so much a part of their lives as children is lacking. Sooner or later many of these women go looking for what they feel is missing, usually upsetting the applecart in the process just as you did. Applying the word "love" to all the old familiar feelings of drama and pain seems perfectly natural to them. Nothing in the relationship they left behind can compare with this thrill. The crescendos of feeling generated by an illicit involvement, such as yours was, are fueled by all the dramatic elements that were present in your childhood experience: uncertainty, secrecy, danger, shame, painful abandonment by the loved one, longed-for reconciliation, deep despair repeatedly alternating with fresh hope, prolonged waiting punctuated by emotion-laden encounters, the struggle of competing desperately for attention, trying to be good enough or attractive enough or loving enough (or all three) to make everything turn out all right, etc.

The history of abandonment in your past is the key to understanding your continuing need in adulthood to earn the right to exist. As children we believe that we are personally the cause of everything that happens around us and to us. If it is pleasant we take the credit and if it is negative we take the blame through the magical sense of omnipotence, which is a natural phenomenon of childhood. We believe that we make the sun come up and go down and that the moon comes out at night to entertain us. If we are left behind by those we need, we believe we caused that, too, through something we did or didn't do. We may never clearly formulate what it was that caused our abandonment, but we carry the burden of having caused it and the fear that we will be similarly devastated again unless we are very, very careful and watchful and good. This explains your motivation in your nursing career as well as in your affair—a powerful need to remedy what was wrong in order to keep yourself safe.

I am so pleased to know that you are working at using one of the suggested affirmations. If used diligently it has the power to heal those old feelings of unworthiness and replace them with the confidence that you are a necessary and beloved part of the universe.

Nine

LETTERS FROM MEN

Ms. Robin Norwood,

I've just finished reading your book and I have benefited from it a great deal, but it has been very hard for me to have to translate "women" to "men" throughout the book. I've been a "battered husband" and now as a "man who loves too much" and a victim of the games of an immature woman, I'm trying to fight this addiction by learning more about this disease. It's very unfortunate that you are not aware that many men who meet women who are troubled, distant, moody and unpredictable find them attractive and then go through the same agony that the women described in your book do. We could also benefit from your work and find comfort in its pages if it was titled and treated as "People Who Love Too Much" or you could personalize your edition and publish "Men Who Love Too Much: When You Keep Wishing and Hoping She'll Change." Otherwise, thanks for the help.

Miguel J.

It was not due to either oversight or indifference that *WWL2M* was addressed specifically to women. I understand women who are relationship addicts very well because I have shared their experience, but I do not really understand the male experience of relationship addiction. Although it may be very similar to the female experience, I sense that there are subtle differences and believe that to assume expertise in one area because it exists in another may be both presumptuous and irresponsible. Although many female writers have captured the very essence of my being with their words, I have not yet discovered a male writer who could accurately describe my experience as a woman. I want to avoid doing men a disservice and therefore am leaving the writing *about* men *to* men. However, I am as grateful that *WWL2M* has been of help to many men as I am that some of them have taken the time to write me about their reactions to the book. All their letters have been a gift to me, and I want to share some of them here.

The letters and comments from men who have read *WWL2M* seem to fall into roughly four categories: men who love women too much; men who are or have been involved with women who love them too much; men who love women who love another man too much; and, finally, gay men who love too much.

In some ways these letters from men can illuminate relationship addiction for all of us in ways that the letters from women cannot. Particularly when the man is, himself, a relationship addict, we can see the disease process with a clarity that is otherwise impossible. This is because the relationship addiction occurs without the cultural reinforcement that is given for such behavior in women. Every woman in this culture is actively encouraged to behave in most of the ways that are typical of a very sick relationship addict: that is, to make another person the focus of her thoughts and actions; to be preoccupied with controlling, changing and improving that other person and to be willing to go to any lengths to do so; to be self-sacrificing and martyred; and to be far more in touch with that other person's thoughts, feelings and needs than with her own. Our cultural encouragement of relationship addiction in women and sanctions against women who do not think, feel and act in these ways makes it almost impossible to assess how unhealthy these attitudes and behaviors are for any individual *until we see them in men*. As sexist as it sounds (and *is!*), only when we can view these relationship patterns in contrast to typical sex-role stereotyping does it become apparent to us how truly sick they are, regardless of the sex of the person practicing them.

The letter that follows rivals any I've received in terms of the seriousness of the relationship addiction described. Both the martyred behavior and the manipulative elements behind it can be seen all the more clearly because the writer is a man.

Dear Ms. Norwood,

Your book was recommended to me by my therapist, who suggested that if I put myself in the place of the women you describe, it might help me through this present very difficult stage in my life.

I can't imagine I'm the first man who has written to you, but with your indulgence, I'd like to tell you my story.

First, let me set the scene: I am twenty-nine years old, six feet tall, one hundred eighty pounds, and considered reasonably good-looking. I do not drink, smoke, use drugs, or have what anyone would call an overbearing or obnoxious personality. I am creative, and for the last three years have worked as a screenwriter. I don't want to sound like I'm bragging, but I also make a lot of money. All these nice pieces seem likely to add up to an interesting and fulfilling existence. But my life is far from that. Although I am heterosexual, throughout my entire teen years and early adulthood there have been few involvements with women, no one I could really call a girlfriend, and no lasting intimacy. The two or three relationships I tried to form with women were very brief, lasting barely three or four weeks.

I guess you might also describe me as one of those "nice, but dull men" from whom a lot of the women in your book run. That's not the way I'd choose to describe myself, but I do seem to be cast in the role of "good friend" to a lot of women, but never in the role of "lover."

Because I am so often rejected as a lover (by women who'd make time to see me as a friend, if you can believe it, sometimes putting me ahead of their real boyfriends) this has given rise to a lot of confusion, stress, and disappointment in my life. Especially as I go to great lengths to be as nice as possible when I meet someone in whom I'm interested. Maybe I'm too nice. Or maybe I'm instinctively attracted to women I know are going to reject me for the flashy, attractive, but ultimately unful-filling men described in your book. Let me tell you about the one big relationship I've had—big in its intensity and effect on me, I should say. I never lived with this woman, or even had sex with her. But for the last four years, all my energies have been steadily trained on her, and it has been, from beginning to end, an unmitigated disaster.

I first met Lynn when we were in college. I had gotten some friendly responses from her, although at the time I was not interested in her. A few years went by during which we were thrown together a little more often, and I began to feel very attracted to her. During this time, she was living with someone, so I could not really pursue her. I went to work after graduation, and two years later when Lynn graduated she went back East to look for work as an actress. Although we now were at opposite ends of the country we remained in touch and there was always a little hope alive in me that someday we'd be able to get together as lovers. Four years ago, after she left a bad relationship, I invited her out to visit me. I knew in my heart she was not interested in a love relationship but I felt that given the chance, I could win her over. I paid for her ticket out, and so began a two-year cross-country relationship, of sorts. While with me, Lynn told me how great it was to get away from the grind of trying to find acting jobs while working as a waitress. As I was doing freelance writing at the time, I suggested to her that she help me out on a script and I would split the fee with her. She was hesitant since she had never done anything like that before, but I was pleased to show her how it was done. We spent a week writing, and our collaboration was very rewarding. When she went back home we were both feeling great about our partnership, and I felt I had shared something very special of myself with her. My imagination is the most personal thing I've got. It's how I make my living, and how I cheer myself up when things go wrong. It excited me to think that I was able to help Lynn use her imagination, too. Now here, I told myself, was a rela-tionship I'd never even dare to dream about—with some-one who turned me on intellectually as well as physically.

And the way we wrote together was much more inspired than if I had done it on my own. This relationship had to work out, come hell or high water and by "work," I meant physical love, commitment and marriage.

Well I'm sure you don't need a crystal ball to reveal that it all ended badly for me. We did go on to write many scripts together over two years. And during the times when there were no scripts to write, I was wiring money to Lynn's bank account. She never asked outright for that, but some of her hints were pretty strong. And I think I was mainly doing it because I wanted to. I envisioned every act of kindness, every script shared, every check sent as another step closer to our eventual permanent union. Please let me say in my defense that I really loved her with every bit of my heart, and believed I should be doing these things. If you love someone, don't you take care of that person? In those two years, I went to see her a lot, and she came to see me just as often. She met my parents, and I met hers. Each year, in fact, right up to Christmas two years ago I got a big box of presents from her parents. It broke my heart the last year I got one, and I had to explain in a nice way to them how I'd prefer not getting any more.

While Lynn was writing with me, she was also involved in a series of love relationships back at home. I tried hard to tell myself that I was just her friend now, but by being true, and proving myself with gifts and support, she'd see that I really loved her and was the right man for her. There came a time when the freelance work we were doing together dried up. I then put Lynn in contact with some people back East who were looking for experienced local writers. Though she was very uncertain, I helped pave the way for her with a company for which she has since gone on to write some very good scripts. In fact, she has become one of their leading writers. But when she was just starting to get work from them, money was still short and she wanted to take an acting class. I paid for it then, and am still paying for it now. The teacher of the class was a muscular, handsome single man, and, to make a long story short, they're getting married this June.

Believe me, Ms. Norwood, when I say hell can be no worse than the three months I've just lived through. I first heard through casual conversation with friends that she was getting married. She explained that she wasn't ready to tell me right away. Nevertheless she told people who regularly talk to me. I had known she was seeing this guy and that they had even moved in together. But everything she told me about him made him sound like a beautiful, but somewhat dull fellow, the kind she'd grow tired of before too long. She even had the gall to tell me a year ago that I should meet him! He liked a lot of the same movies, books, etc. that I liked, and we really had a lot in common. All I could think of was that she was trading me in for a better-looking version of myself. And then there followed a long period of really hating myself. How could it be, I'd ask myself as I stared into my bathroom mirror, that I could help her reach into herself and bring out a wonderful talent she never thought she could develop, and that I could connect with her on that wonderful level, and yet have her pass me by? What was it, I'd scream at my reflection, that she saw in me and hated so? The hair between my eyebrows? The little rolls of fat on either side of my body that won't go away no matter how many sit-ups I do? What? What? What? How can a man be so good to the woman he loves only to have her refuse him?

I used to have that dialogue with myself a lot, and a few days after hearing about her engagement, I had the same dialogue again, but this time with a hunting knife. Yeah, I was quite stupid, and I'm very embarrassed to talk about it now, but I guess I should tell you everything. I looked at myself in the mirror, and every place there was an imperfection, there went a cut. I was entranced by grief, and it wasn't until I saw the blood running down my sides that I realized what I had done, and how much I needed help. But who was there to help me? For three years I loved a woman who lived on the other side of the country, and now, in my worst moment of crisis, I was totally alone. That's when the real fear set in. And that's when I decided to get help.

I Band-Aided up my cuts (I felt too ashamed to go to a doctor) and they healed painfully, but did not scar. The same day I cut myself I went to a therapist who had been recommended by a friend of mine, and together we're making good progress. My first assignment was to read your book, and it's helped me a lot. I try not to think too much about the past, about how I could have changed things with Lynn, made them work out the way I wanted. I don't think I could have had the relationship I imagined with her but perhaps if I had not been so quick to provide for her and stood up for myself more instead, things would have been different. By "different" I mean this whole thing would have ended long ago, and I wouldn't be going through this now.

I was so afraid that I'd never find anyone else like her, someone with whom I could be creative, and wildly in love as well. She seemed like the best I'd ever find and I was determined to hold on no matter how rough it got. I was so busy worrying about things turning bad, it never dawned on me that things weren't that good to begin with.

I'd like to end this letter by saying that things are much better, and that my evenings are filled with wonderful women, and all my problems are solved, but that's not true. Not true yet, anyway. I still ask women out, and some want to get to know me, and some don't. And the ones who do are mostly interested in being friends. They think I'm a great conversationalist, lots of fun to be with, a real nice guy. But there's something missing. Lynn always said there was no romantic "chemistry" between us, and to this day, I still don't know what that means. I don't know any lovers' games, and feel that if I were really in love with someone, I wouldn't have to use them. If you care for someone, you make time to be together, you share your happiness with that person and nothing else matters, right? Where is it written that a man has to be a bastard to get a woman interested? Why keep someone you're fond of dangling and at arm's distance? What I'm attracted to most in women is a kind of boldness and independence. I guess these are the same women who look for distant and difficult men to capture. When a man like me comes along, he's too easy. Too bad.

Well, I may be alone but I'm also alive, and very grateful your book was there to help me in my time of need.

David P.

An unrecovered woman who loves too much automatically shuns any serious involvement with a kind, decent, caring man who is able to be genuinely emotionally present to her, because to develop such a relationship might present an unbearable challenge to her capacity for intimacy. But such a choice should not be confused with the one made by a healthier woman who is unwilling to become deeply involved with another type of man who, because he appears so self-effacing, accommodating and devoted, is also typically described as "nice." Her reasons for avoiding him, whether conscious or unconscious, may be very sound. She senses that behind his ostensible concern for her welfare and his various caretaking behaviors on her behalf, this type of man is covertly manipulating her into a position of indebtedness. In return for all his "giving" she must reciprocate with gratitude and loyalty or else find herself guilty of having "used" him. A healthy woman instinctively senses this trap and avoids it (as does a healthy man when these sex roles are reversed).

When any of us gives and gives to another person, it really amounts to an unacknowledged bribe.

David is a self-avowed "nice" man. He describes his initial attraction to Lynn as owing to her independence. Yet he tried in every possible way—by playing the role of her mentor, by supporting her financially, by being "understanding" throughout her series of liaisons—to make her dependent on him. He has convinced himself that these tactics on his part have been due to a loving concern for Lynn's welfare, but it is apparent that they have in fact been calculated to produce a sense of obligation in her.

When any of us gives and gives and gives to another person who is not responding in kind, we usually do so because we do not trust that we will be able to establish and maintain a relationship with that other person on our own merit. In other words, our "giving" really amounts to an unacknowledged bribe, a covert manipulation designed to make that other person overlook whatever *we* think we lack. When the other person inevitably senses the manipulation and resents it, we can self-righteously respond with shock and indignation because we are out of touch with the true motives behind all our generosity. In our denial we cannot understand why, when we've done so much for this person, we could be treated so badly in return. Where is their gratitude? Why are we resented for our devotion instead of appreciated and loved? The answer is—because we haven't been honest. We haven't been willing to risk rejection by being ourselves, so we've stacked the deck in our favor. Yet, ultimately, all our efforts haven't paid off. Now we're angry and hurt and believe we've been exploited by someone whose best interests were our only concern. Our martyred view of things is very convenient, very self-serving, very pat and very unhealthy—and ultimately very self-perpetuating as well.

Sometimes relationship addicts prefer the fantasy of a relationship over the possibility of involvement with a real, live, interested, responsive and affectionate human being—like the prison wife who prefers the dream about how it will be someday when her man is released over the day-to-day reality of an actual partnership. If we don't know how to relate honestly and intimately we may prefer never to be put to the test. Choosing unavailable persons on whom to focus is a great way of avoiding that test.

I cannot believe that David chose Lynn by accident. Nor do I think it a coincidence that he first was attracted to her *after* she became involved with another man and was therefore unavailable.

David has a pattern of being attracted to unavailable women. In fact, it almost seems that a woman must be unavailable in order for him to find her attractive. That pattern and its roots merit the closest examination, because implied is a fear of any closeness, a fear that is further hinted at in David's choice of women with whom there is no sexual involvement.

The incredible irony of relationship addiction is that at the core of this obsession with another person lies deep fear of intimacy, a fear we never have to face as long as we continue to choose partners who are, for one reason or another, impossible.

The next two letters clearly demonstrate relationship addiction in their precise detailing of the other person's thoughts, feelings, actions, motives, needs, health, etc., combined with a striking lack of attention to the writer's own questionable condition. The physician who writes describes himself as a nice, healthy man who just happened to fall in love with a woman married to a brute. In my opinion, most men who are involved with women who love someone else too much are themselves relationship addicts. They have, after all, become involved with someone who is basically unavailable to them, and they keep wishing and hoping she'll change. Their focus on the problems of the unavailable woman conveniently distracts them from facing their own predicament of loving too much.

Dear Ms. Norwood,
I have just finished reading your book at the request of a woman who loves too much. She was married for eighteen years to a man who psychologically abused her for at least the last twelve of those years. He had

numerous affairs during that time, one being with the au
pair *girl and another with his wife's best friend. The
marriage finally ended and he married a young girl, and
has started a new family. About four years after the
divorce she married a man who is probably worse than
the other one. She went out with him for three years and
ignored all of the danger signals that told her what this
new marriage would be like. He had an affair about six
months into the marriage, and generally treats her very
badly. She said to me, "I feel like I've been his maid for
ten years." They have been close to divorce on about
three occasions, but he always wants to patch it up when
the divorce is imminent and she always agrees.*

*Last spring I had some contact with her when she
did some work in my house (she is an interior designer)
and she told me that things were very bad in her marriage. They were living in separate rooms in the house
and they had both hired lawyers who were arranging the
terms of the divorce. I have known her for seventeen
years and have always liked her, and thought her to be a
nice person. I have never gone out with a married
woman before (and after this never will again) but I
asked her out to dinner since I considered her to be
separated. She accepted and we started a relationship
in which we saw each other almost every day for four
months. The relationship was very close and very stimu-
lating, but at the same time peaceful and comforting
except for the fact that she was still married, but that
seemed to be nearly over.*

*She had two serious problems at the time: first, her
job of the last five years was coming to an end and she
was to start a new job in a month; second, she began to
suffer from serious vaginal bleeding that was not responsive to medications, and her gynecologist said that she
needed a hysterectomy.*

*I only saw her once that week (which was unusual),
and when I called her for dinner she said that she could
not go because she and her husband were going to try to
patch up the marriage. I found this hard to believe after
all the bad things she had told me about the marriage
and her husband. My feeling was that this would never*

work and that she would call me to tell me that soon. Five days later she called to tell me how he stayed out most of the night and would not tell her where he had been, etc. At this point I became a bit upset and told her that this was no different than the past ten years had been, it was unlikely that it would ever change, and that she would continue to be the human doormat. I guess that she did not want to hear this, since, although she agreed with me, she did not call again. I called her at work about a month later and was told that their marriage was working out, which made my mouth dry and my chest heavy. She also said that she was to have the surgery in about a week. I called her in the hospital the night before the surgery, and she seemed happy to talk to me.

Three days after the surgery she called me and continued to call every day for a week or so. I then started to call her also, because I wanted her to make me understand why she behaved the way she did. She said that the pressure of a new job and the trauma of the surgery had influenced her not to get the divorce. At this time she has written to her lawyer to reopen the divorce case, and wants to move out as soon as she is physically able. Her husband treated her very badly during both the surgery and the postoperative period and this seems to have been the last straw. She cannot drive and cannot leave the house, and I have not seen her in two months, and will not see her for another several weeks as she is going to Florida to stay with a friend in order to get out of her house. She has not told her husband anything yet, and says she will not until she becomes physically better, as he will make things miserable for her when she tells him that she wants to leave.

She keeps reassuring me that she will really leave him this time because of the insights gained by reading your book, because of her therapy, and because she has no outside pressure now.

I am not as sure as she is, and feel that she could still revert back to her old patterns of behavior. I love her very much and have suffered much pain when she went back to her husband, but feel if she did ever go back again that I could finally end the relationship once and for all.

In your book there is not much said about the feelings of the nice, healthy man who gets involved with a woman who loves too much. I can tell you that falling in love with one can be a very discouraging and depressing experience.

If I ever do find happiness in this relationship your thoughts will be part of the reason, and if it does not work out your book will make it easier to cope with the situation and to accept it.

Harold B., M.D.

When I wrote Dr. B. requesting permission to use his letter in this book I got this note back.

Dear Robin Norwood,

I can't resist adding a postscript to the letter that I sent you last year. The woman about whom I was writing once again went back to her husband last September. I stopped seeing her but called her in November, and we went out to lunch. This was an excruciatingly painful experience, since I could see that things had not changed between her and her husband. Actually, if I had paid more attention to your book this would not have been surprising to me. She had stopped seeing her therapist because, "There was nothing to talk about any more." That put the cap on it.

I told her that I did not want to see her again, and told her not to write me. She has complied with this request except to send me a note when I sent her a card for her fiftieth birthday in July.

The last year has been very difficult for me, and it has taken all this time for the painful feelings to abate, but things do seem rosier now.

Your letter stirred up some of those old painful feelings, but fortunately they are less intense today.

Harold B., M.D.

This man's not-so-subtle excuses to have further contact with the woman who has been the source of so much emotional upheaval and distress are another symptom of relationship addiction. He describes in detail her inability to stay away from her unfaithful husband while ignoring his own inability to cease contacting her, though she has kept none of her commitments to him.

The doctor's need to save this woman from her husband and from her own destructive choices no doubt makes up a major part of the strong attraction he feels toward her. Until he has acknowledged his own need to play the foil (being stable and devoted in contrast to her husband's irresponsible callousness), I suspect the doctor will continue to ingenuously find excuses to recontact her and enact his role in this ongoing saga.

––––––––––

Dear Ms. Norwood,

I am not going to go into detail, but my first exposure to your book resulted in some painful experiences . . . my girlfriend, or ex-girlfriend, broke off our relationship after reading it. My immediate reaction was that I wanted to send you a letter bomb (not that I am really that violent . . . actually I am very passive; I'd hope for someone else *to do something like that) but what I* actually *did instead was to go out and buy your book for myself. I am only about halfway through it now, but I have already gotten some insight into what Anna, my girlfriend, may have been feeling and seeing in herself. I have gained a great deal of insight into my problems, too. I am an addict, alcoholic and compulsive overeater with a few years in Twelve-Step programs. But at this time I can see that I am going to have to get into therapy if I am ever to feel comfortable with myself. I've been having a full spectrum of confused, painful feelings. Right now I'm angry and bitter! To be truthful with you I really don't know what the pay-off of this letter is, but I felt a need to write you and to thank you, Ms. Norwood. You and your book may have helped save my life!*

Perry H.

Perry's letter is eloquent testimony to the fact that abandonment can produce the same agony in the man who is the object of relationship addiction as it does in the woman who is the relationship addict. Indeed, in many such partnerships it would be difficult to discern who is the more dependent and needy of the two, no matter which roles they each play.

Perry's initial fantasy of violent retribution in the face of his loss belies despairing frustration and confusion about who he should be and what he should do in his dealings with women. He is obviously very immature and very frightened. However, having achieved several years of recovery from his various substance addictions makes him a good candidate for therapy with a professional who is familiar with the etiology and treatment of his particular addictions. Few addicts of any type recover without eventually having to acknowledge their tremendous inadequacies in the realm of personal relationships, but for men in particular, the willingness to seek help in addressing what is often their most damaged and vulnerable area requires great courage.

Dear Ms. Norwood,

Your book is incredible. I read it both for professional and personal reasons. I was astounded. You answered a profound question for me. I have long wondered, "Where in the world have all the women gone?" I am now fifty-six years old.

In past years women flocked around me. The worse shape I was in, the more blighted I appeared, the more they came to cuddle me. I always had women in my life, nurturing me, attempting to make me all better.

That was years ago, when I abused alcohol, was a chauvinist about women, prejudiced against Blacks and Jews, and you name it. I was very popular!! Women came forth from all directions to be with me. But now, I have no women interested in me, no women bubbling around me, seeing it as their duty to "help" me. Today

I even find it difficult to find women who will just be my friend! It must seem to them that I do not "need" them. I may even seem to be a threat to some of them although I have as much to give to a relationship as I need to get from it.

But now, with the help of your book, I can have women in my life again!! When I meet a new, interesting woman, I will relate how I had many women interested in me when I was a sick alcoholic, prejudiced and obnoxious, and that now that I'm healthier there are very few. I will tell her about your book. I will tell her how I changed my life, how I rid myself of much blight but at the same time lost my "charm." Maybe she'll get interested. And maybe I'll get to have a nice lady friend!
                                                                    Earnest L.

When I received Earnest's letter I responded to it, and some months later I wrote him again, this time requesting permission to use his letter in this book. The agreement form he returned to me included this note at the bottom.

Your book helped me to find a truly great woman! I'm married to her now!
                                                                    Earnest

I sometimes suspect that most women in this culture are co-dependent (and most particularly co-alcoholic), and I know that these co-dependent women are desperate and determined in their search for someone to save and to change. Healthier women are by definition not desperately in search of a partner, period. So naturally Earnest was in great demand at the height of his disease and not much in demand at all in his recovery.

His letter and the note that followed later are not included here to imply that reading *WWL2M* helps arrange happy marriages. They are here simply to show that there was at least one woman who found him sufficiently attractive in sobriety to marry him.

———————

Dear Ms. Norwood,

I have just finished reading your book, which I thoroughly appreciated and needed. I have recently ended, or had ended for me, a relationship with a woman for whom I cared very deeply. Her behavior during the course of our relationship baffled me a bit but nevertheless I still loved her. Now I've read your book and her behavior and prior history make more sense to me.

I still feel this woman may play some role in my life or I in hers and would appreciate your input so that I may do a better job of relating to her in the future. I'm currently seeing a therapist over this. I was able to get Andrea into counseling but I think the therapist did not recognize Andrea's problem. Andrea found counseling threatening, left it and left me.

My concern for Andrea is serious and I write this letter in earnest. I would like you to help her or help me help her.

Terrance R.

In my opinion no one, ever, has any business looking for a therapist for another person. Whenever we are tempted to do so we would be well advised to examine our motives very closely. While we may tell ourselves that our concern is primarily for the other person's welfare, we usually have a definite "agenda" of results that we want therapy to accomplish for that person and we are looking for the therapist who will produce those results. What is operating here is anything but a disinterested concern for another's well-being. The motive is self-interest operating under the guise of "being helpful."

Even if none of this were true, finding a therapist for someone else simply doesn't work. The decision to go into therapy is an intensely personal one and cannot legitimately be made to please another person. In order for the therapeutic process to work, the client must have a keen desire for self-knowledge and must freely make a commitment to pursue that goal. Without that kind of incentive, therapy simply cannot succeed.

It is obvious that behind Terrance's concern that Andrea see a therapist is his hope that she will become, in the process, more amenable to his attentions. Much as he might wish for such a turnaround in their relationship, if *he* wants to recover the only therapy with which Terrance should be concerned is his own.

Dear Ms. Norwood:

I have been a man who attracts women who love too much and I can affirm the daily misery in which both partners in such a relationship live.

My wife Pam and I met twenty-two years ago this month in what, according to your book, was a typical meeting. A friend of mine had picked up his latest heartthrob for their date and Pam was with her. They all came to where I was playing pool because my friend wanted me to pay attention to Pam so he could concentrate on the other girl. I was cold, distant, aloof, rude and only interested in playing pool, but after some badgering by my friend Al, I went out with them. After a couple of hours we dropped the girls off and I went home and promptly forgot all about Pam. About three days later Al began telling me how much Pam wanted to see me again and although I remember not being interested, I also remember being impressed that any girl wanted to see or date me. I don't remember exactly how we happened to see each other again but I do remember kissing her and instantly falling madly in love. That began what has been twenty-two years of misery for both of us, and our four sons seem to have taken this unhappy life-style even further than we have. Just as countless other fools before me, I have spent these last years mindlessly wreaking havoc in my family and especially with my wife. What she and I did together could provide a blueprint for creating a tortured life. It has made me physically sick to recall events in our lives. Accepting my responsibility for my actions has been an unavoidable nightmare and I don't have a way to express the depth of my remorse. I began to learn I had to change myself when I was involved in a course called "Understanding Yourself and Others." There I heard another man in the course coldly and dispassionately describe the circumstances of the death of one of his children and I saw that he was myself in another fifteen years. I was terrified, sick, overwhelmed and at the same time determined to change. It did not happen in a therapy session; it happened through hearing and feeling the experience of someone I'd met only twenty-four hours earlier. He didn't even feel moved by what he was saying, yet I did.

The impact of that evening precipitated a series of changes I absolutely had to make in order to continue to live with myself, but these changes reversed the roles my wife and I had played for so long. Instead of being cold, aloof and unfeeling, I was suddenly full of emotion. My wife, in turn, withdrew.

Now, with this role reversal our relationship has dramatically deteriorated. Just changing roles hasn't relieved or reduced anyone's anguish but it has helped us to understand what each other's experience of the relationship has been. After having caused so much suffering, I now feel like her victim.

Two weeks ago my action for divorce was filed, and (characteristic of someone unable to make a decision) it happened by "accident." My attorney filed it because he believed I'd paid his retainer. I hadn't. Not paying it was my unconscious way of avoiding responsibility for my own life. It's embarrassing but true that I learned I'd filed for a divorce from my wife who read it in the newspaper the next morning. I don't want to divorce her. I want us to grow healthier together and at the same time I know that can only happen if both of us make a commitment to facing ourselves individually. I know I

*need to face the formless, haunting anxiety that has
always plagued me. This is a personal responsibility and
it is unavoidable for me whether I am married or not.*

*So, no matter what happens between Pam and me,
I'm thankful that you and others are inspiring a change
in my life that helps me be a better human being.*

Walt S.

Many of us women who have had partners like Walt dream
that the man in our life might experience an emotional breakthrough such as he reports. Yet he also reports that his relationship is in worse trouble than ever, which makes it sound as if his
wife really doesn't want to be close to him. His commitment to
changing sounds so sincere that it is easy to overlook the fact
that emotional abuse has been a long-standing theme in this
marriage and that physical abuse is at least alluded to (although
Walt never actually admits to having physically abused his wife
and children).

Whether or not this was a situation in which just emotional
or also physical abuse was present, the pattern of relating
between these two partners is best understood by applying the
phases in the syndrome of violence to their interactions. The
phases are these: First, after an episode of abuse there is usually
a resolution on the part of the abused partner not to endure any
more abuse—in other words, she threatens to leave the situation.
The strength of that resolution to leave is fully matched in degree
by the remorse expressed by the abuser, *the motive of which is
not to lose control of the victim.* All of Walt's protestations
about having seen the light are a part of this cycle. The apologies
and promises to change are made so eloquently and convincingly
(and the abused partner is usually so addicted to the abuser)
that this courtship phase almost always results in the couple
being reunited. Then a honeymoon phase follows during which
the abuser's behavior is above reproach. During this period the
abused partner feels strong and powerful, convinced that she
has gained control of the man and the situation. Slowly, how-

ever, tension begins to build, and sooner or later the abuse both recommences and escalates, reaching a level more damaging than the last episode. This outbreak is followed again by remorse, penitent apologies and promises to reform accompanied by bouquets of flowers, romantic cards, etc. Frankly, a relationship of greater intensity is difficult to imagine. No woman in a stable, healthy relationship is ever wooed with the single-minded devotion demonstrated by the abuser while in either the courtship or the honeymoon stage. Indeed, except for the physical abuse and/or emotional humiliation, the abusive relationship best fits our culture's idea of how "real love" is expressed. The begging, the pleading, the flowers and letters and desperate phone calls, the threats of suicide or murder or both unless there is a reconciliation—all these are typical components of the abusive relationship in the courtship phase, and all of these manipulations are romanticized by our culture as indicative of "true love."

The abused partner finds these behaviors not only reassuring but deeply flattering, as indeed they are meant to be. Now she is sure that the tables have turned and because she is so desirable to him and so necessary to his life, she has power over him. She will be able to control him. That need to control him is usually her strongest motive for being in the relationship, but because of its driving intensity and the powerful emotions it generates in her she believes herself to be "in love." So, for a while he pleads and supplicates and she holds sway over him and feels the exhilaration that comes with having him where she wants him. But sooner or later the tables turn again. No matter which of these two partners is emoting while the other reacts with cold indifference, the capacity for intimacy is unchanged; the drive to manipulate and control each other, to *win*, continues unabated.

If Walt's wife is indifferent to his promises to change even though he is now taking classes and talking about his feelings, she may be so either because she is trying to prolong the courtship phase or because she has finally stepped off the merry-go-round they have been riding together for so many years. If she has, indeed, stopped performing her part of the dance they've done together, then only time will tell if Walt is pursuing recovery for the impression it will make on Pam or truly for his own sake. Yes, he is very persuasive—but abusers always are. It is their stock-in-trade in the courtship phase, and causes the abused partner to feel disloyal and unfair to the remorseful abuser by not lovingly supporting these promises to change.

When people are sincerely working on their own recoveries they become quiet.

When people are sincerely working on their own recoveries they become quiet about their struggles toward self-healing. For example, a man I know who went in and out of Alcoholics Anonymous (and in and out of sobriety) for years would, during his periods of attendance, always make sure everyone in his family knew when he was going to a meeting. "Well, I'm off to my A.A. meeting!" he would announce as he left the house. Sometimes he went to a meeting and sometimes he went out and drank instead. When he finally accepted in his own heart that he was a sick alcoholic, dying of his disease, he went back to Alcoholics Anonymous for his own sake. He attended meetings regularly for many weeks before his family even knew he was doing so. He was no longer going to Alcoholics Anonymous to convince them of anything. He was going to save his own life.

Recovery in men, as in women, occurs when it is pursued for its own sake, for the peace of mind it promises, rather than for the effect it will have on the marriage. Otherwise "recovery" is just another move in the marital chess game, another step in the deadly dance performed by two partners locked in a strangling embrace of obstinacy.

Incidentally, the way Pam and Walt met and became partners is an instructive example of how there are no accidents in relationships. On their first meeting, to put it very simply, Walt did nothing to make their time together pleasant. Pam was probably already an old hand at being on the receiving end of obnoxious behavior long before she ever met Walt. He represented the attractive possibility that she could change him into someone who treated her better. When Walt, after openly advertising that he was callous and indifferent, found this person who was nevertheless attracted to him on these terms, he promptly "fell in love." Pam, no doubt, quickly went to work on trying to change him while he now had every justification for digging in deeper and rebelling against her efforts. This behavior, interspersed with occasional episodes of shaping up if he had gone too far and was in danger of losing her, simply increased in intensity over the twenty-two years they have been together. But their dance was begun the moment they met.

Dear Ms. Norwood,

I read your book just about one year ago. I wanted to share my progress of the past eleven months with you. I am a forty-year-old gay man who has loved too much. I was in and out of therapy for seven years, trying to work through my relationship problems. Over a period of nearly eighteen years I had serial affairs with inappropriate, unavailable men. Frankly, therapy provided what I called "Band-Aid" results—temporary easing during crisis periods but never really addressing and healing the core issues.

After reading your book, I thought long and hard and realized that not only were the men I had been involved with unavailable or inappropriate but so was I. It took a little more thought to focus in on my addiction and to reason out what was contributing to my unavailability not only for others but essentially for myself. I realized that I was addicted to sex and the search for love. I had or have many of the same symptoms as a drug abuser or an alcoholic, only my escape had been sex. Last year on June seventeenth I went to my first Twelve-Step program meeting for Sexual Compulsiveness. In the last eleven months I have eliminated my sexually compulsive behavior. In the last four months I have used abstinence as a tool for catharsis; an approach to becoming in touch with myriad feelings and emotions that I had been avoiding for years and years. I have been able for the first time in my life to clearly address family relationship issues, self-esteem issues and romantic obsession issues. I now see the person I have been for twenty-five years. I see, as well, the potential reemergence of the original person I was as a child. Perhaps I can accept him and allow him to flourish into adulthood for the next twenty-five years (or more).

I learned through your book that I was a caretaker in my family from childhood on, never really addressing my own problems or needs or feelings, always hiding or submerging them. I have, in the last eleven months, been strong enough or, if you will, frail enough to ask for help from others and at the same time become my own caretaker. I have learned to "fix" only myself (or to try to at least) and let those close to me try to do the very same for themselves.

The process has not always been easy. It has been slow and painstaking. But I have been developing a patience to deal with life one day at a time. Who knows? Some day in the not too distant future I may even begin to explore dating and its risks and with available, appropriate individuals. In the meanwhile I am loving and accepting myself for who I am.

Michael R.

The role of caretaker in one's family of origin, especially if that family is a severely dysfunctional one, can preclude the child cast in that role from ever really knowing or understanding himself. He is too busy knowing and understanding everyone else and putting out the emotional brushfires that surround him as he is growing up. This unhappy, dramatic milieu fosters first a familiarity with and then an actual need for excitement, struggle and pain. The same heightened emotional tone, fraught with deep secrets and explosive pressures, is then sought in every subsequent relationship and situation. The greater the difficulties of an encounter the more exciting it is and the greater the feelings of arousal it creates. These feelings, compelling in their very familiarity, are powerfully attractive and often mistakenly identified as love. The person who was shaped by his childhood experiences of overwhelming pressure is now actively creating and perpetuating that pressure in his present patterns of relating. That these highly dramatic, frustrating and even dangerous kinds of encounters can be so much a part of homosexual as well as heterosexual interactions goes without saying. Indeed, because our society makes secrecy such a necessary element in homosexual interactions, their dramatic elements are particularly heightened.

Michael was very fortunate in being able to recognize both his sexual behavior and his behavior in relationships in general as addictive. His consequent involvement in a Twelve-Step program is, I believe, also very fortunate and appropriate. It is an approach that is being followed by more and more homosexuals as well as heterosexual individuals who, like Michael, are admitting to the addictive quality of their sexual behavior. (This is not to imply that homosexual relating in and of itself is necessarily indicative of the presence of sexual addiction. Rather I want only to point out that sexual addiction is a condition that needs to be addressed by some homosexuals and heterosexuals alike.)

The life-threatening possibility of contracting AIDS through compulsively pursued sexual encounters with partners of either gender finally puts the *addictive* pursuit of sex in a clear light. We are able now to understand and address it not as a freely chosen albeit unconventional lifestyle but as the progressive and potentially fatal disease it is.

Finally, Michael's commitment to a period of total sexual abstinence in order to allow his buried emotions and experiences to surface is a very wise and courageous decision. We all must let go of the "drug" that has served as a buffer between ourselves and our pain if we want to heal whatever it is in us that has been damaged.

———

The next several letters speak clearly for themselves and require no additional comment from me.

Dear Robin,
A female friend gave me your book to read some months ago. I didn't think much of it, seeing it as a morbid collection of horror stories. Shortly thereafter, I became involved with a woman who was separating from her alcoholic husband. In my forty-four years I had never met anyone who I believed would be the ideal partner for me until I met her, even though I've been married three times! I knew that she was confused and uncertain, that she had a number of unresolved issues in her life besides her marriage/separation and that she needed time. I was patient, caring, tolerant and supportive. I knew early on that I loved her. She said of me that she had never known anyone who was so sensitive to her thoughts, feelings and to her very being. My senses (instincts/intuition) had never been so heightened as they were with her. I had the most powerful feelings of unconditional love I had ever experienced (parenting aside). Then she told me that she needed time away from me: We could not be lovers, but could be friends.
I immediately sought therapy to deal with letting go. I realized that she was attracted to a more macho-type male than I; one who was somehow unavailable. She confirmed this for me. I bought your book to reread in order to learn more about her. I took it with me on vacation along with some of the other books you had recommended. I read and cried for a week, and came home early. I had discovered me: an adult child of an alcoholic, a man who loves too much. I had always

thought I was reasonably normal and healthy and now I am devastated to recognize what my life has been.

Since my last divorce six years ago, I have involved myself in a variety of therapeutic experiences. Instead of learning all of life's lessons about relationships the hard way as I had for the preceding twenty years, my learning and changing became accelerated. I have been in and out of therapeutic experiences for twenty-five years. For the past five years of my life I have felt very stable and healthy. I have a masters degree in counseling psychology and have been a college professor for the past decade.

Now I know I am in serious trouble. I had never examined my problems with relationships in the context of growing up with alcoholism. I had been willing to accept this recent breakup as an opportunity for continued personal growth. But I discovered a frightening disease called loving too much. I am now emotionally unstable, in serious trouble, and I need help. I will start attending an Adult Children of Alcoholics meeting this week. With all that I know about psychology I somehow missed my own diagnosis, but now that I understand what has made me the way I am I feel most comfortable with that direct approach to my problem.

Frederic J.

Dear Robin—
Susie calmly told me one night in bed that she no longer agreed with my negative assessment of life and was not willing to spend her energy trying to live with my discontent and lack of openness and feelings. Her words—combined with a recent trip to the emergency room with our daughter, a trip which we discovered was totally caused by her anxiety toward me—finally pierced my armor. I could do nothing but agree. I read your book—and got pierced some more. It has been a long time since I've cried as much as I did reading WWL2M. I am now seeing a male psychologist and am hopeful of changing my attitude on life.

Benjamin D.

Dear Ms. Norwood:

I am a twenty-two-year-old college student about to graduate and start law school in the fall. I have an alcoholic father and a nonsupportive mother. I recently went through a breakup with a girl I loved very much. We are very different people and were about to start counseling together to work out our problems. But she broke up with me before our sessions began and I decided to go it alone. My counselor hadn't read your book yet, but she knew what my problem was. I have a long history of being drawn to women who have problems because I feel like they need me too much to break up with me. My counselor was telling me that I needed to be with someone who was my equal, but I continued to feel like it was my fault that these relationships were not working out. Thanks to WWL2M I now know that is not the case. I have a long road to "recovery" but I felt better after reading just the first two chapters of your book.

The reason I am writing is to let you know that there are many men out there who have this problem. Almost all my male friends do. We call it the "Nice Guys Finish Last Syndrome." No matter what we do, we always end up with a girl who hurts us. We can't seem to get it right because if we try to have a relationship with a "woman who loves too much" she finds us boring and unchallenging. On the other hand, if we involve ourselves with a woman who has the characteristics of most of the men in WWL2M, we meet with disaster of equal proportions since these women treat us badly. In a sense we have it tougher than "women who love too much." Anyway, it is comforting to know that I am not alone in this struggle. With the aid of my new insights, of my counselor and my friends I know I am going to make it.

Glenn R.

With Glenn's letter we come back to the sex-role issue. Who has a harder time with relationship dependency—a man whose behavior runs contrary to the cultural prescriptions for his sex or the woman whose behavior is culturally reinforced? Obviously members of both sexes struggle with this problem but from different vantage points. Trying to compare and contrast their degrees of suffering is probably not as productive as acknowledging that the suffering is present in both sexes and is not dependent on which role either sex is playing. Indeed, even when the roles are interchangeable the incapacity for intimacy remains constant. That incapacity is the deeper source of pain as well as the problem that requires a deeper level of healing. As long as our attention is on the state of our relationship with another person at the expense of developing our relationship with our own inner self, the capacity for intimacy will not increase. Man or woman, we must accept and love that inner being in us before we can tolerate another person coming close enough to know us and to love us.

Ten

LETTERS FROM WOMEN WHO ARE RECOVERING

The title of this final chapter is not meant to imply that only those women whose letters follow are actually recovering from relationship addiction. Most of the other women whose letters you have read are also in various stages of recovery. The three letters that follow simply serve to illuminate further some of the paths that recovery may take and what it can feel like to the woman who finds herself on one of these paths.

The first of these letters describes the changed quality of interaction that can occur between partners when the one who has previously been carrying the burden of making the relationship work stops trying so hard to do what is not, after all, her sole responsibility. As she improves in her attitude toward herself she makes room for improvement in the situation as well. Put another way, we don't get stepped on if we aren't already lying down.

In the counseling profession, marriages and families are often compared dynamically to a dangling mobile with each of its parts representing the people involved. The ways in which the people are interconnected with one another and the balance that is thereby created make up the structure as a whole. Should one person in the family shift position the balance of the entire structure is automatically changed. This phenomenon is succinctly described by Merrilee's letter.

Hello!
I've just completed your book about loving too much. What an eye-opener! My sister recommended it to me—and the next week a close friend wrote to say I

should read it—so, I made it a priority and am very glad
I did. I see things so very differently now! I called to join
a new group that's forming for Adult Children of Alco-
holics. My sister and I saw ourselves in most of the
stories. I've also noticed since reading the book that my
husband (a recovering alcoholic) has often said, "What
do I need you for, anyway?" if I'm not doing something
he wants—and then I'd actually tremble in fear of not
being needed because that meant I wouldn't be kept
around—even though I've always worked outside the
home, cooked, cleaned, taken on his financial debts from
before we married, etc., etc., etc.! Last week when he
asked me what he needed me for I simply replied, "I
don't know, what?" Later that evening he said I'd be a
"solo" again if I didn't get more lunchmeat for his
sandwiches. I felt a mixture of fear and exhilaration
when I replied simply, "Oh?" Later he asked me if I still
loved him.

As you can see, the way is opening for me to become
what I've always hoped to be—free, whole, and well.
Merrilee S.

When one person in a couple changes there are only three
possible results. Either the partner adjusts correspondingly; or
the person who changed first changes back again; or the relationship itself dramatically alters. Most of us are threatened by any
change that is thrust upon us, even that which is potentially
positive. Our initial reaction is usually an attempt to restore the
old, familiar conditions with which we are comfortable and can
adequately cope. Further, many of us believe that if someone
really loved us that person would protect us from having to
change, indeed would indulge us in remaining exactly the way
we are. We may interpret it as a lack of love when another's
behavior requires us to examine and adjust our own. Unfortunately, many of us prefer a stagnant status quo to the challenge
of changes that would improve the quality of our lives.

When Merrilee was allowing herself to be ill-treated she

wasn't doing her husband a favor at her own expense. She was passively permitting interactions that were unhealthy for *both* of them. By taking better care of herself she is creating an opportunity for her husband to become a more mature and responsible partner. Whether he can accept this challenge or not has nothing to do with the correctness of her action or her worth as a person. His reaction reflects his ability or inability to evolve as a person in the relationship.

To use the analogy of the "dance" from *WWL2M:* As Merrilee's husband executes one of his usual steps he expects her to perform her corresponding step. When she responds with a new, unfamiliar one he is thrown off balance. Suddenly he finds himself with a partner who is performing a dance he doesn't know. He naturally feels threatened and tries to jog her back into their old familiar routine. If he cannot do so he will either have to summon the humility necessary to learn the steps to her new dance himself or else stop dancing with her altogether and find another partner with whom he can interact in the old familiar way.

The possibility that Merrilee's changed behavior toward her husband may cause their marriage to end must be acknowledged. Each of us takes that chance when we stop doing what isn't good for us in a relationship. But it is my consistent observation that ultimately we are not punished for pursuing our own recovery. Some conditions may change in ways that are, at first, alarming; some people may leave whom we would rather not see go. But in the end life improves in direct relation to the degree that we become more true to ourselves.

The next letter summarizes what this entire book has been trying to communicate regarding the way recovery comes about, how difficult its achievement is, some of its great rewards and the fact that it is always ongoing.

Dear Ms. Norwood,

When I first bought your book I could only read a few pages at a time. It was so powerful for me because I was on every page!

I am forty-four years old and sober two years in Alcoholics Anonymous. Well, after reading and rereading your book, in December everything started churning inside of me. Until then I had no idea how incapable I was of focusing on myself rather than "him." You know how you said that when women like me start to look at just themselves they may find an underlying depression that has been there for years? Well, I sure did and the month of January was the worst of my sober life. But every morning, along with my Alcoholics Anonymous books, I would read the section of your book where you guaranteed me that if I followed what you said, I would recover from this illness, too (the same as they promised me in Alcoholics Anonymous that if I went to meetings and I didn't drink I would get better).

Well, I spent January praying, talking to my sponsor and others in Alcoholics Anonymous, going to meetings, and it felt like I was just getting worse. I didn't want to drink, I didn't want to die. But the pain was so horrible I couldn't imagine living. It felt like all the pain of my life was coming out and I began to feel anger such as I have never known.

Finally, one day when I said my morning prayers, I admitted I was utterly and totally defeated and I guess I finally surrendered everything to God.

That was the day I first realized that I needed to go not only to Alcoholics Anonymous but Adult Children of Alcoholics meetings as well. Both my parents are alive and drinking still. Then with help of friends I finally admitted I needed more help than meetings and through a series of circumstances ended up with a woman therapist who is absolutely wonderful. And she suggested I go to a five-day Adult Children of Alcoholics workshop. I debated and debated whether to leave my two teenage children for a week but decided if I had been led this far it was meant for me to go. Well, I went last week. I dealt with all that anger and with all that pain underneath.

Ms. Norwood—I can't even begin to tell you how wonderful I feel today. I feel more solid, like my inside and outside are closer together than ever in my life.

When I was a girl the woman next door used to sing while she worked and I used to listen to her and want that happy feeling so bad in my family and in me. Well, I'm not singing yet, but I'm laughing, I'm even humming a bit. I was truly such a gentle child and for the first time in my adult life I'm beginning to feel that the gentleness is still there and it's an important part of me. They told me at the workshop to put a picture of me as a child where I can see it every day. I have it on my mirror next to my I.D. bracelet from the alcohol rehabilitation hospital I went to two years ago. It helps to remind me every morning to be gentle with myself.

After three marriages (the last two to the same man—the first one of fourteen years to my children's father) and three divorces (I didn't start drinking until my first divorce ten years ago) I am now involved with a wonderful man. He's divorced and six years sober in Alcoholics Anonymous. He lives two hours away so we only see each other on weekends, which gives us both time alone. We are both working for a healthy relationship but at times it isn't easy, because being healthy is so new to both of us.

I have to tell you about your "Oh . . ." comment that you refer to in the "don't play games" section of WWL2M.

One night he was an hour later than usual in calling me. Well, I started feeling anxious, abandoned, angry, but instead of calling him and playing the victim (I'm real good at that role), I got out your book. There I sat, Indian style on my bed, practically rocking from that old compulsion to call him and blast him with my silence, but reading the section on game playing instead, when the phone rang. As he began to apologize, I said, casually, "Oh, that's okay, I'm fine," and started just chatting. He was so surprised that he exclaimed, "You are?" *The rest of the conversation went fine.*

Afterward I wondered if I had done it perfectly but decided that whatever else, at least I got out the "Oh."

Now, whenever I use that word or hear it I have to smile.
It is now five days later and I just reread what I have written. I must tell you, I feel pretty vulnerable revealing all these thoughts to you and I don't even know you. But it's worth the risk because I feel that to not share with you after all would be selfish on my part.
I'm not very good with good-byes. Any kind makes me feel sad. But I do think I will close for now.
Sara P.

Sara's letter illustrates several important facets of recovery. The degree of pain she had to endure before she became willing to surrender her relationship addiction to the same Power that had healed her alcohol addiction is typical of women who love too much. We don't easily give up our own efforts to control the uncontrollable. Also typical is the fact that once Sara completely surrendered, her path to this next recovery quickly followed. It's important to understand that looking frantically for the answers is not the route to recovery. Becoming totally willing to recover, no matter what, is the necessary first step. Then the route to recovery reveals itself.

In recovery, retaining poise becomes a higher priority than either arousing pity or taking revenge.

When Sara managed, in spite of her anxiety, pain and anger over the late phone call, to simply say, "Oh . . ." rather than trying to punish the man with whom she's involved, she achieved a major victory in her recovery. Retaining her poise became a higher priority than either arousing pity or taking revenge. Naturally, her new behavior and the unfamiliar response it generated were a little unsettling. We all need some practice in the lines of conduct that are part of recovery before they become a comfortable part of us. At first these new patterns of interaction can feel cold, unfeeling, abrupt or anticlimactic. If in the aftermath of this unaccustomed kind of exchange we find ourselves struggling with self-doubt, as Sara did, we can benefit from talking to another recovering person. Such a person can objectively evaluate what happened and reinforce our attempts to practice recovery.

Finally, Sara's feelings of vulnerability after communicating so openly with me deserve attention. An automatic result of the recovery process is that we relate to others in a more genuine, more open, less defended and self-protective way. To do so creates in us a sense of greater vulnerability. This is compounded by the fact that recovery also gives us heightened awareness of all our feelings right along with a greater capacity for handling them. Sara's feeling of vulnerability is as much a hallmark of her recovery as is her courage to write so honestly (and then *send* the letter) in spite of the risk she feels. Sharing our experiences in recovery is part of recovery itself.

———

This last letter, very long and rich in detail, seems such a fitting one with which to close. It presents what is a very typical genesis of relationship addiction. Its author poignantly describes many of the feelings and experiences both in childhood and adulthood that are common to those who have grown up in tense, battle-ridden alcoholic homes:

- Alcoholic parents suspecting (sometimes correctly) their children of abusing drugs and making that problem their primary focus and the reason for all the family's troubles while ignoring the effects on the family of their own alcoholism.
- Children actually experiencing relief when transferred from their chaotic alcoholic homes to the comparatively stable and predictable environment of an institution such as a psychiatric hospital or a juvenile detention center.

- The "jailbreak marriage" (to borrow Gail Sheehy's term from *Passages**) as a means of escaping an intolerable home environment.
- The repeated failure of those in the helping professions to assess the presence of alcoholism in the parents of a troubled child. (It is the primary contributing factor in the lives of most disturbed children and adolescents but is very rarely diagnosed even after repeated encounters with principals, counselors, juvenile authorities, etc.)
- The tendency of those from alcoholic homes to develop chemical dependency and/or to marry someone with chemical dependency.
- The "need to be needed" so common in adult female children of alcoholics, which attracts them to men whose lives are unmanageable and prompts them to leave their partner if his condition improves significantly.
- The bitter dramas in which many alcoholic families are embroiled, often spanning decades and generations, with offspring required to take sides in the ongoing battle.
- The need of the adult child from an alcoholic home to feel "in control" in both the personal and professional arenas.
- Alcoholism and co-alcoholism each making life unmanageable.
- The necessity of facing long-held resentments and letting go of them in order for recovery to take place.

This letter also depicts very clearly many typical aspects of the relationship between a physically abusive man and the woman who is unable to stay away from him, especially the repetitive or generational aspects operating in both their lives:

- The presence of chemical dependency in the family histories of both partners in the violent relationship.

---

*See the Recommended Reading list for more information.

- The fact that the abuser was, himself, abused as a child.
- The pattern of extreme chaos and/or violence in the family histories of *both* partners in the violent relationship.
- The escalation of physical abuse during pregnancy due to heightened dependency needs and fears in both partners.
- The progressively addictive nature of the battering relationship.

Most important, though, this letter describes recovery not only from alcohol addiction but from relationship addiction as it operates in the battered woman. Those of us who have worked with victims of domestic violence know how rarely these women are able to walk away and stay away from the men who abuse them. We all know the disheartening regularity with which a battered woman returns to the man who beats her, who may eventually kill her, or she him, as they spiral together in the ever-escalating cycle of violence.

I believe it bears repeating that women who are being abused physically can best be understood and treated when they are recognized as being relationship addicted. They are afflicted with a progressive and ultimately fatal disease that must be taken as seriously by them and those who treat them as any other life-threatening form of addiction. The only women I've personally known to recover from this particularly dramatic and deadly variety of relationship addiction have done so through being involved with one Twelve-Step program or another, usually Alcoholics Anonymous or Al-Anon. As is the case in the following letter, the battered women I've known have all qualified to be members of one or both of these programs, and when they applied the principles therein to their relationship addiction they began to recover.

The reason I've included this letter here rather than in the chapter on battering is because it describes a conversion experience. Many alcoholics (but by no means most) have a similar conversion experience, a deeply spiritual awakening which is both sudden and indescribably compelling, after which they never need to drink again. In this letter we learn how such a conversion experience happened to a relationship-addicted, battered woman. Some of you who read this letter may have difficulty believing it is genuine, that such a healing really happened in the way described here. I have known enough people who have had similar recoveries from other life-threatening diseases of addiction to know that this kind of miracle can and does happen. Since the natural condition of any addict is to be practicing the disease and dying of its consquences, every recovery from any kind of addiction is a miracle whether it comes about through a sudden conversion experience or by a slow, step-by-step process of change. But because Belinda's letter makes so abundantly clear the progressive and ultimately fatal nature of her relationship addiction, her moving account of the astounding nature of her recovery seems to me to be the perfect miracle with which to end this book.

Dear Ms. Norwood,

My name is Belinda E. I am twenty-seven years old and the single mother of a twenty-two-month-old boy. I read your book several months ago and I thoroughly enjoyed it as well as identified with much of its content. I am an adult child of two alcoholic parents, as well as a co-dependent and a recovering alcoholic myself.

Before I can disclose the main purpose of this letter I must tell you a little about my history. I have never before written to anyone who has published a book or who is famous except once when I was a little girl I wrote a letter to Golda Meir for a school project. I tell you this in hope that you will read my entire letter and not discard it as just another letter from a fan or perhaps even a "kook."

I was born the third child and only daughter in a typical middle-class family. Outwardly, we appeared to be no different from any other family, but we were different because my mother was an alcoholic. She was angry, bitter, resentful and verbally abusive. My father stayed away from home much of the time due to his work.

As a young teen I was also angry, bitter and resentful and was in a continuous state of depression. My parents were concerned that I was involved with drugs (I wasn't) and I was sent to various expensive psychiatrists for therapy. The psychiatrists each failed to look into the situation at home, instead focusing all their attention on my behavior as the entire problem. They agreed with my parents (who were paying eighty dollars an hour) that my behavior should be changed, and when their methods failed to produce the desired results, I was admitted to a psychiatric hospital for treatment.

The six weeks I spent in the hospital improved my attitude immensely, not because of the treatment I received there but due to the fact that I was away from the insanity of my home. I found a psychiatric hospital full of "crazies" to be more peaceful than my own home.

After leaving the hospital I was determined to be on good behavior as long as necessary, because I knew I would not have to stay at home much longer. I vowed secretly to leave as soon as possible, and at seventeen I did so by marrying the first boy who would have me.

I felt sorry for my first husband and thought I would be able to help him overcome his shyness and insecurity. We remained married for four years, and during that time he did overcome those weaknesses but not because of anything I did. He became a success in business and shortly thereafter we lost interest in each other and divorced.

My drinking problem began after my divorce. During the next few years my alcoholism steadily became worse. I also continued to manipulate men for whom I felt sorry and who I felt needed me. Twice I asked men of this type to marry me and luckily I was rejected by both of them, but I was devastated each time.

Also during this time my father's alcoholism worsened. We worked for the same large corporation and he was preparing to retire from this company to which he

*had devoted his life. We felt very close and would spend
long hours together drinking and discussing business.*

*After my father retired, my mother joined Alcoholics
Anonymous and moved out of their home. She had a
facelift and then went on a tour of Europe while my
father literally tried to drink himself to death. I was
going out of my mind with worry and frustration.*

*When she returned they began a protracted, bitter
fight over the divorce proceedings. My mother had long
since felt cheated as a woman and had joined a woman's
group for support. It was a vicious, ugly battle, and I
was caught in the middle of it, with each of them looking
to me for support.*

*One night I received a call from my mother that
would change my life forever. She said she had consulted
several authorities in her woman's group along with a
financial advisor, and they each advised her not to
divorce my father because at the rate he was drinking he
would not live another two years and she would stand to
lose $180,000 from the entire estate. Instead she planned
to remodel their home into a duplex and live there with
him but lead a totally separate life until he died. At that
moment I went stark raving mad. All I could do was
scream, "You're sick!" over and over until I finally hung
up. I called my father who was drunk at the time and he
told me he was willing to go along with my mother's
plan. I didn't know which of them I hated more, my
mother for thinking of such a sick, cruel plan or my
father for going along with it. All I knew was that I
wanted to get as far away from both of them as I could,
and at that point I really didn't care anymore if either of
them lived or died.*

*They didn't divorce. Instead, my mother began
drinking again and they reconciled, but I still wanted no
part of their lives and wanted them to stay completely
out of mine. I quit my job and moved away.*

*I had felt so completely out of control for such a
long time that I wanted a job where I would have a lot
of control. I decided to become a police officer. I passed
a battery of physical and psychological tests and was*

eventually accepted into the police academy. (At that time I was a full-blown alcoholic.)

While attending the police academy I met a man named Dave at a Christmas party. I went to the party with another date and didn't really notice Dave. Later that week I met his sister (who had also been at the party) in a shopping mall and she approached me saying Dave had asked her if she knew my phone number. I reluctantly gave it to her. Having left home I was still fearful of strangers, but the girlfriend I was with said to go ahead, that it might be fun to go out with him.

Dave called and we scheduled a date to go fishing. The attraction I felt toward Dave was enormous from the start. His wife had recently left him, taking away his two children. He was so depressed he couldn't work, he drove an old beat-up truck and he was being evicted from his apartment. He seemed to be a sweet, gentle man who was just down on his luck and needed someone to care for him and help him through this difficult time. He told me very little about his family and his past, saying that I would find out soon enough.

Within a week he had moved into my house. I was unable to complete the police academy because Dave needed constant emotional support and my independence was in conflict with his needs. Also my drinking at night was making it difficult to concentrate and perform during the day.

I became pregnant shortly thereafter. I thought I was giving him the family he had lost and that a new child would strengthen our relationship and improve his self-esteem.

Neither of us were capable of maintaining a job for any length of time and over and over I had to ask my parents for financial help, which I loathed doing. They were distraught over my situation as well as extremely critical and I still wanted to be totally independent of them.

Instead of improving our relationship, the pregnancy placed more strain on both of us and Dave's temper became apparent. He was verbally and physi-

cally abusive. I later learned he had been abused as a child by his father.

I drank during the pregnancy, but not very much. I have no doubt I would have drunk to the point of permanently injuring my unborn child had I not become violently ill each time I tried.

A perfect example of the insanity in our relationship happened when I was seven months pregnant. I went into premature labor and was admitted to the hospital where I was expected to lose the child. While I lay there feeling the contractions and being terrified, the doctors and nurses worked frantically, administering drugs in an effort to try to stop the labor. Dave was jealous of the attention I was receiving, saying that I had it made, having people wait on me hand and foot while he had to suffer at home alone with no one to prepare his meals and take care of him. He actually made me feel guilty for being in the hospital and I called his sister to ask her if Dave could please eat over at her house until I could come home.

They saved the baby but I was not to walk farther than the bathroom and was supposed to stay in bed as much as possible until the pregnancy was full-term. I also was to take expensive medication four times a day to keep the contractions from beginning again.

My first day home from the hospital I had to do the weekly grocery shopping because Dave refused to go. And later he asked if I could please stop taking that medication as it was too expensive.

After the baby was born I began to drink heavily again and Dave was absolutely no support in taking care of a newborn infant. It seemed as though his demands for constant attention increased and his temper outbursts became more frequent. I was beaten several times and I had to call the police twice when it was apparent that we were not having just another fight, but rather that my life and the life of my infant son were in real danger.

This continued for several months until I found a job in another area and we moved there. We started seeing a counselor but because Dave felt the counselor and I were against him, we only went to three short visits. Finally, after yet another fight, I called the police and had Dave removed from the apartment.

I lost several jobs in a short period of time because of my drinking, and my family was deeply worried about the welfare of my son. I did my best to care for him but the burden of my alcoholism along with my many other problems pulled me down deeper and deeper into despair. I began seeing Dave again for whatever financial and moral support he would give. He offered a little financial help in return for sexual considerations and the same amount of moral support he had always given.

Unbeknownst to me, my family was planning an intervention* with a counselor where I lived. They contacted Dave, and everyone involved met in the counselor's office to arrange it. Dave was told the intervention plans must be kept a secret from me in order to be effective when put into action, but during an argument the following night he disclosed the fact that he and my family had discussed the need to take my son away from me and everyone had agreed it was necessary. We had a terrific fight and (for the last time) he beat me.

Later that night my brother came over and told me the truth about the intervention. He did so lovingly and with compassion. I agreed to see the counselor on my own terms. I would make the appointment and go there willingly, but not be humiliated in front of my entire family in my own home.

Within five minutes of my first meeting with this counselor she told me in no uncertain terms just what I was and where I was headed. She expected me to be angry but I wasn't. I knew she was telling me the truth. In a way I was relieved because I wasn't alone anymore. Someone else understood that black void where I lived most of the time.

---

*An intervention is a structured confrontation during which family and friends relate some of the situations to the alcoholic in which his or her drinking has caused problems and emotional pain. This is done with the guidance of an objective person, usually a counselor skilled in helping with this task. The object is to persuade the alcoholic to seek treatment. See Vernon Johnson's book, *I'll Quit Tomorrow,* for greater details about how intervention works. (See the Recommended Reading list for more about this book.)

Within days I was on a plane to a drug/alcohol treatment center in another state. And at the exact time I was on my journey, my father was on his way to an alcoholism treatment center, too. I arrived at a majestic old mansion set in the most beautiful countryside and that home is surely the reason why God made those hills and valleys. There I experienced more love, support and understanding than I had ever dreamed possible in one lifetime. I learned about the disease of alcoholism, and with the help of a fantastic network of counselors and the support of the patients who were just like myself, I worked through many of my resentments concerning my parents.

I refused to deal with my feelings toward Dave though, because I was still holding fast to the fantasy that he would change and our love for one another would see us through.

While I was away Dave moved my belongings into his apartment. He drove up to the treatment center for my last week there and sat through a few sessions with me. He also took several written psychological tests and we listened to the results together.

The counselor told him there was every indication that he, too, had a chemical dependency problem. She also described his emotional immaturity, unrealistic attitudes and violent nature. Dave had little to say concerning any of this, and I, wanting to believe the best of him, disregarded these findings. I knew Dave used pot occasionally, but to my knowledge it had not been a problem. We returned to his apartment and shortly thereafter picked up our son from my mother's house. I was ready for us to be a family again.

Within a matter of weeks Dave's pot use began to be a problem with us. He would never use it at home in front of me, but would sneak away periodically and return stoned and angry with me, like a guilty teenager. I quickly learned not to make an issue of it because he would become angry to the point of violence, and under no circumstances would I risk exposing myself or my son to his violent attacks again. While drinking I had not been able to control myself enough to keep quiet about my feelings, but sober I could sense the destructive power behind his rage and learned to hold in my emotions around him.

It soon became apparent I could not express any feelings which might trigger his anger, so I maintained a cool front with him while expressing my true feelings in private sessions with my counselor and with women like myself in group therapy.

Our son, Patrick, however, was too young to understand the need to control the expression of his feelings. One night after I had put Patrick to bed, I decided to go to the store for some soft drinks. I went down the stairs and pretended to leave by slamming the door, but actually hid in the entryway so that I could sneak up on Dave and surprise him as a joke. Patrick started crying from his room and immediately Dave began screaming threats and obscenities at him, not knowing I was still in the apartment. I stayed hidden to see what would happen next. Dave went into Patrick's room and hit him with such force that I could hear it from downstairs. Numb and in shock, I remained hidden. Dave returned to where he had been sitting in the living room with Patrick screaming hysterically in his crib. Dave began his stream of threats again, stormed back into Patrick's room and was standing over the crib hitting him as I ran into the room to stop him. I grabbed my son and left. After driving aimlessly around with no place to go, I returned later that night. Dave was in a rage when we returned, throwing things in my face and making wild accusations. I did not argue back but told him to calm down. He went to bed angry and I stayed up all night thinking. . . .

I remembered the countless times he apologized in tears for hitting me and the many promises of "never again." My self-esteem had been so low that I was willing to risk believing in him, and time after time I forgave him, only to have it happen again. But I was not willing to risk anything when it came to the safety of my child. And that episode shattered what little hope I still held of our remaining a family. The following day I told my counselor about it and we began to plan my escape.

I first had to find a job. Dave wanted me to work

(for the money it would provide) but he didn't want me to have any outside contacts or friends. His mother resented me for not working, saying I should be supporting my man. (She is an adult child of an alcoholic and has had four husbands, all of whom have been physically abusive or alcoholic or both.) My only outside contacts were with the people at the treatment center and in Alcoholics Anonymous. Dave resented even these.

I searched for a job and was confident one would appear soon. Two weeks prior to my six-month sobriety anniversary (which was also the date by which I hoped to be able to move out) a very strange feeling came over me and stayed. It was similar to the feeling of déjà vu, and it grew in intensity with each passing day. I felt as though everything I was doing I had already done before: I knew what people were going to say before they actually said it; I even knew when the telephone was going to ring before it rang. I thought this was extremely strange and I mentioned it to a few people, but at the same time it was a nice feeling, as if I was going to be forewarned against any unusual or dangerous happenings.

One week into this the feeling was extremely strong. Dave and I were supposed to go over to his mother's house that evening for a family dinner and something told me not to go. Ordinarily I would never ask Dave to go without me because to do so was sure to cause a fight between us, and I could not risk another fight with him. But the feeling was so strong I couldn't ignore it. Miraculously I found the right words to say to him which did not trigger his suspicion or anger and he agreed to go alone. After he was gone, I put Patrick to bed for the night and settled down on the couch for a nap.

(Before I continue, I must tell you I am not a religious fanatic. While I was at the treatment center I reestablished contact with God through the help of a caring chaplain who worked there, but my conception of God was similar to that of a small child. Each night I simply prayed that His will be done in my life and that was and still is the extent of my religion.)

When I awoke from my nap the feeling of prescience was so great that I became extremely frightened. I had experienced something similar to this on previous occasions, always in conjunction with bad or negative happenings, but never with such force. Now there seemed to be a massive electrical energy in the room and I sat on the couch terrified. I was afraid that this was God's warning to me that my life would soon end, that Dave would learn of my plans to leave and he would kill me. I knew beyond any doubt whatsoever that if he knew what I was trying to do, Dave would surely kill me in his rage.

Then all at once I saw my entire life as though it were a movie. It was in sequence but it happened all at once in less than an instant. And with it came a knowledge I cannot explain fully. In place of my usual feeling about each person in the movie, there was an understanding acceptance toward them all. I saw that we were each victims and that no one was to blame.

When the "movie" stopped, it didn't have an end and I was still afraid that this was my warning about my impending death. I asked God, "Did you bring me all this way to have it end like this?" and immediately my attention was drawn to a painting on the wall.

I had received the painting from a friend with whom I had worked several years before. I brought it with me each time I moved because I always thought it pretty, but otherwise never felt much about it. Now it was as though I were seeing that painting for the first time. And as I looked at it, wordlessly I was assured, "This is how the movie ends." It was a sudden feeling and a sudden knowing.

The painting is an autumn scene with golden trees and soft hills. In the distance is a blonde woman with a small child by her side, walking away from the viewer and toward the horizon on a long, narrow path. I was astonished to realize it was a picture of me and Patrick walking here in these beautiful hills that surround us! I had received the painting years before I ever knew I would have a child or live anywhere but in the flat country with no hillsides that had always been my home.

I was no longer frightened, but I was numb. I was happy, grateful and overwhelmed! This was so unreal I couldn't believe it was happening.

Then the strangest experience of all occurred. I was told several things, but again not in words, and it was not in a progression of thoughts either. It was as if a large package of knowledge was instantly implanted firmly and deeply into my mind. (I realize I must sound like a nut. Please know I'm not, and I swear to you every word of this is the truth.)

I was told, "You must show others what I have shown you. There was a reason for everything that has happened in your life. Your suffering has not been without purpose. By sharing the experiences in your life, you will help others recognize themselves in your pain, so that they may change their direction and seek My guidance. You must do it with honesty, compassion and the sincere desire to help others, not for any financial benefit to yourself. If it is done as I have asked, your rewards will come."

I couldn't believe what I was being asked to do! I am not so egotistical that I think my life has been very different from any other person's who was raised in the same environment. In fact, I'm sure many people have had a far more difficult time than I. And many people would believe I have been spoiled throughout most of my life because my family has always had an ample amount of money. When I told this to God, He answered, "It is more the reason for you to do as I ask. Money played no part in your unhappiness as a child."

Today, I am the woman in the painting. Patrick and I have walked away from Dave, leaving him in the care of God and sincerely wishing for him every happiness. We love him and in many ways we will miss him, but I know we must leave him behind for our future is over the horizon.

Now I am attempting to do what was asked of me, and I don't know how to go about it. I enjoy writing but I know I have neither the talent nor capability to write a book or manuscript that would do justice to the task at hand. I know nothing about any aspect of the media or even where to begin to find out about it. The only thing I knew to do was to write to you, tell you my story and hope you feel the desire to become involved in this project. Perhaps you can give me some advice or suggestions as to what you think I should do.

Please believe I am not a "kook." There is much about my life I am not proud of and many things I have done which I would rather not expose, as I am a very private person, but I must do what was asked of me and I believe it is a small price to pay in exchange for a healthy life for myself and my son. But most importantly, I must do this if it will help others who would otherwise be as trapped as I was.

Thank you for reading this. I had asked God in the beginning to please help me say the right words to you and I feel He has.

If this letter has reached you, physically and spiritually, please contact me with your response. I hope to hear from you soon.

Belinda E.

Dear Belinda,

I hope that together we're doing what God had in mind when you wrote your letter. Thank you for giving the gift of your story to all who read this book.

LIST OF
RESOURCES
(ALPHABETICALLY)

Adults Molested As Children United
P.O. Box 952
San Jose, CA 95108
phone (408) 280-5055
or Childhelp USA 1-800-422-4453

A program of Parents United. Purpose is to provide support and therapy to men and women unable to cope with the trauma of having been sexually abused as children.

Al-Anon Family Group Headquarters
One Park Avenue
New York, NY 10016
phone (212) 683-1771

Relatives and friends of persons with an alcohol problem. Membership includes Alateen for members twelve to twenty years of age whose lives have been adversely affected by someone else's drinking problem, usually a parent's.

Alcoholics Anonymous World Services
P.O. Box 459, Grand Central Station
New York, NY 10163
phone (212) 686-1100

(In their own words) International fellowship of men and women who share their experience, strength and hope with each other that they may solve their common problem and help others recover from alcoholism and achieve sobriety.

Anorexia Nervosa and Related Eating Disorders (ANRED)
P.O. Box 5102
Eugene, OR 97405
phone (503) 344-1144 or (503) 686-7372

Information and referral service for those with questions regarding eating disorders and their treatment.

Co-dependents of Sexual Addicts
P.O. Box 14537
Minneapolis, MN 55414

Serves as a support group for the families of "sexual addicts."

Daughters and Sons United
840 Guadalupe Parkway
San Jose, CA 95110
phone (408) 299-2511
or Childhelp USA 1-800-422-4453

Sexually abused children and their families. Affiliated with Parents United.

Debtors Anonymous
316 Fifth Avenue
New York, NY 10001

Debtors Anonymous is a fellowship of men and women who share their experience, strength and hope with each other that they may solve their common problem and recover from compulsive indebtedness. We study the literature of Alcoholics Anonymous to strengthen our understanding of compulsive disease. We can identify with many of the situations described therein by substituting the words "compulsive debt" for "alcohol."

Families Anonymous
P.O. Box 528
Van Nuys, CA 91408
phone (818) 989-7841

Parents, relatives and friends concerned about drug abuse or related behavioral problems. Self-supportive, self-help group patterned after Al-Anon and Alcoholics Anonymous programs. Assists families in overcoming overprotectiveness of drug abusers and developing a better understanding of their problems.

Gam-Anon International Service Office
P.O. Box 967
Radio City Station
New York, NY 10101
phone (212) 391-0911

Husbands, wives, relatives and close friends of compulsive gamblers. Seeks to help members better understand the compulsive gambler and learn to cope with the problems involved.

Gamblers Anonymous (GA)
1543 West Olympic Boulevard, Suite 533
Los Angeles, CA 90015
phone (213) 386-8789

Men and women who have joined together in order to stop gambling and to help other compulsive gamblers do the same.

Incest Survivors Resource Network, International Friends Meetinghouse
15 Rutherford Place
New York, NY 10003
phone (516) 935-3031

Refers incest victims to local support groups. Affiliated with Parents United.

International Advisory Council for Homosexual Men and Women in Alcoholics
    Anonymous
P.O. Box 492
Village Station
New York, NY 10014

Provides information for gay and lesbian alcoholics and those who counsel them regarding regular groups of Alcoholics Anonymous specifically composed of homosexual members. Affiliated with Alcoholics Anonymous World Service.

Nar-Anon Family Group Headquarters
P.O. Box 2562
Palos Verdes Peninsula, CA 90274

For the families and friends of drug users. Applies the principles of recovery developed in Alcoholics Anonymous and Al-Anon.

Narcotics Anonymous (NA)
P.O. Box 9999
Van Nuys, CA 91409
phone (818) 780-3951

Recovering addicts throughout the world who offer help to others seeking recovery. Uses Twelve-Step program to aid in rehabilitation.

National Council of Child Abuse and Family Violence
1050 Connecticut Avenue N.W., Suite 300
Washington, DC 20036
phone (202) 429-6695
Toll-free number providing referral service 1-800-222-2000

Is concerned with the cyclical and intergenerational nature of family violence and abuse. Provides information, education and referral.

O-Anon
General Service Office
P.O. Box 4305
San Pedro, CA 90731

O-Anon is a fellowship of friends and relatives of compulsive overeaters. O-Anon is not part of but does work in cooperation with Overeaters Anonymous. Our purpose is threefold: to offer comfort, hope and friendship to the families and friends of compulsive overeaters; to give understanding and encouragement to the compulsive overeater (whether eating compulsively or not); and to learn to grow spiritually by working the Twelve Steps ourselves (as adapted from Alcoholics Anonymous).

Overeaters Anonymous (OA)
2190 West 190th Street
Torrance, CA 90504
phone (213) 320-7941

Men and women who meet to share their experiences, strength and hope in order to recover from the disease of compulsive overeating. This "lifetime program of action" follows the Twelve Steps and Twelve Traditions of the Alcoholics Anonymous Program.

Parents Anonymous
6733 South Sepulveda Boulevard, Suite 270
Los Angeles, CA 90045
Toll-free phone number in California 1-800-352-0386
Toll-free phone number outside California 1-800-421-0353

Parents Anonymous is a self-help organization that provides safe, supportive weekly meetings where parents under stress can discuss their problems with their peers and with trained volunteer professionals. The organization is free and open to all parents who are overwhelmed, isolated or afraid of their anger toward their children.
This is not a Twelve-Step program. However, anonymity and confidentiality are guiding principles.

Parents United
P.O. Box 952
San Jose, CA 95108
phone (408) 280-5055

Individuals and families who have experienced child sexual molestation. To provide assistance to families affected by incest and other types of child sexual abuse by providing crisis and long-term support.

Recovery, Inc.
802 North Dearborn
Chicago, IL 60610

The Association of Nervous and Former Mental Patients, founded in 1937 by Dr. Abraham Low. Uses the text, *Mental Health through Will Training,* published by the Christopher Publishing House, West Hanover, MA 02339.

Sex Addicts Anonymous (SAA)
P.O. Box 3038
Minneapolis, MN 55403
phone (612) 339-0217

Purpose is to provide a support group for sexual addicts that follows a program adapted from the Twelve-Step program of Alcoholics Anonymous in dealing with sexual behavior. (Sexual addicts are described as people who compulsively repeat sexual behavior that is often abusive, exploitive and damaging to their lives at home and at work.)

Sexaholics Anonymous (SA)
P.O. Box 300
Simi Valley, CA 93062

Individuals wishing to stop their sexually self-destructive thinking and behavior such as fantasy, pornography, incest or criminal sexual activity. Group believes that the sexaholic is addicted to lust and sex as others are to alcohol or drugs; this behavior is often followed by guilt, remorse and depression and may damage relationships with family and peers. Conducts programs based on the Twelve-Step recovery program used in Alcoholics Anonymous to help members achieve "sexual sobriety."

VOICES–Victims of Incest Can Emerge Survivors
P.O. Box 148309
Chicago, IL 60614
phone (312) 327-1500

Purpose is to create a communication and peer support network for victims of incest and those affected by it.

RECOMMENDED READING

In addition to those books suggested in *WWL2M*, here are a few more that I find myself constantly recommending to those who are already well on their way to recovery:

1. Cady, H. Emilie. *HOW I USED TRUTH*. Unity School, 1916.
2. Cady, Emilie. *LESSONS IN TRUTH*. Unity School, 1894.
3. Goldsmith, Joel. *PRACTICING THE PRESENCE*. New York: Harper & Row, 1958.

   This little book is a constant reminder, page after page, that our real work is always with ourselves. For those who feel they truly "get" what Florence Scovell Shinn writes in *THE GAME OF LIFE*, this book is the next step in training one's consciousness. I also recommend any other book by Joel Goldsmith.
4. Silverstein, Shel. *THE MISSING PIECE MEETS THE BIG O*. New York: Harper & Row, 1981.

   A delightful little cartoon story of the long and often difficult journey toward becoming whole.
5. Greene, Liz. *RELATING: AN ASTROLOGICAL GUIDE TO LIVING WITH OTHERS ON A SMALL PLANET*. York Beach, ME: Samuel Weiser, 1977.

   Whether or not you understand astrology (or care to), Greene's book is worth reading. She applies the principles of what is usually referred to as Jungian psychology to relationships with a clarity and depth I've not seen matched.

In addition to the above recommended titles, the following books were mentioned in letters and text.

1. *ALCOHOLICS ANONYMOUS,* Third Edition. New York: Alcoholics Anonymous World Services, Inc., 1976.
2. Black, Claudia. *IT WILL NEVER HAPPEN TO ME.* New York: Macmillan, 1982.
3. Carnes, Patrick. *OUT OF THE SHADOWS: UNDERSTANDING SEX-UAL ADDICTION.* Minneapolis: CompCare, 1985.
4. Johnson, Vernon. *I'LL QUIT TOMORROW.* New York: Harper & Row, 1980.
5. Sheehy, Gail. *PASSAGES.* New York: Dutton, 1976.

INDEX

352   *Index*